P9-DGU-262

Your
Practicum in
Psychology

Your
Practicum in
Psychology

A Guide for
Maximizing Knowledge
and Competence

Edited by
Janet R. Matthews and C. Eugene Walker

American Psychological Association • Washington, DC

Copyright © 2006 by the American Psychological Association. All rights reserved. Except as permitted under the United States Copyright Act of 1976, no part of this publication may be reproduced or distributed in any form or by any means, including, but not limited to, the process of scanning and digitization, or stored in a database or retrieval system, without the prior written permission of the publisher.

Chapter 8 was coauthored by an employee of the United States government as part of official duty and is considered to be in the public domain.

First Printing, October 2005
Second Printing, October 2009

Published by
American Psychological Association
750 First Street, NE
Washington, DC 20002
www.apa.org

To order
APA Order Department
P.O. Box 92984
Washington, DC 20090-2984
Tel: (800) 374-2721; Direct: (202) 336-5510
Fax: (202) 336-5502; TDD/TTY: (202) 336-6123
Online: www.apa.org/books/
E-mail: order@apa.org

In the U.K., Europe, Africa, and the Middle East, copies may be ordered from
American Psychological Association
3 Henrietta Street
Covent Garden, London
WC2E 8LU England

Typeset in Meridien by World Composition Services, Inc., Sterling, VA

Printer: Data Reproductions, Auburn Hills, MI
Cover Designer: Naylor Design, Washington, DC
Technical/Production Editor: Tiffany L. Klaff

The opinions and statements published are the responsibility of the authors, and such opinions and statements do not necessarily represent the policies of the American Psychological Association. Any views expressed in Chapter 8 do not necessarily represent the views of the United States government, and the author's participation in the work is not meant to serve as an official endorsement.

Library of Congress Cataloging-in-Publication Data

Matthews, Janet R.
    Your practicum in psychology : a guide for maximizing knowledge and competence / Janet R. Matthews and C. Eugene Walker.—1st ed.
       p. cm.
    Includes index.
    ISBN 1-59147-328-4
    1. Clinical psychology—Study and teaching (Internship)—United States. 2. Clinical psychologists—Training of—United States. 3. Mental health personnel—Training of—United States. 4. Practicums—United States. I. Walker, C. Eugene (Clarence Eugene), 1939–   II. Title.

RC467.7.M38   2005
616.89'0071—dc22   2005015452

British Library Cataloguing-in-Publication Data
A CIP record is available from the British Library.

Printed in the United States of America
First Edition

Contents

CONTRIBUTORS   *vii*
PREFACE   *ix*

1 How to Maximize Your Training Experience   3
   Theresa A. Wozencraft

2 Characteristics of a Helping Relationship   23
   B. Max Price

3 Getting Started and Developing Rapport   41
   Janet R. Matthews and Lee H. Matthews

4 Confidentiality and Other Ethical Issues   61
   Elizabeth Swenson

5 History of Treatment of People With Mental Illness   81
   Carol Terry

6 A Review of Psychopathology   105
   Leonard S. Milling, Phuong M. Chau, and Mary Alice Mills-Baxter

7 Psychological Assessment   129
   Lee H. Matthews

8 Interventions: Empirically Supported Treatments   157
   Morgan T. Sammons and Peter E. Nathan

9 The Use of Medicine in the Treatment of
   Mental Disorders   187
   Bruce K. McCormick

10 Special Issues in Working With Children   209
   Jean C. Elbert

11 Mental Health Professions   237
   Janet R. Matthews and C. Eugene Walker

MEDICAL ABBREVIATIONS GLOSSARY   *253*

INDEX   *269*

ABOUT THE EDITORS   *281*

Contributors

Phuong M. Chau, MA, Department of Psychology, University of Kansas, Lawrence

Jean C. Elbert, PhD, Department of Psychology, California State University, Northridge

Janet R. Matthews, PhD, ABPP, Department of Psychology, Loyola University, New Orleans, LA

Lee H. Matthews, PhD, ABPP, Department of Psychiatry and Neurology, Tulane University Health Sciences Center, New Orleans, LA

Bruce K. McCormick, PhD, private practice, Shreveport, LA

Leonard S. Milling, PhD, Department of Psychology, University of Hartford, West Hartford, CT

Mary Alice Mills-Baxter, BA, Department of Psychology, University of Connecticut, Storrs

Peter E. Nathan, PhD, Department of Psychology, University of Iowa, Iowa City

B. Max Price, PhD, private practice, Oklahoma City, OK

Morgan T. Sammons, PhD, U.S. Navy Bureau of Medicine and Surgery, Washington, DC

Elizabeth Swenson, PhD, JD, Department of Psychology, John Carroll University, University Heights, OH

Carol Terry, PhD, Department of Psychology, University of Oklahoma; private practice, Norman, OK

C. Eugene Walker, PhD, Department of Psychology, University of Oklahoma, Norman

Theresa A. Wozencraft, PhD, Department of Psychology, University of Louisiana, Lafayette

Preface

You may be wondering how we decided to write this book and how we selected the topics to be included in it. We have collaborated on numerous projects over the years, including a previous book for the undergraduate practicum course. We learned a great deal from that previous experience that we wanted to bring to our new collaboration. We each teach an undergraduate psychology practicum course. One of us found our previous book to be a good match for the course; the other ultimately did not. As we discussed the differences in our courses, we discovered that there is truly a breadth of experience being offered to undergraduate psychology students who have the opportunity to take this type of course. We also discussed this course with colleagues who offer it at other colleges and universities. We discovered that many of them would have liked to have a book for their practicum students, but either they were unaware of any available books or they had found the few available books did not meet their needs. Most of them either used a series of assigned readings, such as reprints of journal articles, or just provided information orally to their students.

We therefore decided to look at our previous book and then develop one that would be an even better match for the variety of undergraduate courses in this area. Each chapter of this book is written by a different author or authors. We view the chapters as being analogous to having a guest lecturer for each topic. Just as there are differences in style among guest lecturers, so there are some differences in style among the chapters of this book. The authors were asked to write for an undergraduate psychology audience on specific topics relevant to the practicum experience.

Some of the chapters are designed to provide you with summary material from courses you may have already taken. This material may also provide a useful background for those of you who have not had these specific courses. An example is the chapter on psychopathology. We have found that even if you have previously completed a course in abnormal psychology, you will benefit from a review before actually having contact with "real" people in the field. The chapter on psycho-pharmacology is not intended to make undergraduate students into physician assistants. Rather, we find that students who are placed in psychiatric settings frequently hear the names of medications but have little or no background in understanding their general purposes. You may have known someone who was taking one or more of these medications, but that history does not necessarily mean you have a broad understanding of its uses and potential side effects. This chapter is designed to familiarize you with the uses of the major medications about which you are likely to hear at your placements. The same comments relate to the chapter on psychological testing. Although many undergraduate psychology departments offer a course in tests and measurements, these courses are seldom required. Field placement students are likely to hear the names of various tests in team staff meetings where they observe or even possibly have the opportunity to observe a psychologist administer some of these tests. In a particular practicum placement, the tests used may be highly specific to that population (e.g., children or persons who are organically impaired). This chapter is intended to give you a general introduction to the topic.

There is some question among psychologists about the application of a professional ethics code to students who are serving primarily in the role of observer. It is our view that students of psychology should be held to the same code as professionals in psychology when it comes to situations involving ethics and that they need to begin to learn this as early in their careers as possible. Much as undergraduates are taught to observe the Ethics Code of the American Psychological Association (APA) research ethics regarding whether they are conducting their own studies or assisting professors in a research lab, students need to know the remainder of the current Ethics Code of psychology when they are in an applied setting. Strict adherence to proper ethics is especially important when other human beings (or animals) are affected. Material from the Ethics Code is explained using simple vignettes that we hope will make sense to you and allow you to have a stronger appreciation of what you observe in these settings.

Although undergraduate students are certainly not making thera-peutic interventions, they may find themselves talking individually with patients on an inpatient psychiatric unit in much the same way as psychology techs do. It is useful for them to understand the characteristics of a helping relationship and how to establish rapport even if they are not providing clinical services. Coverage of methods of intervention proved to be among the most difficult of the topics addressed in this book. Because there are so many methods of intervention currently in use, it is impossible to summarize all of them in a general book of this type. The chapter on intervention is therefore used to illustrate a broad domain by describing just one approach as used with four common forms of emotional disturbance. Because children present unique issues, we have a separate chapter dealing with them. As the geriatric population continues to grow and more facilities for geriatric patients are developed, a separate chapter for this population may be warranted. In order to limit the size of this book and on the basis of our collective experience with this course, we chose not to have such a chapter at this time.

Psychology departments train students to become psychologists. There are many other professions that are related or similar to psychology in applied settings. Our chapter on mental health professions is not an exhaustive one. It is intended to help you understand the background of some of the professionals you may encounter during your field placement as well as perhaps to stimulate you to search for further information about some of these career options.

We thank all of our chapter authors for their diligence in sending us material and making revisions in a timely fashion. Special thanks go to Susan Reynolds in APA Books who remained in contact with us to keep us on schedule and let us know what was needed to finalize our project and bring this book to print.

Your
Practicum in
Psychology

Theresa A. Wozencraft

How to Maximize Your Training Experience

1

The purpose of this chapter is to address pragmatic issues related to maximizing your training experiences. You will learn the following by reading this chapter: (a) what to consider insofar as site selection is concerned, (b) how to establish yourself in your practicum, (c) ways to adapt to and find your niche in your new work environment, (d) ideas for optimizing your relationship with your supervisor(s), and (e) the utility and potential content of a practicum contract. I hope that you will take advantage of these ideas to make the most of your investment of time and energy in the practicum enterprise.

Using Training Needs to Guide Site Selection

Considering the type of practicum site at which you will receive your training is very important. Even if you are assigned to a site, your faculty practicum supervisor will often ask for your input and preferences. Whether you select the site yourself or you are assigned to a site, it is a good idea to think about your training needs. This will allow you to match your needs with what various sites have to offer.

DISCERNING YOUR TRAINING NEEDS

Many factors can influence your training needs, but perhaps most important of those factors is your future goal. If your postbaccalaureate goal is to obtain employment, then there are several actions you can take to help with the determination of your training needs. For example, you can interview one or two individuals who make hiring decisions for the type of position(s) you would like to obtain to determine the types of experiences and skills that successful candidates will possess. Alternatively, you can interview a person employed in the type of position(s) you desire. Preparing a resume and asking a faculty member to review it to recommend some areas for further development is another source of information. A faculty member can assist you with determining the type of training experience that will help you gain the skills and knowledge you need to be a more successful candidate for employment in your chosen area. For assistance with resume preparation, check with your university career center to determine the types of services available. University career centers also frequently offer assistance with interviewing skills development.

If attending graduate school is your postbaccalaureate goal, learning more about the types of experience and skill that graduate programs prefer in candidates is important. This information can be obtained from several sources. These include reading the literature that graduate programs provide, examining their application forms to determine the types of experience about which they inquire, and asking students who are currently in the program what types of experiences they and their peers had when they applied. Consider also your own unique preferences, but remember that it is generally more beneficial to have a broad range of experiences than to seek an experience limited to a certain problem area or age group. Being exposed to service provision at a broader level provides a firmer foundation for future career decision making by increasing your awareness of the many opportunities in the field (Faiver, Eisengart, & Colonna, 2004), and it enhances your marketability to a wider range of graduate programs or employers.

MAJOR TYPES OF PRACTICUM SITES

The major types of practicum settings are listed here to familiarize you with them. Sites may first be broadly divided into inpatient and outpatient settings. Inpatient, correctional, or residential settings are those in which the patient resides either temporarily or permanently and include medical and psychiatric hospitals, physical rehabilitation centers, residential centers for those with developmental disabilities, shelters for displaced youth, youth or adult prisons, and substance abuse treatment programs. Outpatient settings are those in which the client visits for a period of less than a day and include government-run mental health agencies, privately funded mental health clinics, private practices, social service agencies (e.g., those supported by United Way), partial incarceration programs, delinquency prevention and early intervention programs, and outpatient programs administered by the inpatient settings listed above.

INFORMATION RESOURCES FOR SITE SELECTION

There are numerous means by which you may obtain information on a practicum site (Wozencraft, 1997). Many departments have information on the practicum sites that are frequently used by students; this information may be available in a written format or through meeting with the faculty practicum supervisor. In addition, students who have been or are currently on a placement can provide up-to-date information. The site itself can provide information to you. However, before approaching the site for information, it is advisable to use your on-campus resources to gain as much information as possible so that you need only to approach the site staff for answers to questions unanswerable by others or to clarify conflicting information received from one's sources. Keep in mind that you should call for an appointment before going to the site to ask for additional information. This will help to assure that you can be seen and that you are perceived as professional and respectful of the schedules of others. It is appropriate to ask for an appointment with the staff supervisor and to limit your visit to 20 to 30 minutes, unless the supervisor wishes to meet for a longer period of time. If you have done your homework, you will need no longer than this to clarify issues.

By the end of the information-gathering period, you should have a sense of these aspects of a training site according to Boylan, Malley, and Scott (1995):

- site personnel (credentials, disciplines, theoretical orientations represented, employment stability, and formal supervision training);
- types of services (case management, crisis intervention, psycho-educational and skills training, short- and long-term therapy, and family, group, or individual therapy);
- professional associations of the site (accreditations received and affiliations with other agencies);

- site-based learning opportunities (inservices, staffings, and rounds);
- client population characteristics (socioeconomic status [SES], gender, ethnicities, and ages);
- service support (computer facilities, clerical services, office space, professional library, and supplies and equipment);
- opportunities to participate in ongoing research or grant writing; and
- quality and quantity of supervision (individual or group, observation, and cotherapy).

TRAINING SITE SELECTION CRITERIA

Once you have obtained the information you need to make a decision, you will be in a position to consider how well your training needs and the site's opportunities match each other. No match will be ideal, but you can still obtain good training from a site that meets most of your needs. For undergraduates, a good placement will provide the opportunity to observe service provision to a broad range of clients with a wide range of problems and to observe professionals from various disciplines with various theoretical orientations. You may in fact have the opportunity to work with only one professional. This situation can provide the opportunity to build a deeper supervisory relationship. A deeper supervisory relationship may allow you to learn more about the supervisor's approach to his or her work with clients (which is based on professional discipline and theoretical orientations used). You may also be given more training opportunities once you have gained the trust and respect of the supervisor. By engaging in the process of examining your needs and the practicum site's strengths and weaknesses, you can make a well-informed decision.

Establishing Yourself in the Practicum

Once the site has been selected, the real work begins. The task of establishing yourself at your site is one that requires a readiness to be adaptive. You will be learning a number of new roles, most notably professional and practitioner (Wozencraft, 1997). You will also have the obligation to learn about your new work environment, including the multidisciplinary staff and agency rules and activities.

TAKING ON NEW ROLES

Professional Role

One of the exciting challenges of beginning the practicum is adopting a professional persona. Professionalism entails your appearance, behavior, and attitudes. Professionalism involves conveying to the service recipient that you are competent, confident, warm, respectful, and task-oriented. The most outward indicator of your professionalism, your appearance, will be discussed first. Your appearance is important, as it is your opportunity to convey your respect to the clients and staff. A professional appearance signifies that you see the clients and staff as important. This is particularly meaningful to clients, who often feel disenfranchised from society.

The type of clothing considered as professional and appropriate varies from setting to setting. For both men and women, it will be necessary to observe the attire of the majority of the professionals at your setting to determine how you should dress. (See the discussion of professional attire in chap. 3, this volume.)

Even more convincing than appearance as a sign of professionalism is your behavior and attitude. Although certainly not an exhaustive list, professional behavior includes promptness, responding calmly and objectively to situations, maintaining a pleasant demeanor, carrying through with your assigned duties, taking initiative to complete a task that is clearly in your realm of responsibilities, and taking responsibility for your errors. Professionals put business ahead of pleasure when they are at work. Another important aspect to consider is that you are a guest at the site. As in any situation in which you are a guest, courtesy is of utmost importance. The type of courtesy the site expects from you is that you graciously accept your role and their mode of operation. Taken altogether, appearance, attitudes, and behaviors that are professional will help you to be respected by staff and clients alike.

Practitioner Role

As a practicum student, you will be challenged to apply the concepts learned in your coursework. This represents a major change in the way that you have been expected to function. You are usually expected to master abstract concepts and theories in your courses. In practicum, you are expected to know how to translate ideas, even abstract ones, into action. Having to switch to this mode is cognitively taxing for the first few weeks. You can ease the transition by reading literature that directly deals with practice, such as assessment and therapy books and manuals. Reading case notes and treatment plans as well as assessment reports can also help you to understand how concepts are applied. You may be surprised to discover how much self-instruction is expected of you. Students are expected to teach themselves as much as possible and then to approach professionals for help with the aspects of the task that they are not able to master independently. This allows the professionals to work more efficiently with you and gives you the opportunity to take initiative and apply the skills and knowledge that you have gained as a college student to the tasks at hand.

Adhering to the American Psychological Association's Ethics Code is also an integral part of learning the role of the practitioner. Your faculty supervisor may have a different code of ethics than your site supervisor if they are from different disciplines. It is your responsibility to adhere to both codes; should they conflict, you can bring this to the attention of the site and faculty practicum supervisors. Learning how to behave in an ethical manner is one of the most important skills you will gain from your practicum. This topic is so important that chapter 4 of this book (Confidentiality and Other Ethical Issues) is dedicated to its further exploration.

The Work Environment

In addition to the internal changes of new roles, you will experience the external changes involved with being in a new work environment. Meeting the demands of the new environment can be challenging as there is much to learn. Not only will you be learning about the practicum site itself in terms of its services, activities, and policies but also about working with both professional and clerical staff. Finally, you will have the opportunity to further develop your competence in working with individuals from diverse backgrounds, whether they are staff or clients.

PRACTICUM SITE SERVICES, ACTIVITIES, AND POLICIES

Becoming familiar with the wide variety of services that most practicum sites offer will help you to develop an understanding of mental health care. As well as providing services to clients, your practicum site will be engaging in many activities that support the provision of these services: staff training, record-keeping, report preparation for governing agencies, program evaluation, and more. You will learn the policies and procedures of site operation, which include information on the types of clients who may be seen, how often and under what conditions they may be seen, and the financial arrangements for service provision. Working effectively within the system is accomplished by knowing how tasks are accomplished and then using that structure to accomplish them. Ask for assistance if you are not sure how to achieve an objective.

MAXIMIZING YOUR TRAINING OPPORTUNITIES

You may initially feel disappointed with your training as many undergraduates are given clerical duties early in their practicum. There are many experiences that you may be allowed to have later in the practicum after you have proved yourself to be responsible, motivated, and interested. Although you may not be allowed to provide services directly to clients, you can seek opportunities to learn about service provision by inquiring about opportunities to sit in on the supervision of more advanced students, or by attending staffings, rounds, grand rounds, and inservices. Although different sites offer different learning opportunities, each is an excellent way to gain exposure to a greater number of professionals and issues.

There may also be occasions to observe direct service provision. In these instances, not only your supervisor but also the client must give consent; if the client says no, the professional must respect the client's right to privacy. If you can't observe direct service provision, you may be allowed to engage in several other activities that give the flavor of clinical work. For example, you can offer to administer or score assessments appropriate to your level of training. Asking for additional experiences and being willing to take the initiative to prepare yourself for those will allow you to enhance your training. Learning to accept *no* for an answer in a graceful manner is also part of your professional training. When a training experience you seek is denied, you might ask your supervisor how you could obtain similar experience at a level more appropriate to your training. Your professionalism, initiative, and effectiveness as well as the comfort level of your supervisor can all impact the types of experiences in which you will be allowed to participate.

RELATIONSHIPS WITH STAFF

You will have a variety of staff members with whom you interact. There will most likely be contact with both professional and clerical staff. How you are to relate to the staff members is best learned from your supervisor; however, some general guidelines apply to most sites. You may be expected to work with several members of the multidisciplinary professional staff. This multidisciplinary professional staff may include psychiatrists, psychologists, social workers, licensed professional counselors, substance abuse counselors, psychiatric nurses, pastoral counselors, and marriage and family therapists. It is the fortunate student who has this arrangement, as the training opportunities are abundant. There will be variability in those learning experiences; one supervisor may expect you to observe, another to participate, and the third may prefer you to review records. Other professionals with whom you may also come into contact include educational diagnosticians, speech therapists, occupational therapists, physical therapists, rehabilitation counselors, recreation therapists, art therapists, music therapists, and court workers, as well as many others. Learning more about these professions can be accomplished at the site as the need arises.

DEALING MORE EFFECTIVELY WITH DIVERSITY IN STAFF AND CLIENTS

How might our differences affect the way we relate to each other and perceive each other? Consider the following scenario. You are an African American woman in your 20s interacting with a male Hispanic client in his 30s. Your supervisor is a European American woman in her 50s who is a lesbian. You might ask yourself questions such as

- What are my beliefs about men, Hispanics, European Americans, and persons who are homosexual?
- What stereotypes have I grown up with about these groups?
- How might the client or supervisor view me as an individual from a group different from his or her own?
- How might the client's cultural background impact the choice made about type of assessment or intervention?

Differences between groups can create situations in which discomfort develops between individuals because of a lack of understanding or acceptance of these differences (Ladany, Brittan-Powell, & Pannu, 1997). Working effectively with people who are different from you in terms of culture, ethnicity, race, religion, gender, lifestyle, sexual orientation, SES, and age is critical to success in the field of psychology. To be prepared to work effectively with a diverse staff and clientele, you must learn how to take into consideration which differences exist between groups, when they exist for any given individual within a group, and how the working relationship may be affected by those differences that do exist (Atkinson, 2004). This task can be further complicated by your own acceptance of myths and stereotypes about people who are different from yourself. Even when you strive not to be prejudiced, you can still retain deeply ingrained beliefs that affect your interactions with others.

Given that whole texts are dedicated to understanding diverse groups, it is obvious that information provided here offers assistance with only a few aspects of diversity and gives only a limited view of the complexity of each aspect of diversity. Additional readings are necessary, and several are recommended at the end of this chapter. Some general considerations about gender, ethnicity, and culture follow.

Gender

Gender role expectations may influence your relationships with your supervisor, clients, and staff members. Stereotypical role expectations among European Americans place women in the expressive role and men in the instrumental role. Women are expected to enact the expressive role by being nurturing, emotionally responsive, cooperative, sensitive to the needs of others, and dependent. Men are expected to enact the instrumental role by behaving in an assertive, dominant, competitive manner. In addition, men are expected to demonstrate logical and rational thought in the service of their achievement and goal orientation (Berk, 2004; Sigelman & Rider, 2003).

You may want to consider how your gender role beliefs influence your expectations of yourself and others around you as well as how other's beliefs may influence their interactions with you. For example, a female practicum student may have the experience of a male client making a sexist remark or asking her out on a date. Either of these situations deserves a professional response. In the former case, you can choose to ignore it or to state respectfully that you prefer not to hear that sort of remark. In the latter case, it is important that you explain that the professional nature of the relationship prohibits your dating anyone who is a client. This rule applies even when you are not actually a treating professional but rather an observer or student in the setting. You can state that the training facility and the university do not allow this practice. In addition to gender role beliefs among those from the same culture, one must also consider how gender role expectations vary from culture to culture. This can help you to understand what leads a client or staff member to behave toward you in a certain way and lessens the chance that you will misperceive it. Don't hesitate to consult with your supervisor for advice about how to handle these situations. If you believe that a supervisor is treating you in a gender stereotypical manner or in a sexually harassing fashion, consult with your faculty practicum supervisor for advice (Lamb & Catanzaro, 1998).

Ethnicity and Culture

Generally speaking, ethnic and cultural group differences can exist in ideologies and values and in their attendant behaviors. Such values include, but are not limited to, (a) present, past, and future orientation, including how much importance each is given in daily life situations; (b) interdependence versus independence; (c) scheduling of time versus more spontaneous use of time; (d) locus of control for life events; and (e) the nature of social relationships (Dana, 1993; Lee, 1999). It is important to understand these differences as well as the more obvious differences such as religion, dress, food preferences, customs, and holidays. There are several ways you can become more culturally competent and aware of diversity (Lee, 1999). Reading about diverse groups introduces you to general trends found for a particular group. Spending time with people from different backgrounds, engaging in events held by those groups, and exposing yourself to the art, literature, and food of various groups can all help you to understand cultures other than your own.

In working with those individuals who have a different background, it is important to strike a balance between culture-general and culture-specific values (Lopez, 1997). This means that you must take into account the values that are specific to the culture in comparison to the values that most cultures share (culture general). An example of a culture-general value is the valuing of life by all cultures; whereas a culture-specific value is the specific circumstance that allows the taking of another's life (e.g., the death penalty or infanticide). Additionally, you should ascertain which values from the culture of origin the person subscribes to in daily life. Ethnic minority group members may adopt some of the cultural values of the majority group as well. Thus you should view every person as an individual who has his or her own unique set of values acquired from one or more cultures to which he or she has been exposed. For example, if a client is chronically late, the lateness is typically interpreted as a form of resistance to therapy. This is based on the European American upper-middle-class value of strict adherence to time schedules (Dana, 1993; Lee, 1999). You should take into account the client's values concerning strict adherence to a time schedule. The lateness may not be a form of resistance to therapy; rather it may be that adherence to strict time schedules is not important or even counter to the person's beliefs about time. Because of value differences such as this, you can see how important it is to understand a person's culture in order to understand the person with whom you are working.

Student–Supervisor Relationships

THE ROLES OF THE SUPERVISOR

The purpose of the supervisory relationship is to provide training to the supervisee while ensuring that the client receives the best possible service. The supervisor must fulfill many role obligations, primary among which are teacher, consultant, and evaluator (Veach, 2001). Your supervisor will teach you those things that you are not able to teach yourself and will eventually serve as your consultant as you gain the skills and knowledge needed to become less dependent on the supervisor's assistance. Your supervisor can suggest readings that can help you to develop the knowledge and skills you need to be successful in your practicum. In addition, your supervisor is responsible for evaluating your performance and giving you feedback that promotes your professional growth. At times, these roles may overlap or even conflict with each other. Thus, your supervisor must be able to provide a variety of services to you while keeping each type of service in balance with the overarching goals of training.

THE ROLES OF THE SUPERVISEE

You, the supervisee, must simultaneously enact a number of roles (Baird, 2005; Nelson & Friedlander, 2001). As a supervisee, you are expected to accept direction and guidance that is sought or offered. You should share both your strengths and weaknesses with your supervisors in service of receiving this guidance. The supervisee also accepts the role of professional. As discussed previously, the role of professional includes personal, ethical, and interpersonal behaviors and attitudes that follow the dictates of the profession. In the role of volunteer, you are expected to provide a variety of services with a skill level commensurate with your education and training. Fulfilling the obligations of all these roles can be cognitively and emotionally stressful and tiring; however, with time and experience, you will no doubt find yourself adapting well. When you are experiencing difficulty with adapting, your supervisor will be able to assist you in working through your concerns in a productive manner. Last, you retain the student role in which you continue to report to a faculty practicum supervisor and are evaluated periodically on your performance by the practicum supervisor, faculty supervisor, or both.

POTENTIAL PROBLEMS AND SOLUTIONS

Just as supervisors may experience problems balancing their roles, so may supervisees. Problems in the supervisory relationship can emerge when a supervisee has unrealistic expectations of a supervisor, struggles with role ambiguity, or experiences role conflicts (Nelson & Friedlander, 2001). Common examples of each potential problem area are provided to assist you in dealing more effectively with these issues. One common but unrealistic expectation is that the supervisor will teach the supervisee all he or she needs to know and will be readily available to the supervisee on a frequent, on-demand basis (Nelson, Gray, Friedlander, Ladany, & Walker, 2001). The realities of the site supervisor's duties prohibit this; nearly all supervisors have supervision as only a small percentage of their total responsibility as a staff member. Most supervisors would like to spend more time with supervisees but simply cannot. Therefore, you may be expected to learn independently, with the role of your supervisor being to assist you with that which you did not understand on your own. A scheduled supervision period can help to assure that you have predictable access to supervision.

Role ambiguity is a problem frequently experienced by beginning supervisees because they do not have experience with the roles they must fulfill. This leads supervisees to question what they must do to fulfill their role obligations (supervisee, volunteer, and student). To avoid role ambiguity, you must clarify what is expected of you in each role. Because what is expected may change with time or across supervisors, it is a good idea to ask your supervisor(s) to describe his or her expectations about each role you must fulfill as a supervisee and then to periodically reassess these expectations. Another way to decrease role ambiguity is to have a practicum contract or supervisory contract that spells out your major responsibilities (Nelson & Friedlander, 2001). These contracts are discussed later in this chapter.

Another type of problem supervisees may experience is role conflict, which is caused by role expectations being incongruent with each other. For example, there can be conflicts between the expectations placed on you in your roles as volunteer, student, and supervisee. You are expected to be knowledgeable as a volunteer while at the same time to be in need of knowledge as a student. As a supervisee who is evaluated on your performance, you may be concerned with the degree of competency you are perceived to demonstrate and thus the grade that will be recommended. This may lead you to underutilize the student role and not ask about issues that you should ask about so that you may be evaluated as independent and competent. However, your ability to recognize when you need supervisory assistance is usually evaluated as well. Therefore, the conflicting expectations of the various roles you undertake can be problematic. However, when you are caught between roles, your faculty practicum supervisor or site supervisor will be available to help you clarify what you need to do.

Practicum Contracts

Although not a requirement, a practicum contract is nonetheless recommended because it allows the requirements of the practicum to be spelled out clearly for all parties involved. It also formalizes the agreement between you, your faculty practicum supervisor, and your site supervisor. The faculty practicum supervisor may have a standard contract with the practicum site. This contract may outline the agreement between the university and the site in very general terms or it may specifically address training expectations, such as hours to be completed, activities to be included, and type and amount of supervision to be received. Your syllabus may also contain this type of information. If there is no contract or a general contract, the site supervisor must be made aware of any specific training requirements, and it would be appropriate to inquire of the faculty supervisor whether you or the faculty supervisor communicates this information and the preferred mechanism for that communication. If your faculty supervisor prefers a specific contract, it may take one of many forms. The content of a practicum contract varies by the goals of the contract. A sample of a basic contract that delineates what is expected of the faculty and site supervisors as well as the basic training requirements is provided as Appendix 1.1 at the end of this chapter. Some contracts include not only a list of responsibilities of each of the parties but also a list of practicum activities (Boylan et al., 1995). Other contracts may be focused on the learning goals of the student and the activities that will be used to meet those learning goals (Baird, 2005; Sweitzer & King, 2004). More than one contract can be used because your learning goals with the site supervisor may be different from your learning goals with the faculty supervisor. Regardless of its form, a contract can be a useful tool for clarifying expectations and decreasing misunderstandings.

Summary

- Your training needs should dictate the type of practicum site you choose. What resources are available to you to determine your training needs?
- The roles of practitioner and professional are new for most practicum students. What appeals to you about each role? What concerns do you have about adopting each role?
- Adapting to a new work environment takes considerable energy. How will you maximize your success in making that adaptation?
- What are your resources for dealing more effectively with diversity? Which resources are you most likely to use and why?
- The supervisory relationship is a major contributor to the learning experience. Which supervisor roles are the most important to you? Which supervisee roles will be easiest for you to fulfill? Which will be more challenging? Elaborate on your answers.
- What are the steps you might take in handling a conflict with your supervisor?
- What is most important to you in a practicum contract? Design a contract that includes these elements.

Additional Reading

Atkinson, D. R. (2004). *Counseling American minorities* (6th ed.). New York: McGraw-Hill.

Baird, B. N. (2005). *The internship, practicum, and field placement handbook: A guide for the helping professions* (4th ed.). Upper Saddle River, NJ: Prentice Hall.

Boylan, J. C., Malley, P. B., & Scott, J. (1995). *Practicum and internship: Textbook for counseling and psychotherapy* (2nd ed.). Philadelphia: Accelerated Development.

Faiver, C., Eisengart, S., & Colonna, R. (2004). *The counselor intern's handbook* (3rd ed.). Belmont, CA: Brooks/Cole.

Matthews, J. R., & Walker, C. E. (Eds.). (1997). *Basic skills and professional issues in clinical psychology*. Needham Heights, MA: Allyn & Bacon.

Sue, D. S., & Sue, D. (2002). *Counseling the culturally diverse: Theory and practice* (4th ed.). Hoboken, NJ: Wiley.

Sweitzer, H. F., & King, M. A. (2004). *The successful internship: Transfor-*

mation and empowerment in experiential learning (2nd ed.). Belmont, CA: Brooks/Cole.

Travers, P. (2002). *The counselor's helpdesk*. Belmont, CA: Brooks/Cole.

Woody, R. H. (1997). *Legally safe mental health practice*. Madison, CT: Psychosocial Press.

Appendix 1.1
Sample Practicum Contract

PRACTICUM CONTRACT FOR _____

_____ will need to obtain a minimum of XX hours of practicum experience and a minimum of XX hours of direct client contact. I would suggest that _____ obtain between XX–XX hours per week of practicum duties. I ask that all training experiences be provided in accord with the Ethics Code of the American Psychological Association located at www.apa.org/ethics. The site supervisor is asked to provide 30 minutes per week of individual or group supervision. The site supervisor is also asked to complete a set of evaluation forms at midterm and at the end of the semester to help _____ gauge his or her strengths and weaknesses and to assist with the assignment of a grade reflective of his or her performance. Toward that end, the site supervisor is asked to observe directly the work of the student at least once a week. I ask that the site supervisor review these evaluation forms with _____. The university provides (does not provide) liability coverage for student trainees. Dr. _____ can request a verification of coverage letter for your agency's records at your request.

I agree that I will be able to provide the practicum experience and supervision outlined in the practicum contract. If I am or my site is unable to meet these requirements, I agree to call Dr. _____ (faculty practicum supervisor) so that alternative arrangements may be made for the student. Dr. _____ agrees to provide the evaluation forms, group supervision, and verification of liability insurance as well as other types of institutional and training support that it is within his or her purview to provide.

_____

Signature of On-Site Supervisor

_____

Signature of Supervising Faculty Member

_____

Signature of Student

References

Atkinson, D. R. (2004). *Counseling American minorities* (6th ed.). New York: McGraw-Hill.

Baird, B. N. (2005). *The internship, practicum, and field placement handbook: A guide for the helping professions* (4th ed.). Upper Saddle River, NJ: Prentice Hall.

Berk, L. E. (2004). *Development through the lifespan* (3rd ed.). Boston: Pearson Education.

Boylan, J. C., Malley, P. B., & Scott, J. (1995). *Practicum and internship: Textbook for counseling and psychotherapy* (2nd ed.). Philadelphia: Accelerated Development.

Dana, R. H. (1993). *Multicultural assessment perspectives for professional psychology.* Needham Heights, MA: Allyn & Bacon.

Faiver, C., Eisengart, S., & Colonna, R. (2004). *The counselor intern's handbook* (3rd ed.). Belmont, CA: Brooks/Cole.

Ladany, N., Brittan-Powell, C. S., & Pannu, R. K. (1997). The influence of supervisory racial identity interaction and racial matching on the supervisory working alliance and supervisee multicultural competence. *Counselor Education and Supervision, 36,* 284–294.

Lamb, D. H., & Catanzaro, S. J. (1998). Sexual and nonsexual boundary violations involving psychologists, clients, supervisees, and students: Implications for professional practice. *Professional Psychology: Research and Practice, 29,* 498–503.

Lee, W. M. L. (1999). *An introduction to multicultural counseling.* Philadelphia: Accelerated Development.

Lopez, S. R. (1997). Cultural competence in psychotherapy: A guide for clinicians and their supervisors. In C. E. Watkins Jr. (Ed.), *Handbook of psychotherapy supervision* (pp. 570–588). New York: Wiley.

Nelson, M. L., & Friedlander, M. L. (2001). A close look at conflictual supervisory relationships: The trainee's perspective. *Journal of Counseling Psychology, 48,* 384–395.

Nelson, M. N., Gray, L. A., Friedlander, M. L., Ladany, N., & Walker, J. A. (2001). Toward relationship-centered supervision: Reply to Veach (2001) and Ellis (2001). *Journal of Counseling Psychology, 48,* 407–409.

Sigelman, C. K., & Rider, E. A. (2003). *Life-span human development* (4th ed.). Belmont, CA: Brooks/Cole.

Sweitzer, H. F., & King, M. A. (2004). *The successful internship: Transformation and empowerment in experiential learning* (2nd ed.). Belmont, CA: Brooks/Cole.

Veach, P. M. (2001). Conflict and counterproductivity in supervision—when relationships are less than ideal: Comment on Nelson and Friedlander (2001) and Gray et al. (2001). *Journal of Counseling Psychology, 48,* 396–400.

Wozencraft, T. A. (1997). Finding a training placement and making the transition from student to trainee. In J. R. Matthews & C. E. Walker (Eds.), *Basic skills and professional issues in clinical psychology* (pp. 13–38). Needham Heights, MA: Allyn & Bacon.

B. Max Price

Characteristics of a Helping Relationship

2

Getting Started

As a practicum student in psychology, you are likely to have many questions about this new experience: What am I expected to do in the practicum? What is my role as a practicum student? What type of clients will I be assigned? How can I be helpful to the clients? What should I do if such and such happens? What skills do I need to be an effective helper?

It is normal to have these kinds of questions and to feel anxious about what you are going to do. I can still remember my first practicum experiences: I was anxious to do good, I profited from good supervision and group discussion, and I learned a great deal from this hands-on experience.

You are not expected to attempt formal therapy sessions with patients. You are not expected to be a professional therapist. Your supervisor will help you define your role(s). You will likely be asked to spend time with a patient as a friend or companion. The basic skills needed to be an effective helper in an undergraduate practicum are similar to the skills needed to be effective in all helping relationships, including counseling.

In this chapter, I deal with the question of the basic skills necessary in helping relationships and give you guidance in improving your communication skills.

Definition of Helping

Carl Rogers, the father of client-centered therapy, gave this definition of a helping relationship: "By this term I mean a relationship in which at least one of the parties has the intent of promoting the growth, development, maturity, improved functioning, improved coping with the life of the other" (Rogers, 1958, p. 441). Rogers stated that his definition covered a wide range of relationships that usually are intended to facilitate growth. Examples of such relationships are parent and child, physician and patient, teacher and student, almost all counselor–client relationships.

Robert Carkhuff, the founder of the Carkhuff Helping Model, emphasizes interpersonal skills training as essential in becoming an effective helper. Carkhuff states, "The purpose of helping is to engage the helpee (person receiving help) in processes leading to human growth and development" (Carkhuff, 2002, p. 23). Both Carkhuff and Rogers emphasize helping as promoting and aiding growth.

In his skilled helper model, Gerard Egan calls for a basic, practical working model of helping. He declares, "Since all approaches must eventually help clients manage problems and develop unused resources, the model of choice is a flexible, humanistic, broadly-based problem-management and opportunity-development model" (Egan, 2002, p. 25). He further states that since problem management and opportunity development are embedded in all approaches to helping, the skilled helper model "provides an excellent foundation for any 'brand' of helping you eventually choose"(Egan, 2002, p. 25).

In *Helping Others Help Themselves: A Guide to Counseling Skills*, John Loughary and Theresa Ripley define helping as "providing purposeful assistance to other people which makes their lives more pleasant, easier, less frustrating, or in some other way, more satisfying. Most every relationship you have involves the opportunity for helping" (Loughary & Ripley, 1978, p. 1). Using this practical definition of helping, think of the different roles you have. Are you a friend? A brother or sister? Aunt or uncle? Daughter or son? Employer? Employee? Student? Supervisor? Roommate? Club member? Teammate? Lover? Other roles?

Doesn't each of your relationships involve assisting others? You are likely to provide help in several relationships and have daily opportunities to help. Loughary and Ripley (1978) described helping efforts as including informing people, making them feel better, listening to their problems, making suggestions, making arrangements, teaching, explaining, criticizing, and in other ways assisting them.

For you, the question is not, "Do you help?" but it is, "How effective is your helping?" You are likely to be better in particular areas of helping and with particular kinds of people. Some are better listeners. Some are better problem solvers. Some are better in practical actions.

PRACTICE EXPERIENCE

Think of two people that you consider as good helpers. What specific attitudes and actions do they display?

List:

GENERAL RECOMMENDATIONS FOR HELPING BEHAVIORS

1. DO practice empathic listening. Empathy involves listening to another person so that you accurately understand his or her thoughts and feelings. Attentive listening is a special gift to give another human being. Example: I have found that focusing all my attention to listen and try to understand Jimmy is the best helping behavior I can give him.

2. DO show positive regard for the other person. This means acceptance of the other person, valuing that person whether you like or agree with him or her. It also means wanting the best for that person. Example: Phil had an angry, sullen adolescent named Kent for his practicum assignment. Kent did not like counselors and stated his dislike clearly. Phil demonstrated positive regard by accepting Kent as a hurting, confused, and angry young man. He did not try to straighten out Kent. He did not react in anger or let his dislike of this teen's behavior keep him from accepting and caring for Kent.

3. DO be optimistic. This does not mean having a naïve, Pollyanna attitude about everything. It does mean looking for positive outcomes. It is seeing the glass half full not half empty. Positive thoughts and feelings will get you farther than negative thoughts and feelings. Example: Jill was struggling with a statistics course, her least favorite subject. Instead of saying, "I hate statistics; I'm not any good at it. I 'm gonna fail," Jill told herself, "I'm having a difficult time in this class,

but I am going to look at it as a challenge to be met." She took a positive approach of developing a plan of study that included getting help from other students.

4. DO be cheerful. Use humor and laughter based on the other person's responsiveness. Laughter truly is good medicine. Look for opportunities to smile and laugh with the other person during your practicum. Example: Bill took his practicum assignment seriously, but he found opportunity to laugh with Sarah while they were doing a craft project together.

5. DO show hope. Hope involves looking to the future, a belief that change can occur. Hope provides the motivation and energy to keep trying even in difficult circumstances. Example: From Example 2 above, practicum student Phil did not try to talk Kent out of his anger and despair. He did have hope that Kent's life could change, could get better. This hope helped Phil to have faith that he could make a difference in Kent's life.

6. DO give encouragement. Do point out skills, interests and strengths that you see in the other person. He or she may not be aware of these strengths, and your encouragement can make a difference. Teachers often make a huge impact on the lives of their students by being encouragers. Example: I had a teacher in college who told me I was a very good writer. I still remember his comment and his belief in me. It has given me confidence through the years to tackle numerous writing opportunities such as this chapter.

PRACTICE EXPERIENCE REVIEW

Review the above list of helping behaviors. What are your strength areas in helping?

List at least two:

What are helping behaviors you want to improve?

List at least two:

The Nature of Helping Relationships

The next step is to look at the nature of helping relationships that will assist you in your role as a practicum student helper.

HELPFUL VERSUS UNHELPFUL RELATIONSHIPS

Carl Rogers asked the question,

> What are the characteristics of those relationships which do help, which do facilitate growth? And at the other end of the scale is it possible to discern those characteristics which make a relationship unhelpful, even though it was sincere in intent to promote growth and development? (Rogers, 1958, p. 442)

Rogers (1958) cited a study by Heine (1950) that focused on how the person being helped perceived a relationship as being helpful or unhelpful. The subjects were clients who had received therapy from therapists with three different theoretical orientations: psychoanalytic, client centered, and Adlerian. Regardless of the type of therapy, the clients reported similar changes in themselves. Yet when asked what accounted for the changes they had made, the clients were in agreement on the counselor attitudes that they found helpful:

- the trust they felt in the therapist,
- being understood by the therapist, and
- the feeling of independence they had had in making choices and decisions.

The therapist procedure that they found most helpful was that the therapist clarified and openly stated feelings that the client had been approaching hazily and hesitantly.

The clients had a high degree of agreement as to which therapist attitudes they found unhelpful in the relationship. Unhelpful therapist attitudes reported were

- lack of interest,
- remoteness or distance, and
- overdegree of sympathy.

Unhelpful procedures reported included giving direct, specific advice regarding decisions or emphasizing past history rather than present problems.

Truax's studies (Truax & Carkfhuff, 1967) concluded that therapist empathy, genuineness (congruence), and warmth (positive regard) are crucial to the success of the psychotherapeutic relationship. Yet are these qualities important to success in other interpersonal contexts?

Support for these basic qualities was evident in a series of studies by Alsobrook (1962, 1967, 1969). Alsobrook constructed a scale to measure helpful versus unhelpful relationships. He labeled a person who helped his associates feel comfortable, work out their problems, and do their best as a health-engendering person (HEP). Alsobrook described a contrasting kind of person who makes people feel uncomfortable or defensive or causes them to do poorly (Alsobrook, 1962, p. 6). He called this individual a health-depressing person.

Alsobrook's scale measured the degree to which a person possessed a conscious and deliberate concern for the welfare of others, affectional warmth and liking for others, and trust in and belief in others (Newton & Krauss, 1973, p. 321). His studies found that HEPs had a positive impact on others in several relationships. Psychiatric patients assigned to psychiatric aides classified as health engendering improved more than patients assigned to health-depressing aides (Alsobrook, 1967). He also found that college students whose residence-hall roommates were high in health-engendering behavior made a better social and emotional adjustment to college than did students whose roommates scored low on the health-engendering scale.

Newton and Krauss (1973) found similar results in their study at the University of Georgia. They investigated the relationship between the academic and emotional adjustment of 992 freshmen women and the health-engendering behavior of their 32 resident assistants. Resident assistants were students who were in their sophomore year or above and hired to help new students adjust to their first year in college. Results were that freshmen assigned to resident assistants who rated low in health-engendering behavior manifested significantly inferior academic achievement when compared with freshmen assigned to residents of high or medium health-engendering behavior.

EFFECTIVE HELPER CHECKLIST

Loughary and Ripley (1978) described an effective helper as

> more often than not reasonably objective, self-confident and is a person who has developed purpose and direction in many areas of his or her own life. In addition, effective helpers are probably aware of and sensitive to how people react to them. (p. 24)

They said that you are likely an effective helper if you can give mostly positive answers to such questions as

- Can you express a genuine interest in other people?
- Can you listen to others express values contrary to your own without feeling defensive or resentful?
- Can you empathize with other people, that is, understand their feelings without feeling sorry for them?
- Can you usually refrain from giving unwanted or unasked-for advice?
- Can you communicate your displeasure regarding another person's behavior without becoming unpleasant yourself?
- Can you assert yourself without offending others or at least not be upset if they are offended?

Basic Helping Skills

Robert Carkhuff has been a leader in interpersonal skills models for more than 30 years. He has two decades of research in helping skills demonstrations. Carkhuff stated that "various helpers (parents, counselors, teachers, employers) do have constructive effects upon their helpees (children, counselees, students, employees) when trained in interpersonally based helping skills" (Carkhuff, 2002, p. 281). The Carkhuff helping model is presented in his book *The Art of Helping,* now in its eighth edition.

Carkhuff (2002) said,

> We have found that all helping and human relationships may be "for better or for worse." The effects depend upon the helper's level of skills in facilitating the helpee's movement through the helping process toward constructive helping outcomes. These helping skills constitute the core of all helping experiences. (p. 287)

Communication skills, facilitation skills, health-engendering skills, and helper skills all have in common an emphasis on the basic helping skills. Historically, it began with Carl Rogers' three "necessary and sufficient conditions" for change: empathy, unconditional positive regard, and genuineness (Rogers, Gendlin, Kiesler, & Truax, 1967). Carkhuff and Truax's research led them to operational definitions of "accurate empathy, respect and genuineness" (Carkhuff, 1969; Truax & Carkhuff, 1967).

The Carkhuff model (1983) defined helper skills as having two dimensions: responsive dimensions (empathy, respect, and specificity of expression) and initiative dimensions (genuineness, self-disclosure, confrontation, and immediacy and concreteness). The communication skills that I recommend you emphasize in your *helper* roles during your practicum experiences are empathy and respect and genuineness. These are the working definitions I use:

- Empathy is the accurate understanding of another person's thoughts and feelings and accurate feedback responses to that person without adding to or subtracting from the helpee's expression.
- Respect is the helper's communicating a deep respect (positive regard) for the helpee's feelings, experiences, and potentials.
- Genuineness is the helper's being congruent, honest, and sincere in his or her responses to the helpee. The helper's responses are sincere as expressed in words, tone of voice, emotions, body language, and actions.

LEARNING TO DISCRIMINATE BETWEEN HELPFUL AND UNHELPFUL RESPONSES

In *Helping and Human Relations*, Carkhuff (1969) described a ratings scale that he and his colleagues used in rating helper effectiveness. This scale was also used in training helpers to discriminate between effective and ineffective helper responses. In a description of his Gross Ratings of Facilitative Interpersonal Functioning, Carkhuff (1969) stated,

> The facilitator is a person who is living effectively himself and who discloses himself in a genuine and constructive fashion in response to others. He communicates an accurate empathic understanding and a respect for all of the feelings of other persons and guides discussions with those persons into specific feelings and experiences. He communicates confidence in what he is doing and is spontaneous and intense. In addition, while he is still open and flexible in his relations with others, in his commitment to the welfare of the other person he is quite capable of active, assertive and even confronting behavior when it is appropriate. (p. 115)

There are five levels of helper ratings on this 1–5 scale:

- Level 1: The helper responses are *unhelpful.*
- Level 2: The helper responses are *somewhat helpful.*
- Level 3: The helper responses are *more helpful than unhelpful.*
- Level 4: The helper responses are *almost always helpful.*
- Level 5: The helper responses are *always helpful.*

Here is one of Carkhuff's (1969) examples of an excerpt from a helpee in a therapy session followed by different levels of helper responses to illustrate the system for you:

> I don't know if I am right or wrong feeling the way I do. But I find myself withdrawing from people. I don't seem to socialize and play their stupid games any more. I get upset and come

home depressed and have headaches. It all seems so superficial. There was a time when I used to get along with everybody. Everybody said, "Isn't she wonderful. She gets along with everybody. Everybody likes her." I used to think that was something to be really proud of, but that was who I was at that time. I had no depth. I was what the crowd wanted me to be— the particular group I was with. (p. 115)

Consider how these four responses would rate on the 1–5 scale of helper responses described above:

1. Rating: Level 3 (*more helpful than unhelpful*). You know you have changed a lot. There are a lot of things you want to do but no longer can.
2. Rating: Level 4 (*almost always helpful*). You are damned sure who you can't be any longer but you are not sure who you are. Still hesitant as to who you are yet.
3. Rating: Level 1.5 (*unhelpful*). Who are these people that make you so angry? Why don't you tell them where to get off? They can't control your existence. You have to be your own person
4. Rating: Level 1.5 (*unhelpful*). So you have a social problem involving interpersonal difficulties with others. (Carkhuff, 1969, p. 116)

PRACTICE EXERCISE

Here is another example from Carkhuff's work. Read the helpee's statement below, and then give your rating of each of the four helper responses as *helpful* or *unhelpful*. Compare your ratings with the experts' ratings.

I get so frustrated and furious with my daughter. I just don't know what to do with her. She is bright and sensitive, but damn, she has some characteristics that make me so on edge. I can't handle it sometimes. She just—I feel myself getting more and more angry! She won't do what you tell her to. She tests limits like mad. I scream and yell and lose control and think there is something wrong with me—I'm not an understanding mother or something. Damn! What potential! What she could do with what she has. There are times she doesn't use what she's got. She gets by too cheaply. I just don't know what to do with her. Then she can be so nice and then, boy, she can be as ornery as she can be. And then I scream and yell and I'm about ready to slam her across the room. I don't like to feel this way. I don't know what to do with it.

Rate these four helper responses as *unhelpful* or *helpful* on a 1–5 scale.

1. So you find yourself screaming and yelling at your daughter more frequently during the past 3 months.

2. Why don't you try giving your daughter some very precise limitations. Tell her what you expect from her and you don't expect from her. No excuses.
3. While she frustrates the hell out of you, what you are really asking is, 'How can I help her? How can I help myself, particularly in relation to this kid?'
4. While she makes you very angry, you care what happens to her. (Carkhuff, 1969, pp. 118–119)

Now let's see how experts rated these responses. Response 1 was rated at 1.0—*unhelpful*. Response 2 was also rated *unhelpful* at 1.5. Response 3 was rated *very helpful* at 4.0. Response 4 was also rated *helpful* at 3.0. Think about possible reasons these responses were rated the way they were.

In my doctoral dissertation (Price, 1975), I studied how medium or low facilitation (communication) levels affect counselors' influence in getting helpees to change their opinion of themselves on a personality rating scale. I used the Carkhuff global rating scale as described above. I used expert raters to sample audiotapes of 20-minute interviews between interviewers and college student subjects. The expert ratings placed the interviewers (helpers) in two groups: low facilitation skills group of a 1.96 average rating score and a medium facilitation skills group with a 2.41 average rating score. The medium facilitation skills interviewers (helpers) did have more influence in changing subjects' (helpees) self-ratings. My conclusions from this doctoral dissertation and research of other facilitation skills studies are

1. Facilitation skills as defined and rated by Carkhuff and his associates are necessary characteristics of helping relationships, especially in counselor–client relationships.
2. Empathic understanding, genuineness, and respect are necessary characteristics of a helping relationship.

In his book *The Art of Helping in the 21st Century*, Robert Carkhuff (2002) stressed the great need for basic helping skills in the 21st century.

> The basic tenet of the Age of Information is interdependency. This means that we are each dependent upon the other. In this context, the basic helping skills in the Age of Information remain the interpersonal processing skills or helping skills. They enable a person to relate to the experience of others. Interpersonal processing skills include attending skills to involve the helpees in the helping process. Responding skills facilitate exploring by the helpees. (pp. 37–38)

What are the specific responding attitudes and behaviors that will make a difference in practicum students' effectiveness in their practicum roles as friend, companion, health-engendering person, and helper? Attending and responding are two basic skills that will make a difference and are the two helping skills that I recommend and emphasize. Both the Carkhuff model and Gerard Egan's (2002) skilled helper model provide step-by-step, systematic training in helping skills.

Egan (1975, 2002) said that helping is an art and demands practice on the part of the trainee. You can improve your helping ability through practice in the basic helper skills of attending and responding. Both Egan's and Carkhuff's models are similar in emphasis on and training procedures in these two areas.

The first phase is called *prehelping* and involves attending. The first step is attend physically. The next step is attend psychologically.

Attending physically means to give the other person your full and undivided attention. It is focusing on that person. Egan (1975, p. 10) lists the basic elements of physical attending:

- S: face the other person Squarely.
- O: adopt an Open posture.
- L: Lean toward the other.
- E: keep good Eye contact.
- R: try to be "at home" or relatively Relaxed in this position.

I discuss attending psychologically in the following section.

PRACTICE EXERCISE—ATTENDING

Choose a partner and take turns practicing the attending physically skill. Choose a topic such as your thoughts about a practicum. As the helper, take 4 minutes of attending to your partner. Ask that person to give you feedback as to how well you did the SOLER behavior. Reverse roles and repeat the process with you as the helpee.

Physical attending has two functions: (a) It is a sign to the other person that you are actively present and working with him or her. (b) It helps you to be an active listener, that is, to psychologically attend.

What about attending psychologically? Carkhuff stated that observing skills are the most basic helping skills. They involve the helper's ability to see and to understand the nonverbal behavior of the helpee. The helper observes aspects of the helpee's appearance and behavior that help us to infer the helpee's physical energy level, emotional feeling state, and intellectual readiness for helping. These references are the basis for the helper's initial understanding of where the helpee is coming from—attending psychologically (Carkhuff, 2002, p. 71).

Active listening involves attending to both the verbal and nonverbal communication of the other person. Observing and listening to the other person can be quite difficult. The process requires concentration on the other person and suspending your own opinions and judgments.

Your attention is one of the most helpful tools you have. Giving another person the gift of your full attentions is powerful; it is often a rare experience for another person.

A beginning active-listening behavior of attending to verbal messages is developing the ability to repeat back to the speaker what he or she has said to you. It is a beginning step in learning to communicate accurate empathy.

PRACTICE EXERCISE—RESPONDING

Choose a group of three people: a communicator (speaker), a listener, and an observer. The speaker makes a statement about him- or herself but limits it to two sentences in length. The listener repeats the substance of what the speaker said using the formula of "You said that." The observer gives the listener feedback as to her accuracy. Repeat the process until each person has practiced being a listener.

Attending is called the Prehelping Phase by Carkhuff and Egan. Phase 1 is Responding: Respond to the content of what the helpee said by reflecting or communicating back to the helpee what he or she is talking about. Respond to the affect involved by reflecting how the helpee feels about what he or she is saying. Finally, the helper puts the feeling and content together in a response that reflects the meaning of the helpee's experiences. This is accurate empathy. When accurate empathy is provided, the helper's responses will facilitate further exploration of experiences by the helpees (Carkhuff, 2002, p. 42).

PRACTICE EXERCISES IN COMMUNICATING ACCURATE EMPATHY

In initial training in empathic understanding, beginning helpers are trained to use the formulas "You feel _____" and "You feel _____ because _____." Later, they learn to translate these stylized formulas into more natural language—their language.

The following exercises are excerpts from Egan's *Skilled Helper* training manual (1975). They provide you with some practical examples of training in primary-level accurate empathy:

Exercise A: The Accurate Communication of Feeling and Content (One Emotion)

Read the following statements, imagining that the person is speaking directly to you. Respond with primary-level empathy, first by using the formula "You feel _____ because _____." Then formulate a response that includes understanding of both feeling and content, stated in your own language and style as shown in the example that follows.

Law student to school counselor: "I learned yesterday that I've flunked out of school and that there's no recourse. I've seen everybody, but the door is shut tight. What a mess! I have no idea how I'll face my parents. They've paid for my college education and this year of law school. And now I'll have to tell them that it's all down the drain."

Formula response: "You feel awful—helpless, because you've been dropped from school and ashamed because you've let your parents down."

Response in helper's own language: "Your world has come crashing down. It's really painful to be dropped from school, but maybe it's even more painful to face your parents with the fact, after all they've done for you" (Egan, 1975, pp. 49–50).

Practice Example

Read the following example taken from Egan's manual. Take the role of helper and write two empathy responses, one using "You feel _____ because _____" and the second conveying accurate understanding using your natural language.

College student to a counselor: "Last year I was drinking heavily and playing around with drugs. I had to drop three courses and almost ended up on probation. And today, it's practically the opposite. I woke up in my own vomit one morning and said, 'God, this can't go on—I'm killing myself.' Nobody lectured me, nobody pushed me. I began making the right kind of friends. And I pulled myself out of the muck" (Egan, 1975, p. 50).

First response (using "you feel _____ because _____"
formula).

Second response (using your more natural style).

Two possible responses are given below. Compare these with your responses.

1. You feel proud of yourself and your initiative because you were smart enough to get hold of yourself before it was too late.
2. It's great to look back and see that you practically lifted yourself up by your own bootstraps—you were in the pit one year and riding high the next. (Egan, 1975, p.104)

Egan's helping-skills training manual provides systematic training exercises that progress from primary accurate empathy to advanced accurate empathy and checklists on genuineness and respect.

Helping Applied to All Stages of Life: Childhood, Adolescence, Adulthood, and Geriatric Years

The basic helping skills apply to all ages and cultures, but the application of attending, empathic understanding, genuineness and respect do vary based on the developmental level and specific environment of the person.

If your practicum assignment is with preschool or elementary age children, your helping will likely need to include play. Play is the language of children and toys are their words. Attending to a child involves activities that they enjoy. When you let a child choose a play activity, you are participating in the best stress management technique that children have, and that most adults have also. Eye contact tends to be intermittent with children, but they are aware if you are noticing them and giving them your undivided attention.

Your nonverbal behavior will be an important part of your helping with children. Communicate your caring by paying attention to the child; noticing his or her moods; and taking cues from his or her responses to talk or not talk; to include you in his or her activity; or to set boundaries and want you to be an observer before he or she accepts you on his or her own timetable. Learn to be comfortable with periods of silence. Learn to listen and understand the child or teen who doesn't want to talk. Some children feel freer to talk while you walk with them than when confined to an office setting.

Responding behavior with children and adolescents may be concrete actions such as walking, playing catch, offering a snack, repairing a possession, helping with a math problem, or answering a specific question.

Helping adolescents requires flexibility. You may be assigned a very verbal adolescent who enjoys the opportunity to have you listen to him or her. You may have a sullen, angry, depressed, withdrawn young person who will not want to see you and refuse to talk to you. You can still practice attending and responding with an unresponsive teen. He or she is most likely to respond to your showing respect and caring and to your being genuine in your talk and actions. Try to discover his or her interests. Your supervisor will likely be able to provide you some background information that will help you understand the child or adolescent to whom you are assigned.

Most adults will respond to having someone to talk with. Yet some adults are uncomfortable just sitting and talking. They respond better to doing something with you, such as playing a table game, participating in an art or music activity, doing a practical activity, or eating a snack.

Adults with limited intellectual ability need conversations that are at the concrete level. They can talk about their feelings as being happy, sad, mad, or afraid, but they will likely talk about an exact event regarding their feeling. They, like children, will have a hard time generalizing your help to other situations. They are not likely to apply what they have done with you to another situation, even if it is very similar. No matter what adult you work with, being a friend or companion to that adult can be a helpful part of his or her care.

Seek to know adults. Become as familiar as possible with the person's social and religious culture, customs, and traditions. Try to adapt your attending to the behaviors that your helpee is comfortable with. Observe the nonverbal adult. If you attempt conversation with a nonverbal person who acts uncomfortable and rejects your well-intentioned helping efforts, wait for him or her to begin talking or responding to your presence.

With geriatric clients you are likely to find a positive response to your one-on-one time with them. Loneliness and sadness are common experiences for elderly adults who have lost family members and have lost some control over their lives. If an elderly adult lives in a nursing facility or other institution, he or she has lost much privacy. Seek background information from staff or supervisor to determine the person's mental state. If your geriatric clients have significant memory loss with dementia or Alzheimer's disease, he or she will need special care. If a client begins to talk about something in his or her past as if it is happening right now, don't argue or correct. An example is an 85-year-old woman who says to you, "I'm going to find my baby. She's lost and she needs me." I recommend an empathy response such as, "You really miss your baby." Going along with her confused state is more likely to calm her than correcting her with a statement such as, "There aren't any babies here. Your daughter is grown up and can take care of herself." Validation therapy states that going along with the person's delusions or unrealistic statements tends to calm a person much faster than trying to get them "back to reality." Validating a geriatric client's delusions tends to foster cooperation with present programming faster than correcting the person.

If you are assigned to work with persons with mental illness or a mental handicap and you have had no previous experience with such clients, you are likely to be anxious and uncomfortable being around them. Ask you supervisor if you need direction and support. Above all, treat the client with respect and concern. Try to understand the world from that person's viewpoint.

Summary

Characteristics of a helping relationship consist of personality attitudes that you possess to some degree. Helping skills can also be learned. The basic helping skills of attending, empathic understanding, genuineness, and respect have been identified and researched for more than 30 years beginning with Rogers, Truax, Carkhuff, Egan, and other client-centered practitioners. Carkhuff and Egan have developed systematic helping-skills training models that are based on sound research. Carkhuff (1983) summarized research of helping-skills demonstrations over two decades. A total of 164 studies were reported with 158,940 participants. Carkhuff reported that the effect of trained helpers on helpees was 96% positive (2002, pp. 281–282).

The helping-skills models of Carkhuff and Egan have application for helpers in many situations: teacher–student, parent–child, employers–employees, counselor–client, and practicum students in their various helping roles. Providing cheerfulness, optimism, encouragement, and hope are also significant helping behaviors. If you provide these helping skills in your practicum, you are likely to do good and to do no harm.

Have a helping practicum.

References

Alsobrook, J. M. (1962). *A study of health-engendering-people in a campus community*. Unpublished doctoral dissertation, University of Florida, Gainesville.

Alsobrook, J. M. (1967, September). *Health-engendering aides for psychiatric patients: Implications for therapeutic milieu*. Paper presented at the 75th Annual Convention of the American Psychological Association, Washington, DC.

Alsobrook, J. M. (1969). *Effects of college student interaction upon learning and adjustment*. (USOE Project No. 5-0906). Athens: University of Georgia, Department of Psychology.

Carkhuff, R. R. (1969). *Helping and human relations* (Vol. 1). New York: Holt.

Carkhuff, R. R. (1983). *The art of helping* (5th ed.). Amherst, MA: Human Resource Development Press.

Carkhuff, R. R. (2002). *The art of helping in the 21st century* (8th ed.). Amherst, MA: Human Resource Development Press.

Egan, G. (1975). *Exercises in helping skills*. Monterey, CA: Brooks/Cole.

Egan, G. (2002). *The skilled helper* (7th ed.). Monterey, CA: Brooks/Cole.

Heine, R. W. (1950). *A comparison of patients' reports on psychotherapeutic experience with psychoanalytic, nondirective, and Adlerian therapists*. Unpublished doctoral dissertation, University of Chicago.

Loughary, J. W., & Ripley, T. M. (1978). *Helping others help themselves: A guide to counseling skills*. New York: McGraw-Hill.

Newton, M., & Krauss, H. H. (1973, July). The health-engenderingness of resident assistants as related to student achievement and adjustment. *Journal of College Student Personnel, 14*, 321–325.

Price, M. (1975). *Facilitation, expertness, and influence in counseling*. Unpublished doctoral dissertation, University of Oklahoma, Norman.

Rogers, C. R. (1958). The characteristics of a helping relationship. *Personnel and Guidance Journal, 37*, 6–16.

Rogers, C. R., Gendlin, E. T., Kiesler, D., & Truax, C. B. (1967). *The therapeutic relationship and its impact*. Madison: University of Wisconsin Press.

Truax, C. B., & Carkhuff, R. R. (1967). *Toward effective counseling and psychotherapy*. Chicago: Aldine.

Janet R. Matthews and Lee H. Matthews

Getting Started and Developing Rapport

3

When students are preparing to have their first experience in the "real world" rather than in the classroom, they often have questions about how to relate to the people in such a setting. In this chapter, we discuss issues that arise when you interact with supervisors, staff, and patients or clients in applied settings and provide some suggestions about how to address these issues. This chapter is not intended to make you an expert in interviewing or psychotherapy because you will not actually be doing psychotherapy, but it should help you enter the applied world.

First Impressions

In social settings, people are often concerned about the first impression they make. Think about how parents prepare their children for the first day of school. Part of that preparation involves the impression they may make on the teacher and their classmates. The literature in psychology suggests that once a person forms an opinion about someone, he or she often uses that information to selectively attend to future behavior by that person. People tend to remember those actions that fit their impression of that individual and discount those that do not. This information can also be applied to how you are perceived at your placement site. Thus, talking to other students from your program who have previously had a placement at your site before your first day there can provide useful information about what to expect.

WHAT SHOULD I WEAR?

A common question field placement students ask is, "What should I wear to the placement?" For your initial visit to the facility, it is probably best to dress as you would for a job interview. By this, we mean that you should take care in terms of both your personal hygiene and the type of clothing you select. During this initial visit, ask your site supervisor about the recommended form of dress for that particular facility. Some facilities have specific dress codes for all people on their campus, whereas others leave this decision to individual supervisors to monitor their staff. As an example, in almost all psychiatric and hospital settings, wearing "open-toe" shoes (sandals) is not allowed. Likewise T-shirts with writing such as beer slogans or names of rock groups are generally not permitted. Students who are placed in settings where they will be interacting with young children may find that they are asked to dress in more casual clothing than those students who are placed on an adult inpatient psychiatric ward, and those students in private practice offices or in court-related facilities may need to "dress up" more than one normally would for school. If you will be crawling on the ground with young children, for example, and you are female, wearing a dress and nylons is probably not a practical option. However, wearing clothing that could encourage provocative responses from the clients, regardless of how "good" that clothing may be, is also inappropriate. To learn about the appropriate clothing for your site, it is best to schedule a brief visit prior to the day you will actually start your placement and discuss this issue with the site supervisor.

A special issue that we have noted in a number of facilities is body piercings. Some facilities have rules prohibiting visible attachments to the body and require that they be removed during time spent at the facility. Depending on the location and recency of the piercing, you may need to cover the area from which the object was removed with a Band-Aid while at the placement. It is important if you have elected to have piercings to understand that such rules are not personal but rather apply to everyone who works in that facility. Students on field placement usually are required to follow all such rules.

Who Are All These People?

Your experience at the placement site is likely to bring you into contact with people from a variety of disciplines who are responsible to an organizational structure or "chain of command" in the same way that your professors are responsible to the department chair and the chair to the dean. During your initial meeting with your site supervisor, take written notes about the people with whom you will be interacting on a regular basis. In our experience, most site supervisors will give you this information at a first meeting, but if you are not prepared to take notes, sometimes it takes awhile to "catch on" to the organizational structure. If your supervisor does not discuss the people you will be interacting with at the facility during your first meeting, ask about this topic.

Lines of authority are often convoluted. As an example of why it is important to have this information, here is a description of one site placement on an adult inpatient unit. The student interacted with all of the following professionals. A psychiatrist was the administrative physician (sometimes called the medical director) for the unit and was responsible for the psychiatric care and overall administration of the unit. There was a program director and a social worker (board-certified social worker or BCSW) who provided supervision of the two social workers on the unit, although these people reported on a daily basis to the unit nursing director. The unit nursing director (sometimes the title is charge nurse) was a registered nurse (RN, usually with a bachelor's degree in nursing) who was responsible for the supervision of the shift nurses who could be either RNs or licensed practical nurses (LPNs). In addition there were two or three unit psychiatric technicians (techs) who had a high school education. The three directors made up the administrative team for the unit. However, the administrative director reported to the medical director of the hospital; the charge nurse reported to the director of nursing of the hospital; and the program director was responsible to the director of social work for the hospital.

In other disciplines, students had regular assignments on the unit but were supervised by someone at the hospital level. For example, the creative arts therapist (CAT) worked with five groups on the unit during the week (which the student attended on the days that she was there) and with other CAT staff on a rotating monthly schedule to cover the weekends. Depending on the facility, a clinical psychologist (at the doctoral level) may be a part-time consultant, assigned to do only psychological assessment and behavioral interventions and to attend treatment team meetings. In such cases, the psychologist will be responsible to the chief psychologist at the hospital level. At other sites, there may be a full-time psychologist who is involved in the activities noted above as well as doing group or individual psychotherapy. In this situation, the psychologist may have split responsibility, with duties assigned, in part, by the program director. In our example, the site supervisor for the student was a clinical psychologist assigned part time to the unit, and because of this schedule, the student spent some of her time working with the other professionals. Because this student might need approval to participate in specific activities from any of these staff members, it was important for her to understand their interrelationships.

How Do I Build Rapport?

Although there is no list of techniques we can give you about how to establish rapport with every client or patient, we can provide some general principles (Plante, 1999). Many students who elect to take a field placement course have previously been told they are good listeners or that it is easy to talk to them. If this is typical of you, you have already taken the first step toward establishing rapport. *Rapport* is a term often used by applied psychologists to describe the establishment of a positive relationship with their patients. It is the development of interactions that are trusting, accepting, respectful, and helpful. According to Wierzbicki (1999), rapport is "the quality of an interpersonal relationship considered to be an important factor in psychotherapy outcome" (p. 372).

First, be attentive. Reduce distractions whenever possible. Allow enough time for the person to answer a question before moving to another topic and follow up with additional comments or questions that indicate you are listening.

Second, nonverbal cues give much useful information. Attend to posture. This refers to both your own and the patient's. The amount of eye contact you have is important. Notice "how" statements are made. The person who says "I am not angry" in a loud voice with arms crossed and teeth clenched may not be in touch with his or her own feelings. Even where you sit is important. For example, when you are talking or interviewing in a room, try to sit so that you do not block the exit from the room. It is better if the person who gets upset can leave through the door rather than through you and then through the door.

Third, be nonjudgmental. Show respect, acceptance, and empathy. Do not be critical. Do not be either a "know-it-all" or a "friend." Try to be warm and supportive.

Fourth, be an active listener. Ask open-ended questions, not questions requiring only a *yes* or *no* answer. Ask questions that require some detail to answer. Asking questions about what brought the person to the program, how often or how long the person has had a specific difficulty or problem, what the person thinks caused the difficulty and what he or she has tried to do to cope are all ways to gain information. Ask questions to clarify or fill in gaps. Use paraphrasing or briefly summarize what was said to you to ensure understanding and build rapport. It is important for all parties concerned to have an understanding about such factors as confidentiality, the purpose of the student's placement, and how often the student can be expected to be available to visit the placement site.

Privacy and Confidentiality

The interactions you have in applied settings are very different from conversations you have with your friends. When talking to your friends, you may expect that what is said is private and not to be repeated to anyone. In applied settings, however, this expectation of privacy is a requirement. Many facilities require students to sign a confidentiality statement. Rules of confidentiality are influenced not only by the specific facility but also by federal legislation. The Health Insurance Portability and Accountability Act of 2003 (HIPAA), promulgated by the U.S. Department of Health and Human Services, has a Privacy Rule that includes the fact that people working for psychologists should only be given enough information to do their jobs. As a student in the role of assisting a mental health professional, this rule also applies to you. Additional information about issues of confidentiality as well as other ethical issues is covered in greater depth in chapter 4.

Friends may tell you truly personal information. It is likely, however, that they have thought about it before talking to you. By contrast, some of what you hear at the placement may be material the person has never said out loud before. Likewise, when you talk with (or interview) a client or patient for the first time, there are likely to be some distortions or withheld information. This is to be expected, as it is not usual for "strangers" to openly discuss thoughts and intimate details. People in emotional crisis often display patterns of behavior that are exaggerations of their usual modes of interacting. Ask yourself questions such as "Does the person seem unusually dependent?" "Is the person's approach suspicious or surly?" "Is there an element of seductiveness or provocation?" "Is the person tearful, sarcastic, or overly happy even when discussing extremely stressful information?"

What Is Interviewing?

In basic terms, an interview is a conversation with a purpose or goal (Matarazzo, 1965). Interviewing is a skill that requires practice and careful supervision to learn.

The most common form of clinical interview is an initial assessment when a client or patient comes to the clinician because of some problem in daily functioning. Patterned after the question-and-answer format used in traditional medical history taking, such psychological or psychiatric interviews are usually structured according to a sequence of important topics. Hersen and Turner (1985) noted that interviews designed to classify client problems are most common in mental health settings where a diagnosis is required. Interviews focusing on describing clients and their problems in more comprehensive terms usually occur within the context of a full-scale clinical exploration that precedes treatment (Helzer, 1983).

In recent years, the major developments in psychological interviewing have been on structured and semistructured interviews. The terms *structured* and *semistructured* refer to the degree to which the interviewer determines the direction of the clinical interview. The structured interview involves using a format with carefully planned questions. The semistructured interview, however, has a predetermined set of topics to be covered, but the interviewer has more flexibility about how the topics are covered. This trend can be traced to several sources, including the increased reliance on procedures using operationally defined criteria for making psychiatric diagnoses. Such techniques, originally developed to gain epidemiological information, involve having the interviewer ask specific questions that can be replicated by other interviewers. Structured interviews do not eliminate open-ended questions, nor do they prevent interviewers from asking their own additional questions to clarify responses. However, they do provide detailed rules, sometimes called *decision trees,* for informing the interviewer what to do in the event of certain responses. For example, if a client answers *no* to a basic question about some class of feelings or behaviors associated with anxiety, rather than continue with that list, the examiner would move on to another problem area, such as questions on depression. Chapter 7 provides information about additional types of interview techniques.

Being a
Participant-Observer

In most undergraduate classes, students have a well-defined role. They are there to learn. Expectations may include taking notes, responding to questions from the professor, and participating in class discussions. The role of the student at a field placement site may not be as well defined. You are less likely to have a syllabus summarizing this activity than you have for other courses you take. Are you just supposed to observe or are you also expected to participate? If you participate, to what degree do you do so? These are questions to ask your campus professor as well as the site supervisor.

To illustrate these issues, we describe a couple of the sites we use at Loyola University in New Orleans. One placement site is a substance abuse inpatient program of a private psychiatric hospital. In this setting, the field placement student attends unit staff meetings, participates in some therapy groups, and spends time on the unit with or without the psychiatric techs when the patients are at leisure. What is the student's role in each activities? One goal for this specific placement is for the student to become comfortable doing the tech's duties. Most of our students find that initially they are quite uncomfortable in all of these activities. They are unsure about what to say and may not feel they have the background to contribute. Initially, their role tends to be that of observer in these activities. Over time, however, they begin to participate. In staff meetings, they may continue to just observe unless one of the staff members specifically asks them questions about an individual.

In various creative arts therapy activities, however, the students may participate equally with the therapist and patients. In this case, the students may provide some personal information but should still remember that they are not there to receive treatment.

At this site, students also assist the therapist in some of the educational therapy groups. In this case, they may do reading about a topic or assist in a group activity. They may even be given readings by one of the staff members and subsequently lead a group discussion about that subject. As a participant-observer they may discuss some of their own background but must be careful to maintain appropriate distance.

Before providing personal information, students should learn about the policies of the facility on self-disclosure. Some facilities, for example, issue name badges to all staff and students. These badges may have the person's full name or only his or her first name. In the latter case, the facility may have a policy that staff members do not disclose their full names to the patients. If someone asks you a personal question and you are either uncomfortable revealing the answer or are not sure about agency policy about self-disclosure, you should check with your supervisor before providing the information. In the immediate circumstance, it is best to just indicate that you are uncomfortable with that question and want to think about why you are not comfortable before answering the question. By saying that, you are acknowledging the person's question and explaining why you will not answer it at that specific time.

In other placements, the student's role may focus more on being an observer. At an outpatient program specializing in abused and neglected children, for example, students have learned to use a standardized observational checklist. Along with staff members from that program, students observe children and their parents or foster parents. Some of this observation is done from behind a one-way window with the adult and child in an observation room. The students' observations are then compared with those of the regular staff members. At other times, students observe at daycare facilities and in the person's home.

Issues that arise when serving as a participant-observer may vary depending on the patient group. Undergraduate students who are placed with adolescents may find it more difficult to maintain distance because they are so close in age and identify so closely with the issues being discussed. Depending on the age and physical development of the student some adolescents may relate to them as peers rather than as representatives of the staff. Students placed with adults may find that the adults treat them like their children rather than as students or staff aides. It is important in this case for the students to let the patients know why they are participating in the program. Students may acknowledge that the adult has more life experiences than they have but add that they would like to learn.

What Should I Say at the First Session?

The degree of interaction students have with clients or patients will vary considerably among facilities. In some settings the student will always be accompanied by a staff member, whereas in others, the student may have times when he or she is talking individually with someone such as a patient on an inpatient psychiatric unit or a child on a playground. Although there will be a number of staff members in the vicinity, the conversation may be, to a great extent, private. It is important to approach the person with respect. Let this person know who you are and what your role is at the facility. Indicate that you are a student who will be spending time there and specify how often and for how long you will do so. For example, you might say that you are a senior psychology major from Local University working with Dr. Psychologist. You are taking a university course you hope will help you select an appropriate career. You will be spending 10 hours each week for the next three months at this facility. You plan to be there on Tuesdays and Thursdays from 10:00 to 3:00.

Also, talk briefly about confidentiality and the limits of confidentiality. That is, explain that whatever the individual tells you will not be repeated outside the facility. For that matter, you will not even acknowledge to anyone not connected with the person's treatment in the facility that he or she is even there. However, you may discuss information that you learn with your immediate supervisor, and you have a duty to report to your supervisor if the person tells you anything indicating danger to him- or herself or to another person. Explain that you would like to talk to with him or her and learn more about him or her. Then ask if you may talk for awhile. Then begin to have a conversation. If the person indicates that he or she does not want to talk to you, do not take it personally. Ask your supervisor whether you should pursue conversation with individuals who say no.

Starting and Maintaining Conversation

Once you start talking to a client or patient, remember what you have learned about rapport and interviewing. It is natural to be somewhat anxious in this situation. Some people speak rapidly when they are nervous. Pay attention to the speed of your speech. It is easy to overwhelm the person by speaking too fast. Related to rapid speech is asking the person multiple questions without giving him or her a chance to respond. All this is likely to do is confuse the person about what you have said. It may also cause a person who was reluctant to talk to you to decide that decision was a good one and just walk away from you. Although you may be truly interested in learning about this person, do not make the conversation seem like an interrogation. Asking one question after another without any general discussion is likely to lead to a very short conversation. Be aware of both verbal and nonverbal signs that the person is not comfortable. Suppose a person who was sitting quietly and talking to you begins to move around in the chair? You might say, "I notice that you are moving around a bit. Are you uncomfortable with the topic of our conversation right now?"

How you start and continue a conversation will be strongly influenced by the characteristics of the patient. When you are talking to a shy person at your placement, it is really not that different from talking to a shy person anywhere. Maintaining good eye contact and using both a tone of voice and facial expression that indicate your interest in what the person is saying to you can encourage further discussion. With some people, leaning toward them to show you are listening to what they are saying will also be helpful. All of these suggestions, however, are influenced by the culture from which both you and this person come. For example, personal space needs may vary across both cultures and generations. Looking directly at a person is viewed positively in some cultures and negatively in others. A tone of voice you intend to be soft and supportive may have a different meaning to the person than it does to you. Although it is important to consider cultural factors, you should not try to be something you are not. For example, do not try to adopt slang that is not part of your regular speech. However, if you are talking to a senior citizen with a sixth-grade education who is in the early stages of Alzheimer's Disease, you do not want to demonstrate your ability to use five- and six-syllable words. Treat this person with respect but also try to speak in a way that maximizes understanding. If you do not know anything about the culture from which a person comes, you may want to discuss this with your supervisor and do some independent reading before the next time you visit the facility (e.g., Sue & Sue, 2003). Knowledge of these factors will assist you in establishing rapport not only with people at the field placement but also, new people you meet elsewhere.

When a patient asks you a question, do not assume you know why that question was asked or that your initial understanding of that question is correct. For example, suppose you are talking to a person who has a 10-year history of alcohol abuse. After you have introduced yourself to him, he says, "How can you help me when you aren't even old enough to legally buy a drink?" This comment might indicate that this man believes only people who have a history of drinking can help someone who is an alcoholic. It could also indicate that his style of interacting with people is to take control of the conversation, and this comment is his attempt to show who is in change of the interaction. It could indicate that he is sincerely interested in receiving help in the program and wants to get that help from the most qualified person. You are not expected to be a mind reader and know what he means at this point. The main concern you have is not to become defensive about your age or level of experience. Let him know that you realize it is important to him to know how you might assist his recovery. From that point you might then let him know that you are there to learn and to listen. Perhaps over time you will find that some of your life experiences may be useful to him or that just having someone who wants to listen will help him progress through the program. How you interact with clients or patients at your placement will also be related to the instructions you have received from your faculty sponsor as well as site supervisor. On some campuses, your will have been told that your role is to be a companion to the individuals and that you are only there to add to the milieu. In other cases, you will have a paraprofessional role similar to the aides in the program. Make sure that you clarify your role before talking to the program participants.

As you can see, getting the patient to accept you can be difficult. One suggestion that may help is to try to think about this situation from the patient's perspective (Sweitzer & King, 2004). If you have access to the person's records, you may want to read them for background. For example, has this person had a history of prior treatment that was not successful? If so, it is not surprising if the person is a bit skeptical that this program will be any better than the others were. If this is the first time this person has been in this type of program, he or she may be feeling uncomfortable with the loss of control or the suggestion that personal issues be discussed with strangers (Royce, Dhooper, & Rompf, 2003). Schmidt (2002) suggested that a major challenge for students in applied settings is to be able to enter, but not become lost in, the world of the people with whom they interact. Part of this process is for you to be able to view the world from the perspective of the other person without feeling you must accept that world view. If a person has had experiences that are similar to those in your own life, you may find you are reliving your own experiences and making assumptions about those of the patient. In other cases, called overidentification, you become so involved in a person's feelings and reactions that you actually *need* to have the person improve. It is important to know if you have crossed this line of overidentification so that you can then develop some emotional distance from the person. This skill is useful not only at your field placement but in many other life circumstances.

How to Foster Acceptance

Your ability to accept the people with whom you are working at your placement site is just as important as their acceptance of you. Sweitzer and King (2004) found that students who are just beginning the practical part of their training may experience negative reactions to individuals who lie to them, manipulate them to get something, always seem to need more than the student can give them, become verbally abusive or threatening to the student, blame everyone but themselves for their problems, give only one word answers to questions, reject all suggestions made to them, refuse to see their behavior as problematic, make it obvious they don't like the student, or refuse to work with the student. We discuss some of these issues here and refer interested students to the additional reading section at the end of the chapter for more information.

What about the patient who has a history of aggressive behavior? Although there is a low probability of field placement students being victims of aggressive behavior, it is important to keep this history in mind. Facilities accepting field placement students often require them to complete some form of orientation. This orientation process is likely to include information about how to deal with hostile behavior or a sense of feeling threatened if this is something often experienced there. If a person at your placement tells you, "I don't want to talk to you any more; you are making me angry," take that person at his or her word. If you need to move away from the situation, it is always a good idea to back away, facing the person as you leave the area. Children are less likely than adults to give you a verbal clue that it is time to stop interacting with them. With children, the first indication you may have that the child is unhappy with you is when the child attempts to hit or kick you. Fortunately, you are usually larger than the child. You may be able to use that size differential to convince the child to cease this behavior. If you cannot move away or verbally convince the child to stop, you will need to get help from the staff. There are legal liability issues if you touch the child. Even if you think you would not hurt yourself or the child, do not attempt restraint. This warning does not mean that students should only interact with a select portion of the people at their placement. Just as you would when walking through a questionable neighborhood, be aware of signs of difficulty.

Another issue can arise when talking to people at your placement if a person shows signs of being delusional or experiencing hallucinations. Delusional thinking may influence what this person says to you. If the information does not make sense to you, you may ask the person to repeat something but do not continue to do this if the conversation continues in a confusing direction. Repeatedly asking the person to clarify statements is likely to lead to an end to the conversation. Remember, if the person says anything that could be interpreted as indicating something dangerous to either him- or herself or someone else, tell your supervisor (or if your supervisor is not available, another staff person) as soon as you leave the individual. For example, suppose you are placed on an adult inpatient psychiatric unit. You are talking to a 46-year-old woman who tells you that she is planning to eat the glass in which she gets her juice because she "knows" they are planning to use her fingerprints from that glass to obtain her real identity. Although it is unlikely that she will actually eat her glass, it is important that someone in authority knows she has said she has such a plan so they can monitor her potentially self-injurious behavior.

People who are experiencing auditory or visual hallucinations may periodically respond to these internal stimuli while talking to you. It is best to ignore these responses and continue your conversation normally. A common indication that the person is having auditory hallucinations, for example, is to look upward or to the side to locate the source of the voices. You may then tell a staff member about what you observed. Another possible issue that may arise is when a patient on an inpatient psychiatric unit tells you about plans to leave without permission. Although you may have told that person that you will keep their comments confidential, you will also have said that confidentiality does not extend to conditions that are potentially dangerous. Leaving the hospital without permission falls within that exception and should be reported to your supervisor immediately.

What about the case in which someone you meet at the placement wants to maintain contact with you away from the placement? If you are doing a good job interacting with the people at the placement, patients may ask for your phone number so they can call you when they are feeling distressed or when they have additional questions to ask you. Others, who are preparing to leave the site, may want to see you socially. Regardless of the reason the person wants your phone number or address, do not give it. It is important to take the time to explain to the person that although you are not part of the professional staff of the facility, you are obligated to follow the same policy regarding socializing with them as the staff have. You do not want to give the impression that your refusal is personal to them but rather that you would give the same answer to anyone who asked for it in this setting. It is helpful to let them know that you appreciate the fact that they want to maintain contact with you but that such contact will not be possible.

Becoming too attached to a student can be expressed in ways other than asking for a phone number. A child may cling to you and beg you not to leave when it is time for you to go or refuse to talk to anyone but you. In this case, you need to talk to the child and explain that you are pleased that the child enjoys your company but that you spend only a limited amount of time there. Tell the child that staff also care about him or her and have much to offer, and you hope the child will gain from them too. If the child continues to refuse to interact with anyone but you, it may be necessary for you to take the position that even when you are there you cannot spend one-on-one time with this child. Another example is the adult who continues to try to touch you or invade your personal space. One of our former students, for example, reported a situation in which she had been asked by her supervisor to conduct a standardized interview with an adult male patient. This man continued to move his chair closer and closer to her chair as she moved through the required questionnaire. Both his chair and hers had rollers. As he moved his chair closer to hers, she moved hers away from him. She was eventually backed against a wall in the room. This incident led her to request a change of placement. Rather than honoring this request, we had a discussion of other ways she might handle this behavior in the future. How should she have handled this problem? As in the previous example, the student might acknowledge the fact that she appreciated his desire to sit closer to her but also let him know that moving his chair closer to hers was not appropriate. She could tell him that she was not comfortable with his chair being that close to her. If he continued to move his chair, she would tell him if he continued to move into her personal space, the interview would have to be terminated. She would then be explaining her feelings as well as setting appropriate consequences for continued inappropriate behavior. By the end of the semester, the student in our example had not only learned about the placement site but had also practiced appropriate assertiveness skills she could use elsewhere. Both of these situations should also be discussed with the site supervisor.

What Should I Tell My Site Supervisor?

The way site supervision is conducted varies among programs. Usually one person is designated as being responsible for students or students from a specific discipline, such as psychology. Meetings with students are sometimes held in a group format if there are a number of students placed there. Other sites use an individual supervision format. Chapter 1 covers information about this topic; we cover only a few subjects here. Students who find themselves in an individual supervision meeting with a site supervisor may wonder what they are supposed to say. As we mentioned earlier, if a student has heard something that may indicate problems, this should be reported immediately. Regular supervision meetings, however, allow for many other topics to be discussed. Asking the supervisor about the education needed for that career as well as the rewards and frustrations of the career can be very useful. It is also appropriate to ask about readings that may assist you in understanding things you have heard or seen at the placement. If you are participating in specific activities at the site, keep a list of questions you have about them so you can ask your supervisor during regular meetings. If you have heard about special activities or programs at the facility, you may ask your supervisor about the possibility of observing them.

If the placement site is located in a risky neighborhood, ask your supervisor if your hours can be adjusted so that you leave before dark or at a time when many staff members are also leaving so that you are not alone in the parking lot or public transportation area. Many facilities have security available to escort you to your vehicle if requested. Students who feel fearful are likely to have difficulty establishing rapport with either patients or staff. If the student's fears are excessive, the supervisor may help alleviate them.

Just as professors vary in their teaching styles, supervisors also vary in their supervision styles. Some supervisors focus on building on the strengths demonstrated by the field placement student, whereas others seem to operate from the position that students know what they are doing well. These supervisors may use their time with the student to focus on areas needing remediation. This approach to supervision may lead to students feeling they have no skills. Under these circumstances, you may need to ask your supervisor about your strengths. Corey and Corey (2003) divided supervisor styles between those that are generally confrontational and those that are supportive. In this case, the term *confrontation* does not refer to an angry interaction. Rather, these supervisors will tend to spend their time with you considering ways you might do things differently from the way you are doing them. Supportive supervisors are the ones who are likely to focus on your positive interactions. Understanding the difference between these two styles can help you develop a comfortable and productive working relationship with your supervisor.

Supervision may lead to a certain degree of anxiety. In this setting, you are being asked to try new skills or apply what you have learned in a classroom setting to the real world. Part of the role of your supervisor is to give you feedback about your progress. None of us likes to hear we are not performing well. Thus, there is a tendency to avoid discussing problems you are having with individuals or activities. Other students become argumentative when receiving constructive feedback. They try to debate each point made by their supervisor. They may debate the points during supervision or remain quiet at that time but privately or with their friends debate each criticism. This is an opportunity to learn about yourself and your current skill level—use it to your advantage.

What If I See a Client Elsewhere?

It is quite possible that students on field placement will find themselves in a situation of accidentally meeting someone from their placement away from the facility. This seems most likely in such places as the supermarket, movie theater, or other setting where there are many other people. The first issue to consider is whether or not to greet this person. As a general policy, wait for the person to greet you and let the other person's words guide your behavior. If the person says hello, respond appropriately and then move on. It is especially important with children not to use their or the parent's last name. It is not advisable to engage in extended conversation. Suppose you are with some of your friends and they ask how you know that person? In this case, give a vague answer such as, "I'm not sure where we met," and then change the topic of conversation. You are still bound by confidentiality and cannot reveal how you know this person.

What about those cases in which you are still placed at the facility and you will continue to see the person? The same rules apply unless you have observed the person doing something that needs to be addressed at the facility. For example, suppose you are placed in an outpatient alcohol treatment program. You are at a parade and notice that one of the clients from the program is drinking a beer. Do not confront the person there. The next time you go to the placement, tell your supervisor what you observed so that a staff member can confront the person about this behavior.

How Do I Leave
the Placement?

Just as you may have found it somewhat difficult to establish relationships with people at your placement site, you may also find it difficult
to end those relationships. It is important to realize that although you
have not been the "primary professional" for the patients or clients at
your placement site, you have been a regular part of the program for
a period of time. Thus, you need to plan for the exit process. In fact,
in the first session you have with the patient, you should discuss the
time limitations of the relationship.

Leaving the facility involves saying good-bye to both the staff and
the clients or patients. It also involves dealing with your own feelings
of loss. Over the time you spend at a field placement, it is quite common
to develop an attachment to the facility. Some students ask if they can
continue to "volunteer" there after the end of their course placement.
Although some added time may be permitted at certain placements, if
the field placement course is offered each term it may be time for the
next students to arrive. Most sites allow only a limited number of
students because of staff and space needs. Thus, it is important to allow
sufficient time to complete your placement process. If you plan to
ask your supervisor for future letters of recommendation, you should
discuss this request in one of your sessions near the end of the term.
You should also let the clients or patients know a few weeks and then
a few days before your final day the specific time of your last visit.
That way, any issues a person wants to address with you can be handled
within your scheduled hours. This also provides staff and clients with
an opportunity to say good-bye to you.

Some field placement programs have a formal process of feedback
for both the site supervisor and the student. Regardless of whether this
system is used in your program, it is a good idea to provide your
supervisor with feedback about your experience. When doing this,
remember what you have learned during your placement about dealing
with sensitive issues. This is especially true if you have some negative
feedback for your supervisor. Remember that you and your supervisor
are not on an equal power level. If you have strong concerns about
certain aspects of the placement, it may be best to give those to your
campus faculty member rather than the placement supervisor. If your
placement supervisor asks you for feedback about the experience, clarify what the supervisor is asking for in much the same way you did

with the residents of the program before responding. Just as you may feel close to some school faculty members and not to others, you may feel very close to a supervisor at the placement or you may just want to say thank you for the person's time and then leave. Whatever the case, it is important for students to be aware of personal reactions to the end of this experience. Because of the nature of this experience it has a higher probability of generating attachment feelings than the typical class.

Summary

In this chapter, we have discussed the concept of rapport as it applies to students' interactions with both staff and participants in programs where they are placed. Rapport and a developing sense of professionalism begin with determining what to wear for the first visit to the site and continue through interactions with staff and participants as well as during supervision sessions. We included suggestions about how to initiate and continue conversations with patients as well as how to get the maximum benefit from supervision sessions. The role of culture in understanding individuals as well as self-understanding is part of the field placement experience. Common issues faced in these settings include learning the role of participant-observer, how to handle the circumstance of seeing someone from the placement outside that setting, and working with a range of staff members from different disciplines. Special issues to consider when ending the placement experience are also included. We encourage students to view their practicum as an opportunity to learn about the roles of mental health professionals and to grow from their experience.

Additional Reading

Baird, B. N. (2002). *The internship, practicum, and field placement handbook: A guide for the helping professions* (3rd ed.). Upper Saddle River, NJ: Prentice Hall.

Gordon, G. R., McBride, R. B., & Hage, H. H. (2001). *Criminal justice internships: Theory into practice* (4th ed.). Cincinnati, OH: Anderson Publishing.

References

Corey, M. S., & Corey, G. (2003). *Becoming a helper* (4th ed.). Belmont, CA: Wadsworth.

Helzer, J. E. (1983). Standardized interviews in psychiatry. *Psychiatry Developments, 2,* 161–178.

Hersen, M., & Turner, S. M. (Eds.). (1985). *Diagnostic interviewing.* New York: Plenum Press.

Matarazzo, J. D. (1965). The interview. In B. B. Wolman (Ed.), *Handbook of clinical psychology* (pp. 403–450). New York: McGraw-Hill.

Plante, T. G. (1999). *Contemporary clinical psychology.* New York: Wiley.

Royce, D., Dhooper, S. S., & Rompf, E. L. (2003). *Field instruction: A guide for social work students* (5th ed.). Boston: Allyn & Bacon.

Schmidt, J. J. (2002). *Intentional helping: A philosophy for proficient caring relationships.* Upper Saddle River, NJ: Merrill Prentice Hall.

Sue, D. W., & Sue, D. (2003). *Counseling the culturally diverse* (4th ed.). New York: Wiley.

Sweitzer, H. F., & King, M. A. (2004). *The successful internship: Transformation and empowerment in experiential learning.* Belmont, CA: Wadsworth.

Wierzbicki, M. (1999). *Introduction to clinical psychology: Scientific foundations to clinical practice.* Needham Heights, MA: Allyn & Bacon.

Elizabeth Swenson

Confidentiality and Other Ethical Issues

4

An internship or practicum is often the high point of one's undergraduate education in psychology. My students tell me that it is the time when their classroom learning really seems to come together for them. In addition, learning in the field setting helps students to solidify some career decisions and to rethink some others. Students not infrequently report that it was a life-changing experience for them.

Among the most important things to learn and to consider carefully are the ethical issues that you come across in your fieldwork. As psychology students you should be aware that there is an Ethics Code for psychologists. It is officially called the "Ethical Standards of Psychologists and Code of Conduct" (American Psychological Association [APA], 2002). You can download a copy of it from the APA Web site (www.apa.org/ethics/code.html). This Ethics Code, which took effect in June of 2003, is actually the 10th version of the Ethics Code, so it has a long history.

You may wonder if the ethical standards in the Code are mandatory for you to uphold. The Preamble to the Code states that "this Ethics Code applies only to psychologists' activities that are part of their scientific, educational, or professional roles as psychologists." Further it states that "membership in the APA commits members and student affiliates to comply with the standards of the APA Ethics Code" (APA,

2002, p. 1061). If you are a student affiliate of the APA the answer is obvious. Yet what if you are not a student affiliate? The best strategy is that if you are a psychology student in a practicum class where you are supervised, either onsite or in your class, by a psychologist, you should follow the Ethics Code. Your supervisor also has ethical responsibilities involving your work. When you are concerned about a possible ethical violation, your first responsibility is to talk with your supervisor.

Psychology is not the only profession with an ethics code. In your professional life after college or even now, you may have an interest in the codes of related helping professions such as counseling (American Counseling Association, 1995), social work (National Association of Social Workers, 1999), marriage and family therapy (American Association for Marriage and Family Therapy, 1991), or even psychiatry (American Medical Association, 1998). The Web sites for these codes are included in the reference section. It is interesting to see how similar they are in the ways they approach common ethical situations.

In addition, two Web sites have links to a number of professional ethics codes: http://www.iit.edu/departments/csep/publicWWW/codes/codes.html (from the Center for the Study of Ethics in the Professions at the Illinois Institute of Technology) and http://kspope.com/ethcodes/index.php (from the Web site of Kenneth Pope, a clinical psychologist and prolific writer on ethical issues in psychology). It might be interesting to take a controversial subject like sex between a mental health professional and a former client and see how the different ethics codes deal with it.

Making Ethical Decisions

When people come across a situation in which they need to make an ethical decision, they tend to rely on their innate sense of what's right and wrong, what their parents taught them, or some overarching principle such as the golden rule. In a professional setting, you need to go about this decision making in a more deliberate way. There are two important sources of information, both of which are contained in the "Ethical Standards of Psychologists and Code of Conduct" (www.apa.org/ethics; APA, 2002).

Under the heading of General Principles are basic principles that represent the moral values of the psychology profession. These principles are (a) Beneficence and Nonmaleficence (do good and do not do harm); (b) Fidelity and Responsibility (be faithful to your clients and duties, and act in a responsible way); (c) Integrity (be honest); (d) Justice (be fair to all people); and (e) Respect for Peoples' Rights and Dignity. These principles are aspirational, meaning that psychologists strive to meet them. You may have encountered these principles before in the biomedical ethics context, where they are prominent (Beauchamp & Childress, 2001).

The second source of ethical information for psychology is found in the part of the Code titled Ethical Standards. These standards apply specifically to the work-related behavior of psychologists. The standards are enforceable, meaning that they are not optional for psychologists. Although written for members of the APA, they have been incorporated into the laws and regulations of many states. As a psychology student working in an internship or practicum that is primarily psychology related, you should be familiar with the ethical standards and strive to follow them.

Often the solution to an ethical dilemma in your work is not apparent from reading the ethical standards. In this case, you should follow the steps listed below:

1. Identify the ethical dilemma or problem.
2. Consult professional colleagues. These people should be your site supervisor and your university professor.
3. Generate alternative possible solutions.
4. Consult the ethical standards for one or more standards that shed some light on the solutions.
5. Consider the general ethical principles as they might apply to the problem.
6. Make a decision.

In the following sections of this chapter you will have opportunities to apply this decision-making model for yourself.

Confidentiality

This may be your first exposure to the issue of client confidentiality. Confidentiality is a primary obligation of psychologists. This obligation means that generally all of the information about a client, including anything a client says or anything about a client that could reveal the client's identity, must be kept confidential. There is nothing more fundamental to a therapeutic relationship than confidentiality. It is what breeds trust between the psychologist and the client, and what makes the professional relationship work. As a student of psychology, this means that you as well as your supervisor assume the obligation of confidentiality, no matter what internship setting you are assigned to. Read all of the code standards carefully in Section 4, Privacy and Confidentiality, for the protection of privacy and the instances in which it might be breached ethically. It is particularly important to be familiar with the standards referred to in the text.

There are some limits on confidentiality. They are listed in Standard 4.05, Disclosures, and are discussed later in this chapter. The limits of confidentiality include a risk of harm to the client or others and the need to consult a professional colleague on treatment. Both Standard 4.02, Discussing the Limits of Confidentiality, and Standard 10.01, Informed Consent to Therapy, stress that discussion of confidentiality with the client take place as early as is feasible. You should obtain instructions from your supervisor on how to go about discussing this.

CASE 1: SHOULD YOU GREET AN ACQUAINTANCE?

Heather's internship is in a drug and alcohol outpatient treatment center. She has permission to sit in on an open 12-step meeting. In the meeting is her family's next-door neighbor, Martin, a young man whom she would like to date. He looks at her without apparent recognition. It seems as if he does not want to be recognized. What should she do?

In applying the decision-making model, the ethical dilemma is whether to go up and talk to Martin, perhaps reminding him of their relationship. Heather could do this or she could ignore him, treating him like any other patient in the group. These are the most obvious alternatives, although there are others. This is an issue of confidentiality but also may be construed as one of a multiple relationship, more about which will be said later in this chapter. Doing anything to promote the personal relationship at any possible expense of Martin's treatment is prohibited by the Ethics Code in Standard 3.05, Multiple Relationships, which is discussed later in this chapter. Section 4, Privacy and Confidentiality, of the Ethics Code obligates psychologists to respect confidentiality. As previously noted, although there are limits to confidentiality in the Code, such as for consultation or protection from harm (Standard 4.05, Disclosures), none of these apply here. The general ethical principles of beneficence, nonmaleficence, and respect for dignity indicate that anything that might harm Martin should be avoided.

Heather should consult her supervisor as early as feasible about the problem.

CASE 2: DECIDING NOT TO GREET A FORMER PATIENT

Heather has completed her fieldwork experience and is at college finishing up the last semester of her senior year. In a nearby coffee shop where she is working on her senior project paper, she sees Madison, a patient from the substance abuse facility where she was placed. Her natural inclination is to say "Hello" and ask Madison how he is doing these days. She especially wonders, although would never ask, if Madison is still "on the wagon." She hesitates before making contact and then decides it would not be wise.

This is a good decision. Most psychologists adhere to the principle of not speaking outside the therapy office to a client unless they speak first. Tell the client this when you discuss confidentiality in the first session. The obligation to preserve confidentiality continues after both the psychologist and the patient have gone on to other endeavors. Some people believe it lasts forever. The conservative approach would be to follow this advice.

CASE 3: PROTECTING A PATIENT'S PRIVACY

Tom is working with children in a teaching hospital setting. The staff has decided that students who are doing internships for academic credit may have limited access to patients' records on a need-to-know basis. Tom has used this privilege carefully. While playing pool with a child with Apert's syndrome, the mother of another child in the playroom asks Tom, "What's the matter with her?" Tom says he does not know but feels guilty because he does in fact know the diagnosis. (Apert's syndrome is a rare genetic disorder in which a child is born with all the bones of the head prematurely fused, resulting in a peaked shaped head, shallow eye pockets, other abnormal facial features, and fusion of the fingers and toes. These give the child an odd appearance.)

Tom is correct in protecting the patient's privacy. If it bothers him to deny knowledge, it might be better for him to respond that he cannot discuss patients with other people. This is a good problem for Tom to discuss with both his supervisor and with the professor supervising his academic work for the course. If there is a class with several internship students in other settings, it would not be a violation of privacy for them to discuss together how to deal with this type of question.

CASE 4: DISCUSSING CONFIDENTIAL MATTERS WITH A SUPERVISOR

On his way home from the hospital, Tom encounters his site supervisor on the elevator. Tom begins to describe the events at the hospital that were difficult for him. His supervisor says that the elevator is not a good place to discuss patients because others are present in this small space and "even the elevator walls have ears." He recommends that they stop for a coffee in the hospital cafeteria.

Tom's supervisor is wrong to think that one public place is any better than any other for discussing a patient and the problems she presents. It is a small world. The person at the next table might be an uncle of the patient and listen to every word that is said. An appropriate place to discuss problems concerning a patient would be a private office or the classroom with other practicum students.

CASE 5: DISCUSSING AND REPORTING SUSPECTED CHILD ABUSE

In her practicum at a day care center in an economically deprived part of town, one of Meghan's tasks is to organize children's art work into individual portfolios. Meghan is struck by the drawings of a four-year-old boy who depicts a child being hit by an adult with a piece of wood. In another picture a child is shown with a gag, tied to a chair. Meghan decides to investigate further by talking to the child about the pictures. The child says that he is drawing pictures from his own life at home. She notices unusual-looking bruises on his arms.

Meghan should have talked with her supervisor about the drawings before setting out on her own investigation. The suspicious appearance of the bruises and the words of the child require the supervisor to report this to the child protection agency in the city. Mandated reporting is the law in all states and many other countries to protect children, and with growing frequency, older adults and people who are mentally challenged from harm. Is Meghan required to report this too? This depends on the law in her area, but it may possibly require her too to report her suspicions as an intern in this setting. In many cities it is possible to call a kids' hotline anonymously. This may be the best choice for a student. Is there an issue of confidentiality here? Yes there is. Yet Standard 4.05, Disclosures, clearly states that disclosures can be made to protect the child. Legally, Meghan may have no choice here. Yet as a student, she must discuss this with her supervisor before making a decision. Her clinical supervisor will make a report with her.

Duty to Warn, Protect, or Disclose

Confidentiality can be breached ethically in a number of ways. Two of these are the duty to warn and the duty to disclose. Both of these are in the list of appropriate disclosures contained in Standard 4.05b(3), Disclosures, protecting the client and others from harm.

CASE 6: DUTY TO WARN OR PROTECT THIRD PARTIES

Prosenjit Poddar was a student at the University of California at Berkeley. He also was a client in the university's counseling center. During the course of his counseling, Poddar told his treating psychologist that he intended to kill Tatiana Tarasoff, his former girlfriend. The psychologist, feeling that Poddar was a danger to Tarasoff, called the police, who questioned and released him. Subsequently, Poddar did kill Tarasoff. The Tarasoff family sued the University of California, including the psychologist, arguing that the psychologist had a duty to warn or to protect Tarasoff.

This is a real case (*Tarasoff v. Board of Regents*, 1976). The duty to protect a third party from serious harm became law in California as a result. Many states follow California law, not because they are obliged to but because California courts often set the pace for developing tort law in other states. Now most states have a law that requires psychologists to do something to warn or to protect known third parties from harm. Several questions remain, including how to warn or protect in an effective way (wasn't calling the police enough to protect Tarasoff?) and what to do if the third party or parties are not identifiable. This latter case arises when a person has a sexually transmitted disease and engages in anonymous sexual activity with multiple parties.

CASE 7: DUTY TO INFORM WHEN DEALING WITH A MINOR

Matthew, a bright 16-year-old college student, discloses to his counselor that he needs to finish school in a hurry and get on with his life. He is HIV positive and does not expect to have a long life, particularly because he does not believe in traditional medicine. Matthew also talks about his multiple sex partners all over the region.

The psychologist needs to disclose this information, but to whom? None of the sex partners are known to the psychologist or apparently to Matthew either. The psychologist has a duty to try to impress on Matthew how dangerous his behavior is to others, not unlike playing Russian roulette. In addition, Matthew is a minor. As such, at the beginning of the counseling, Matthew had to be informed that if he talked about being dangerous to himself or others, his parents would be told. A similar result would follow if a minor client disclosed to the psychologist that he or she was going to rave parties and using ecstasy on the weekends.

CASE 8: DUTY TO DISCLOSE AND PROTECT THE LIFE OF THE PATIENT

Allen, a college student, has been a client of Dr. Moore's in psychotherapy for acute depression for the past month. Recently he has been talking about how life is not worth living any more. He has just broken up with his girlfriend of two years and is not going to class or taking exams. Dr. Moore asks Allen whether he has thought about suicide. Allen replies that suicide is constantly on his mind. He has a plan and a time frame for implementing it. He knows it will be effective in ending his life.

Dr. Moore has a duty to disclose this information and to have Allen placed in an inpatient mental health facility for involuntary treatment. This action is necessary to save Allen's life. The disclosure may be made to another professional and/or to Allen's family. Depending on the state, the psychologist may actually do the involuntary commitment and may be legally obligated to do so.

CASE 9: AN OBLIGATION TO PROTECT CHILDREN

Arnold is shadowing a child-protection caseworker for part of his practicum. He knows that in the course of his duties he will see some parts of children's lives that will shock him. He also is well versed in confidentiality issues. He knows that he is not to reveal what he sees or hears and that in this setting this will be a heavy burden at times. Today Arnold is visiting a home where it has been reported that children are not attending school regularly. Arnold enters the home with his supervisor and immediately smells pot. To his amazement, his supervisor does not seem to notice. She talks with the children's mother about how important it is for the children to attend school after the mother offers multiple excuses for her children's attendance problems. Arnold and his supervisor leave the home and discuss how it is that parents would not think that going to school is more important than seeing a particular television program or celebrating a birthday. Arnold does not know what to do.

Arnold has an obligation to tell his supervisor about the pot odor. Maybe she just doesn't recognize it. Confidentiality does not preclude his talking with his supervisor about his observations. It is important for him to do so. Quite possibly the children are living in a harmful environment. Information to keep children safe is not confidential information.

Multiple Roles and Boundary Violations

While you are in your practicum setting it is important to maintain a professional relationship with your clients. When a relationship is both professional and in some way personal, then this is a multiple relationship or a violation of professional boundaries. You may end up working with professionals who have overlapping lines of responsibility. This does not constitute a multiple relationship for you, but it is important for you to determine to whom to take specific concerns. If you cannot figure this out for yourself, be sure to ask.

Standard 3.05, Multiple Relationships, defines a multiple relationship as one in which the primary role is professional and at the same time there is a secondary relationship with either that person or someone closely associated with or related to the person. If the secondary role is reasonably expected to "impair the psychologist's objectivity, competence or effectiveness" or one in which the patient could be exploited or harmed, then the psychologist is not behaving ethically. This is the test to use to determine if a multiple relationship is unethical. This is a controversial ethical standard. There are thoughtful and principled psychologists who believe that personal relationships with clients can be helpful to the client. Others believe that the potential for harm and exploitation is always present and not easy to catch before it is too late. The question to ask is whether the secondary relationship activity is a result of your own needs or the needs of the client. As a psychology student, however, it is important to monitor your interactions with your clients to be sure that an unethical multiple relationship does not develop. Behaving conservatively means that personal relationships with clients in your practicum setting should be avoided.

CASE 10: BOUNDARY ISSUES
WITH A PATIENT

Jeralyn's practicum placement is in a mental health treatment facility that specializes in art therapy. She has especially enjoyed working with Rachel, a high school senior. Rachel is applying to colleges for next year. While painting, Jeralyn and Rachel spend a great deal of time talking about the life of a college student. Because they both really like the actor Matt Damon, Rachel asks Jeralyn if she'd like to come over to her house on the weekend and they could rent *Good Will Hunting*. Jeralyn is not sure she should accept the invitation but does not know why she feels this way or what to say.

Once Jeralyn has spent a social evening with Rachel at her house, she may have lost the ability to have a professional relationship with her in the future. This is not as serious for a student as it might be for a professional psychologist, but it is still a boundary issue. Assuming that Jeralyn has been therapeutically helpful to Rachel, this shift from a quasi-professional to a friend could be harmful in some subtle way. Friends are not always as accepting of each other's behavior as psychologists are of their clients'. She should tell Rachel that she would like to come over but that she is not allowed to do so, that the agency policy forbids this. A student should have contact with a client in a professional setting under supervision. There should be no contact outside of this.

CASE 11: FOLLOWING RULES
WITH PATIENTS

Todd has been a practicum student in a children's hospital. He is supervised by a play therapist. His role is not only to use play to normalize the environment but also to do some medical play to help the children understand and accept their illnesses and their medical procedures more fully. Todd is particularly fond of Eric, a 7-year-old who has been in the hospital for 2 months. Eric's parents rarely visit him because they live in another state. It just so happens that Todd is from the same hometown as Eric. When the semester is over, Todd decides to do volunteer work on this hospital division a few hours a week so he can continue his friendship with Eric. When Eric leaves the hospital to return home, Todd gives him his home phone number and asks him to check in once in a while.

This sounds like a difficult case because it does not seem that there is a realistic possibility of harm or exploitation here. Todd's interest in Eric is only for Eric to give him a call on occasion, if he would like to. Todd should not follow up on this by initiating the calls himself. Although not obviously unethical, some placement sites may have rules prohibiting students from giving their telephone number to the people they meet there. Students should always learn the rules and not act on impulse.

CASE 12: PROHIBITED SEXUAL RELATIONSHIPS

Lisa's practicum placement is on an adolescent and young adult inpatient mental health division in a teaching hospital. She is supervised by a psychologist. Her job is to visit with patients and provide them with recreational activities. As part of her training, she has been able to observe, with the patient's or the parent's permission, some psychological test feedback as well as some therapy sessions. In the course of her practicum, Lisa is smitten by Lance, one of the patients. The chemistry between them is palpable. They decide that as soon as Lance is discharged into outpatient care they will begin dating. A sexual relationship develops immediately thereafter.

As a psychology student, Lisa should know that this activity is forbidden. Standard 10.05, Sexual Intimacies With Current Therapy Clients/Patients, makes this clear for psychologists. Students need to follow this standard too. Standard 10.08, Sexual Intimacies With Former Therapy Clients/Patients, prohibits sexual intimacy with former clients for at least two years and then only under "unusual circumstances." Standard 10.08b sets forth the factors to be considered in making this post-2-year decision. Note that Standard 10.06, Sexual Intimacies With Relatives or Significant Others of Current Therapy Clients/Patients, extends this prohibition to relatives or significant others of therapy clients. To round out this set of sexual intimacy standards, Standard 10.07, Therapy With Former Sexual Partners, prohibits psychologists from doing psychotherapy with past sexual partners.

Informed Consent

You may be familiar with informed consent to being a participant in a research project. Informed consent is just as important when dealing with psychological treatment, including psychotherapy and assessment. The basic standard is 3.10, Informed Consent.

CASE 13: OBTAINING INFORMED CONSENT

Sophia is assisting her psychology supervisor in running a group for high school students who have test anxiety. The students discuss their symptoms and relate to those of others in the group with suggestions and empathy. Sophia tells a neighbor's son to drop in one evening and join the group. He thinks it might be fun and interesting, so he decides to do so. After a few minutes in the group he becomes afraid that he will have to participate in one way or another and runs out.

Even for group therapy, informed consent is necessary. For a minor, a parent's consent is needed, and the minor must give assent. According to Standard 3.10a, consent must be obtained after explaining the therapy in reasonably understandable language. The consent should be documented (Standard 3.10d). A minor needs to be given a careful explanation and have his preferences and best interests considered before obtaining parental consent and minor assent (Standard 3.10b). Standard 10.01a, Informed Consent to Therapy, outlines everything that must be covered in the informed consent including the nature and anticipated course of therapy, the limits of confidentiality, and the opportunity to ask questions and obtain information. Informed consent is also necessary in assessment, Standard 9.03, Informed Consent in Assessments.

Assessment

In your practicum you may have access to psychological tests. You may even be asked to administer them to clients. There are often ethical issues in assessment, many of which are addressed in Section 9, Assessment, of the Code. Some of these are apparent from reading the cases that follow.

CASE 14: MAINTAINING TEST SECURITY

As part of her practicum placement and in her psychological testing class, Miranda has learned a little about the MMPI–2 and its scoring. The results, diagnoses of emotional disorders, are interesting to her. She has access to some test forms and a manual scoring template and thinks it would be interesting to give the test to some of her neighbors in the dorm and to study the results. Of course she plans to get the permission of her supervising psychologist first.

There are several ethical issues here in this short vignette. First of all, only qualified users with a particular level of competence can administer psychological tests. The MMPI–2 is a simple test to administer and score but complicated to interpret. With diagnosis as the end result of the interpretation, the results can be damaging. Therefore, this test requires the highest level of training to interpret. The psychologist should not have let the student borrow the test. Standard 9.07, Assessment by Unqualified Persons, deals with this issue. In addition, maintaining test security (Standard 9.11) is a major issue when dealing with psychological tests. Tests lose their reliability and validity when they are indiscriminately exposed to the public.

CASE 15: CONFIDENTIALITY OF TEST RESULTS

Andrew is in a mental health agency for his practicum. His supervisor has let him sit in on the administration of a Stanford–Binet Intelligence Test. He has also been able to watch the test being scored and has been informed about the results. A woman claiming to be the child's mother approaches Andrew and asks if he knows anything about tests that may have been given to the child. Andrew, feeling quite confident that this is the mother, talks about the test, the scoring, and the results.

Andrew, obviously, is not qualified to discuss these results with anyone other than his supervisor, even if he were positive that this was the mother, and the custodial parent, of the child. There is a privacy and confidentiality issue here as well as ones of test security and competence. Andrew's offer of information went well beyond what was in the scope of his responsibilities and duties as a practicum student.

CASE 16: ACTING AS A TRANSLATOR

Sarah works in the same agency as Andrew. She double majors in psychology and Spanish. Geraldo, a 14-year-old Latino boy, is brought in for assessment. He does not speak English very well. The psychologist, who assumes that Sarah is fluent in Spanish from her college courses, asks her to translate when she administers the Rorschach inkblots and the Thematic Apperception Test. Sarah does her best, but the emotion-generated rapid speech of Geraldo often leaves her guessing about the meaning of his sentences. Sarah does not want to disappoint the psychologist, from whom she would like a good evaluation, so she does her best and does not qualify her translation.

Sarah means well, but by not saying she is unable to translate accurately, she is doing a disservice to Geraldo and invalidating the results of the tests. It is a difficult issue to give a psychological test to someone whose native language is not English and for whom there may not be test norms that apply to the results. Standard 2.05, Delegation of Work to Others, specifically references interpreters. The psychologist is responsible for ensuring that the translation is done with competence.

This would be an ethical problem for the psychologist because Sarah is not competent in the use of Spanish for this purpose and knows little about the tests.

Competence

It is mandatory for psychologists to work only in their areas of competence. Standard 2.01, Boundaries of Competence, extends the competency requirement beyond academic skills and knowledge that are obtained by education and experience to a clear understanding of factors associated with diversity of all types. It is necessary for psychologists to either obtain the education and experience needed to work with diverse populations or to refer clients to those who have this expertise. Standard 2.03, Maintaining Competence, requires psychologists to be up-to-date in their fields. Most state licensing boards require psychologists to complete continuing education courses to maintain their licenses. These continuing education courses are intended to assist psychologists to maintain their skills.

CASE 17: REMAINING WITHIN BOUNDARIES OF COMPETENCE

Adam is using his training in applied behavior analysis to work on language skills with an 8-year-old autistic girl, Marty. The child's foster mother, understanding that Adam is a psychology student, asks him for a favor. The child's biological mother needs to get counseling and parenting lessons so that she can regain custody of Marty. Adam has no counseling skills that he knows of, although his friends tell him that he a good listener. He could use the extra money.

Counseling the mother is outside Adam's area of competence. He should talk this over with his supervisor so that he knows how to handle similar requests that might arise in the future. Many people think that psychology students have special skills. Had Adam's supervisor assigned him the task of counseling the mother and teaching her about parenting, the supervisor may have violated Standard 2.05, Delegation of Work to Others. This standard requires that psychologists delegating work seek to ensure that the person to whom the work is delegated is competent to perform it and that the person does not have a multiple relationship with the client.

An interesting aspect of competence is known as emotional competence. Standard 2.06, Personal Problems and Conflicts, requires that psychologists who have personal problems that might interfere with their work get professional help and decide if they should continue or take a break from their work. These problems include such things as illness, stress, and difficult life events.

CASE 18: APPROPRIATE PRACTICUM PLACEMENT

Julia's practicum placement is in a shelter for runaway teenage girls. One of her jobs is to monitor groups that deal with reasons for running away and with planning for the future. Some of the girls will return home; some will go to foster homes; and some will enter a program to make them independent. Julia was particularly interested in this placement because she had a difficult childhood herself with emotionally abusive parents. As a teenager she had thought many times about running away but did not have the courage or resources to do so. One of the girls in the group tells a story about her life at home that Julia related to too well. This story stuck a chord in Julia. Suddenly she broke down in sobs and ran out of the group.

Julia's supervisor should have interviewed Julia carefully about her background and reasons for wanting to be with this client population before accepting her as a student here. At this time, Julia needs to explain her behavior to her supervisor and ask to be relieved of this job. Julia may also have had this reaction triggered by events in her life outside of the practicum. She should not have been placed with this vulnerable group of girls so close to her own age. Julia should explore with her academic supervisor other tasks or placements she can have to fulfill her academic requirement.

Supervision

There are many ethical issues in the supervision of practicum students. One that has already been discussed is the standard about delegating tasks to others. Others are discussed in the cases that follow.

CASE 19: EXPLOITATION AND INAPPROPRIATE RELATIONSHIPS

Angela loved her placement in a program for binge disorders. She was part of a regular meeting, assisting Dr. Hit, a licensed psychologist, who was the group leader. After each group session they would meet and go over the events of the group. The supervision meeting almost always began with some comment by Dr. Hit on Angela's personal appearance. This made Angela so uncomfortable that she started wearing baggy clothes and no makeup to her practicum. Yet when she did this, Dr. Hit's comments on her appearance became an even more prominent focus of the meetings. Soon, despite Angela's efforts to turn the conversation around, Dr. Hit began asking Angela about her weekend activity and whether she had a boyfriend. The meeting settings changed too. They went from Dr. Hit's office to a coffee shop to a restaurant for dinner. Angela felt that this was inappropriate but did not know what to do and especially did not want to run the risk of a bad evaluation.

Fortunately, Angela has an academic supervisor and a small group of other practicum students to ask for advice. Two Code standards are particularly applicable here. Standard 3.08, Exploitative Relationships, states that psychologists may not exploit supervisees. Dr. Hit may be a lonely individual who enjoys Angela's company, even though Angela does not enjoy his but is afraid to say no. Is this behavior the first step on a slippery slope? Standard 7.07, Sexual Relationships With Students and Supervisees, prohibits this relationship from becoming sexual. This is also a good example of the abuse of power by the supervisor, a clear violation again of Standard 3.05, Multiple Relationships. In addition to the ethical issues raised here, Dr. Hit's behavior may qualify as sexual harassment under federal guidelines describing the hostile work environment.

Another important ethical principle is that supervisors have an obligation with respect to prompt and appropriate feedback on a supervisee's performance.

CASE 20: APPROPRIATE SUPERVISION AND FEEDBACK

Howard is in a practicum placement that deals with domestic violence. Services include a group home, classes to help victims get back on their feet again, a support group, and a hotline. Howard particularly enjoys working on the hotline. He has little training for the job because his supervisor feels that Howard has an intuitive focus and understanding of his work. Howard's general orientation to these situations is that women who have been abused should fight back. He has been heard to say on the hotline "Get the gun away from him and shoot him!" and "Cut the balls off that guy while he's asleep." Howard's supervisor knows that Howard is responding inappropriately to the women who call in, but he is also amused by the comments Howard comes up with.

Standard 7.06, Assessing Student and Supervisee Performance, requires Howard's supervisor to give him feedback on his work in a "timely and specific process" (APA, 2002, p. 1068). It also requires the supervisor to evaluate Howard on his actual performance. Howard is behaving inappropriately, and the supervisor needs to meet with him regularly and review his work. This situation also involves a possible violation of Standard 2.05, Delegation of Work to Others, because without specific training, Howard is not competent to do these jobs.

What to Do if You Find an Ethical Violation

The APA Ethics Code is quite specific about what to do if you discover that a psychologist is violating the Code. Standard 1.04, Informal Resolution of Ethical Violations, requires that if a psychologist sees any possible ethical violation by another, it should be brought to the attention of the alleged violator unless confidentiality rights are involved. If this informal attempt to resolve the problem fails, then Standard 1.05, Reporting Ethical Violations, requires a psychologist to take further action appropriate to the situation. In doing so, the psychologist must balance this obligation against any harm that is done or any confidentiality rights of a client. You should discuss possible ethical violations with your onsite or academic supervisor.

Summary

In this chapter, I have covered some of the most frequently cited ethical issues and dilemmas that arise in practicum settings. Other areas that the Code covers that should be of interest to students are Section 7, Education and Training, and Section 8, Research and Publication. It is most helpful to read the entire Code to put them in context.

Listed in the additional readings at the end of this chapter are three psychology ethics textbooks by Corey, Corey, and Callanan; Keith-Spiegel and Koocher; and Pope and Vasquez as well as two specialized books, one in research ethics by Sales and Folkman and one in industrial and organizational ethics by Lowman. The book by Fisher, who was the chair of the revision task force, is an explanation of the 2002 Ethics Code. The book by Nagy presents good case examples and is suitable for student use.

The Canadian Psychological Association Code of Ethics, found at http://www.cpa.ca/ethics2000.html has some interesting similarities with and differences from the APA Code. I have included this information because some students may decide to attend one of the APA-accredited graduate programs located in Canada after their undergraduate education and because there is a close relationship between U.S. and Canadian practitioners through their participation in the same licensing board organization.

In this chapter you have been introduced to several ethical issues that are relevant to your practicum experience. These issues include confidentiality, multiple relationships and appropriate boundaries, and informed consent. Not every ethical dilemma can be resolved by the Ethics Code. The General Principles and your onsite and academic supervisors are valuable additional resources.

Additional Reading

Corey, G., Corey, M. S., & Callanan, P. (1998). *Issues and ethics in the helping professions* (5th ed.). Pacific Grove, CA: Brooks/Cole.

Fisher, C. B. (2003). *Decoding the ethics code: A practical guide for psychologists*. Thousand Oaks, CA: Sage.

Koocher, G. P., & Keith-Spiegel, P. (1998). *Ethics in psychology: Professional standards and cases* (2nd ed.). New York: Oxford University Press.

Lowman, R. L. (Ed.). (1998). *The ethical practice of psychology in organizations*. Washington, DC: American Psychological Association.

Nagy, T. F. (2005). *Ethics in plain English: An illustrative casebook for psychologists* (2nd ed.). Washington, DC: American Psychological Association.

Pope, K. S., & Vasquez, M. T. (1998). *Ethics in psychotherapy and counseling.* (2nd ed.). San Francisco: Jossey-Bass.

Sales, B. D., & Folkman, S. (Eds.). (2002). *Ethics in research with human participants*. Washington, DC: American Psychological Association.

References

American Association for Marriage and Family Therapy. (1991). *AAMFT code of ethics*. Washington, DC: Author. Retrieved August 8, 2005, from http://www.aamft.org/about/revisedethicscode

American Counseling Association. (1995). *Code of ethical standards of practice*. Alexandria, VA: Author. Retrieved August 8, 2005, from http://www.counseling.org/gc/cybertx.htm

American Medical Association. (1998). *Principles of medical ethics, with annotation especially applicable to psychiatry*. Washington, DC: Author. Retrieved August 8, 2005, from http://www.ama-assn.org/ama/pub/article/7665-4727.html

American Psychological Association. (2002). Ethical standards of psychologists and code of conduct. *American Psychologist, 57*, 1060–1073. Retrieved August 8, 2005, from www.apa.org/ethics

Beauchamp, T. L., & Childress, J. F. (2001). *Principles of biomedical ethics* (5th ed.). New York: Oxford University Press.

National Association of Social Workers. (1999). *Code of ethics*. Washington, DC: Author. Retrieved August 8, 2005, from http://naswdc.org/pubs/code/code. asp

Tarasoff v. Board of Regents of the University of California, 551 P.2d 334 (Cal.Sup.Ct.1976).

Carol Terry

History of Treatment of People With Mental Illness

5

As we enter the 21st century, most mental health professionals would probably agree that the treatment of "mental illness" has come a long way from the ancient practice of trephining to let alleged devils escape through one's skull or from the more contemporary use of enemas and bloodletting to "cure" mental illness. To help psychology students early in their training understand how the treatment of mental illness has evolved and what direction the future of treatment is likely to follow, in this chapter I trace the evolution of treatment, primarily in the United States, discuss current trends in mental health treatment and policy, and then project how the future of psychological treatment is likely to evolve further in the 21st century.

From Tolerance and Torment to Treatment

In ancient and even medieval times, individuals who today would be diagnosed with illnesses like schizophrenia or bipolar disorder were sometimes accused of being possessed by

demons or designated witches. These rather primitive conceptualiza-
tions of the bizarre and unusual thoughts and behaviors associated
with serious mental illness led to all sorts of cruel treatments, such as
drilling holes in the skull to release demons (trephining) and drowning
or burning individuals to destroy so-called witches. In some communities, people with mental illness roamed the countryside, and other
citizens sometimes gave them food, but often they were not allowed
inside the city walls, especially at night. Fortunately for those afflicted
with serious mental illnesses, supernatural explanations and shunning
eventually were replaced with a more logical and humane emphasis
on how moral and healthful practices influenced both the mind and
the body.

Today, most of us live in cities populated by thousands or tens
of thousands of people. Major urban areas of the 21st century have
populations in the millions. It may be hard to imagine that in 1790
only six cities in the United States had 8,000 or more people living in
them or that these cities contained only about 3% of the U.S. population
(Grob, 1994). In the 17th, 18th, and early 19th centuries, our society
was mainly an agricultural one with very small groups of families and
individuals. Religion, largely the Protestant ethic, influenced all aspects
of life, including how those deemed "insane" were cared for.

So it shouldn't be surprising that given the "small-town" and somewhat puritanical nature of early America, the "insane" of the 18th
century were mainly taken care of by family, neighbors, and their
community. Community members felt a moral obligation to care for
the "insane" members of their community. Many communities even
collected money to be given to families to assist them in the care of a
family member with mental illness. There really were no organized
"treatment" institutions until the very late 18th century and even then
very few.

Unfortunately, there were a few, perhaps well-meaning, individuals who attempted to cure the "mad" of the day with what would now
be considered barbaric methods or even torment. In the 18th century,
Benjamin Franklin suggested trying to shock "mad people" and subsequently Dr. John Birch, an English doctor, claimed to have cured a
suicidal singer from depression in 1787 by delivering a series of shocks
to her head (Zacks, 1997). Although this may seem a precursor to
current day ECT (albeit without anesthesia), other procedures of the
day seem to have no logic behind them whatsoever and to bear no
relation to current day treatments. For example, in the 17th century,
some British and French doctors delivered transfusions of sheep's blood
into "mad" humans. Their "logic" was that the "docile" temperament
of the sheep would be transmitted to the humans through the blood
transfusions. When a French doctor killed a "wife beater" with this

method and was convicted of murder, this procedure, not surprisingly, lost its appeal (Zacks, 1997). Bloodletting, a procedure used by various societies since the days of Hippocrates in the 5th century, was used well into the 19th century to "balance" bodily fluids. Rather than curing the "insane" it often killed its recipients. Other purgative procedures were likewise popular well into the 19th and even the 20th century, such as emetics and enemas. Fortunately, most members of our society with mental illness were simply cared for in a custodial fashion by family members and spared the rather strange, and at times tortuous, methods of the day.

As the industrial revolution began in the United States from the late 18th to the mid-19th centuries and immigrants began to flood the United States, the population, particularly in urban areas, grew exponentially. For example, by the mid-19th century, the population of New York City grew to about half a million; four other cities' populations were 100,000 to 250,000; and the population of 20 cities ranged from 25,000 to 100,000 (Grob, 1994). In addition to the population growth, wage labor and urbanization altered the ways families and communities operated and the ability of communities or families to care for their "insane" members at home. The education and welfare of citizens tended to be transferred to public institutions. Unfortunately for people with mental illness, this resulted in many members of this population being cared for in poorhouses or prisons, particularly in urban areas. About the same time, the preindustrial view of people accepting their fate began to change. "Faith in reason and science and in the ability of humanity to alleviate problems and change its environment slowly began to influence theories of insanity and prevailing practices" (Grob, 1994, p. 25).

It really wasn't until the very late 18th century into the 19th century that large numbers of physicians began to "treat" mental illness in a humanitarian manner using psychological and medical treatments. "Psychiatry" as a profession began about this time. Psychiatrists' main roles were as the prestigious "superintendents" of the "asylums," the facilities that began to be established to "treat" or "cure" mental illness. These asylums grew in numbers throughout the 19th century. Psychiatrists' goal was "cure," and their methods were often based on innovative ideas of the day often learned from European physicians. Physical and moral causes of insanity were both discussed, although moral causes were emphasized. One psychiatrist of the day, Edward Jarvis, explained that "malignant and evil passions, anger, hatred, jealousy, pride and violent temper"' along with more "social and economic mobility" contributed to increased rates of insanity in the 19th century (Grob, 1994, p. 61). The first asylums housed very few patients and often catered to the affluent, and the psychiatrist worked closely, albeit as somewhat of an authoritarian figure, with patients. These early asylums, such as the McClean Asylum in Massachusetts and the Friends' Asylum in Pennsylvania, purported to have high "cure" rates, although these claims were likely exaggerated. Treatments varied, but common treatments of the day included engaging patients in recreation and employment, using restraining devices to control violent patients, and still utilizing bloodletting at times in the hopes of curing the insane. Camphor and opium were used as sedatives. At the McClean Asylum, patients earned increasing levels of privileges and freedoms contingent on improvements in their condition.

Unfortunately, with the increasing population in general, the milieus of early asylums changed from small communities of 10 to 30 in the very early 19th century to hundreds and even over a thousand in some institutions by the end of the 19th century. By the end of the 19th century, asylums, first established to reform the inhumane warehousing of the "insane" in poorhouses or prisons, were now overcrowded and ill equipped to implement the models of milieu treatment that the early psychiatrists had envisioned. Aged residents and individuals with chronic mental illness began to be cared for in a more custodial than treatment environment. The vision of mental health advocates, such as Dorothea Dix, William Tuke, and Philippe Pinel, and the goals of early, well-respected psychiatrists, such as Thomas Kirkbride and Benjamin Rush, for treatment and possibly cure of the insane were ultimately not reached in the asylums. By the turn of the 19th century, the once prestigious position of "asylum psychiatrist" was no more, and psychiatry largely looked toward new avenues of treatment in the 20th century. Alternative roles in private practice became even more desirable as populations in U.S. mental hospitals grew to unmanageable proportions. For example, by 1989 there were 425,000 patients living in state hospitals. In the 20th century, it was typical for more than 1,000 patients to be housed in one hospital.

The Rise and Fall of Psychoanalysis and Other 20th Century Treatments

Psychiatry entered the 20th century somewhat disillusioned by the failure of its pioneers to find cures for mental illness and by their asylums coming under the scrutiny and criticism of consumers and the public for their overcrowded, custodial conditions. Other physicians, particularly neurologists, were becoming increasingly involved in treating other types of mental conditions that were more amenable to outpatient treatment (such as hysterics' conversion reactions). The theories and treatments of neurologists, especially Sigmund Freud's psychoanalysis, were capturing the attention of psychiatrists, who heretofore were more involved in asylum care. So, in the early 20th century, much of psychiatry's attention, and thus the treatment of mental illness, turned to the patients with neuroses who had problems in living, rather than those with serious and persistent mental disorders. This broadened the scope of psychiatry as well from just attending to the patients with more severe mental illness for whom the treatments of the day appeared less promising. The focus of treatment in asylums shifted to treatment in the community.

The development of treatments by Freud and his colleagues (e.g., Jung and Adler) was followed by the development of other theories and treatments. Many of these new theories and therapies seemed to develop in reaction, at least in part, against the ideas of intrapsychic and unconscious processes that were the focus of the Freudians and neo-Freudians. Behavior therapy established its roots as early as the 1920s with the work of John Watson and his colleagues and continued to grow with an emphasis on operant conditioning by B. F. Skinner in the 1950s. Behavior therapy focuses primarily on environmental antecedents for behavior and the consequences that affect behavior. This discipline, in its most radical or extreme form, discourages any consideration of intrapsychic processes or even of cognitions as causing problematic behavior to develop. Radical behaviorists believe that by making changes in the environment of an individual (e.g., stimulus controls and consequences) problematic behaviors can be effectively modified. With the advent of behavior therapy, there continued to be a deterministic philosophy underlying the theory of problematic behaviors and conditions (e.g., phobias), but there was also a dramatic shift in treatment away from the intrapsychic and unobservable toward the environment and observable behavior. In the early 20th century, however, despite the advent of behavioral theories and treatments, psychoanalytic and psychodynamic treatments did continue to dominate psychiatric treatment. It is also important to mention that during the early 20th century (the 1930s), the treatment of children with psychiatric problems began to command the attention of psychiatry.

During the first half of the 20th century, a shift began from treatment being delivered by physicians alone to the expansion of such roles to include other professionals, such as nurses, social workers, and psychologists. This expansion of roles was particularly notable after World War II and wasn't without its share of conflicts. For example, in the 1950s and 1960s, there was a series of negotiations between the American Psychiatric Association and the American Psychological Association (APA) over whether psychologists should be allowed to do psychotherapy. Psychiatrists generally felt that psychotherapy was a medical procedure that should only be conducted by physicians. Other mental health professionals were less outwardly in conflict with the psychiatrists, even though they also were conducting psychotherapy with patients. For example, social workers and nurses were essentially doing psychotherapy with patients but called their work casework and counseling to avoid coming into conflict with psychiatrists. Psychiatrists ultimately lost this battle. In the 1940s and 1950s, psychologists began to conduct more psychotherapy; however, their primary role in the mental health field remained in the venue of psychological assessment and testing.

The 1940s and 1950s saw further developments in both psychological and biological treatments for mental disorders. Carl Rogers's *Client-Centered Therapy* was published in 1951, and B. F. Skinners's *Operant Conditioning* was published in 1953. Both of them were psychologists. Rogers's ideas represented a clear movement away from the determinism of psychoanalysis and behaviorism. His approach held a more optimistic, individualistic philosophy of treatment that centered on assisting "clients" with the realization of their "phenomenal self" (Rogers, 1951, p. 146). In addition, Rogers was one of the early pioneers of psychotherapy process research, emphasizing the importance of understanding of what essential ingredients of therapy were helpful to his clients.

About the same time that Rogers's humanistic understanding of personality and treatment of individuals were being developed, other biological treatments for psychiatric disorders were being tried. One of the more dramatic procedures that developed was the lobotomy. The first lobotomies were overseen by Antonio De Egas Moniz, a Portuguese psychiatrist in the mid-1930s. His procedure involved taking out parts of the prefrontal area of the brain. When Walter Freeman and James Watts began doing lobotomies in the United States, the procedure became more popular and even earned Moniz the Nobel Prize in Medicine in 1949. Tens of thousands of lobotomies had been performed around the world by the early 1950s (Zacks, 1997). Yet, the claims by these physicians of patient recovery were largely unfounded. By the 1960s, this procedure was considered to be primitive, ineffective, and harmful and was abandoned by the medical community in favor of new psychotropic medications. However, some renewed interest in very specialized brain surgery for difficult to treat individuals has occurred recently. For example, in serious obsessive–compulsive disorder that is untreatable through traditional means, a specialized psycho-surgery called a cingulotomy has been used successfully (Baer et al., 1995).

Several other treatment approaches that were also popular in the early- to mid-20th century but have since been abandoned were hydrotherapy and insulin coma therapy. Hydrotherapy involved immersing patients in baths of water as an alternative to crueler practices of the day. Although hydrotherapy was essentially a placebo, it was popular well into the 20th century. In Germany, hydrotherapy was used at the Sonnenstein Asylum in the early 19th century (Shorter, 1997). In the early 20th century in the United States, the Boston Psychopathic Asylum used a variety of treatments, including hydrotherapy (Grob, 1994).

Insulin coma therapy was first tried in the 1920s by a Viennese physician, Manfred Sakel. At the time, Sakel was working in a private clinic in Berlin treating primarily people with morphine addiction. He discovered that administering a small dose of insulin to people with addiction reduced their morphine cravings. In 1933, Sakel began using insulin therapy at a clinic in Vienna to treat individuals with schizophrenia. However, Sakel's claims of producing remission rates of about 70% with these patients were not taken seriously by the psychiatric community even when he demonstrated the practice in the United States. It wasn't until another Viennese physician, Joseph Wortes, observed Sakel's treatment and then introduced the procedure himself in the United States, that insulin therapy began gaining a fairly wide appeal. There really weren't any effective treatments for mental illness at this time, and promising treatments, no matter how seemingly barbaric today, were often tried. Insulin therapy produced a brief coma in patients who were then fed sugar to bring them out of their coma; this "treatment" resulted in death for about 1 in 100 patients. By the early 1960s, there were over 100 insulin treatment units in American psychiatric hospitals (Shorter, 1997). Of course with the advent of effective psychotropic medications, insulin coma therapy became obsolete. Other unsuccessful "treatments" that were used in the first half of the 20th century included giving large doses of caffeine to individuals with catatonic schizophrenia and inducing fever in people with serious mental illness by injecting them with the typhoid antitoxin (Shorter, 1997).

Procedures like the lobotomy and insulin coma therapy ended up being "dead end" treatments. However, other biological treatments, some of which would be precursors to current day psychotropic medications, were being tried. Although these early attempts at "cure" failed, psychiatrists' along with chemists' efforts finally paid off by the mid-20th century.

Medication, Deinstitutionalization, and Community Care: Did We Go Too Far?

The 1950s and 1960s were an exciting time in psychiatry, particularly in the treatment of chronic, severe mental illnesses, such as schizophrenia, depression, and mania. It was during these decades that psychotropic medications that could effectively treat mental illness were developed and systematically evaluated. Thorazine (a phenothiazine first used in anesthesia) was first tested in the early 1950s and allowed many patients with chronic mental illness to move from the back wards of mental hospitals to life in the community. Several studies showed Thorazine to successfully reduce acute psychosis in individuals with schizophrenia. In the 1960s, antidepressant medications, such as imipramine, were developed to treat chronic, intractable depression.

Psychotropic medications were not only developed for the treatment of people with serious mental illness. In the 1960s, the first benzodiazepines, Librium and Valium, were manufactured for problems like anxiety. Prior to their addictive potential being recognized, these medications were distributed widely. In fact, by 1970, 1 in 5 women and 1 in 13 men were using tranquilizers and sedatives, primarily the benzodiazepines, prior to their decline in use by the 1980s (Shorter, 1997). When Prozac was approved by the FDA in 1987 for the treatment of depression, the market for psychotropic medications soared, and psychiatry's return to a profession focused on biological treatments for people with mental illness came full circle.

At the same time that these revolutionary medications were being administered to formerly untreatable patients, large bonds were being passed around the country to improve conditions in mental hospitals. Ironically, during this same period, improvements in treatments available in the community were also being legislated. The passage of the Mental Retardation and Community Mental Health Centers Act in 1963 was key in mandating community treatment while also providing federal funds for community mental health centers. Unfortunately, as we can see today, the scope of community mental health centers has never been sufficient to adequately care for the number of people with serious mental illness in our communities, particularly when substance abuse problems are involved. Yet, the ideal of treating individuals with severe and persistent mental illness with a combination of medication and therapeutic interventions in the community is an admirable one.

Unfortunately, this ideal has not been realized given the state of community mental health since its inception in the 1960s.

Psychiatric personnel working in the public sector are the lowest paid in the mental health field, although their clientele are often the most resistant and difficult to treat. It is very strange and ironic that many of the clientele whom the 19th century psychiatric community hoped to treat in hospitals rather than poorhouses or prisons have now returned to these very places for their mental health treatment as many psychiatric hospitals have gradually closed their doors for good. In a recent *New York Times* article, "Out of the Asylum, Into the Cell," a psychiatrist, Sally Satel (2003), pointed out that jails in the United States now contain three times more citizens with mental illness than are found in U.S. psychiatric hospitals. The same report noted a startling statistic: The Los Angeles county jail houses 3,400 prisoners with mental illness. Satel deemed this jail, "the largest psychiatric inpatient institution in the U.S." (2003, p. A15). Satel further points out that 16% of U.S. prison inmates suffer from serious and persistent mental illnesses such as schizophrenia and bipolar disorder. It is clear that our current system of treating individuals with the most seriously debilitating mental illnesses is inadequate at its best and dangerous at its worst.

The reality of the problems in the community treatment of people with the most severe mental illness does not mean that such treatment is never, or even rarely, successful. Yet, for community programs to be successful, they must be adequately funded. For example, a model of community mental health treatment was developed in Madison, Wisconsin, in the late 1960s by Leonard Stein and his colleagues (Grob, 1994). This program successfully taught independent living skills to psychiatric patients through psychosocial rehabilitation. However, once the program's involvement with a patient stopped, the person tended to relapse in the community. A later project by the same researchers in the early 1970s was called "Training in the Community" and emphasized an extensive array of community services. These services included help with basic living skills (e.g., how to take a bus and how to budget money), assistance with finding jobs and housing, providing social support, and involving the patient's family in his or her care. Although this program appeared largely successful in reducing rehospitalizations of patients when compared with control groups not receiving the services, the cost of the community treatment was about equal to inpatient care (Grob, 1994). Yet, it could be argued that quality of life in the community would be better than quality of life in a state institution, and that if costs were equal, then most individuals would choose life in the community.

Current attempts to provide "wrap around services" in community mental health treatment facilities also provide hope toward improved coordination for treatment for people with the most serious mental illness in our society. These services attempt improved coordination of care among the variety of professionals who typically treat individuals with serious and chronic mental illness and attempt to reduce the need for inpatient care. The difficulties with community treatment, however, continue to lie in the great expense of involving the number of community resources needed to successfully maintain treatment gains as well as the longstanding dependency of those with chronic mental illness on the system of care. Community mental health treatment realistically cannot eliminate the need for persons with severe and persistent mental illness to have long-term care, but community treatment centers have not been provided with adequate funds to provide long-term care.

The Movement Toward "Self-Help" and Briefer Therapies

During this same period when psychotropic medications became available, community mental health was being emphasized, and deinstitutionalization was being tried, there was more of a push for therapy for other mental health problems that did not require hospitalization or medication. In fact, when community mental health centers were initially established, more people sought treatment for nonchronic and less severe mental health problems than for chronic and severe mental illness (Grob, 1994; Shorter, 1997). An amendment to the initial Community Mental Health Centers Act was actually passed in 1968 to place requirements on mental health centers to provide long-term treatment for people with serious mental illness and to offer short-term crisis intervention for those without chronic mental illness.

The 1960s and 1970s saw a significant shift in attitudes in our society. Many individuals were trying to break out of stereotypical roles and to challenge traditional societal and familial expectations. The zeitgeist was on developing a healthy psychological self, beyond mere physical health or job success or contentment in a marriage or in one's family. Such dramatic changes in the attitudes of Western societies in the 1960s and 1970s also impacted attitudes about the treatment of mental illness or "problems in living." Although psychodynamic and psychoanalytic therapies still dominated outpatient psychiatric treatment, there was a movement toward less deterministic and more self-directed treatments, such as client-centered therapy. Clients developing both an awareness of and a realization of their self (in Rogers's sense of the word) became a popular focus of therapy. In addition, group treatments became more popular. For example, during the 1970s, encounter groups, which encouraged members to "let out" feelings and to "be real," were very popular, especially among young adults. Peer support groups also became more popular during this time.

Crisis intervention centers also multiplied during the 1970s. They provided a variety of community assistance through hotlines, rape intervention, battered women's shelters, and crisis intervention units (Brown, Shiang, & Bongar, 2003). The services provided by crisis intervention facilities were short term by their nature. It is interesting that the crisis intervention model of service delivery was somewhat portent of the briefer modalities of treatment that would begin to dominate treatment in the final decades of the 20th century. The crisis intervention model would also be extended to "critical incident stress debriefing" interventions developed to treat victims of traumatic events, such as natural disasters and catastrophes (e.g., the Air Florida Flight 90 disaster in Washington, DC, in 1982; the bombing of the Federal Murrah Building in Oklahoma City in 1995; and the terrorist attacks on the World Trade Center and Pentagon in 2001).

Critical Incident Stress Debriefing (CISD) was developed by a former firefighter and paramedic in response to his own experiences with traumatic events. The main goals of CISD are to reduce acute stress after the experience of a trauma, to help frontline workers better manage their stress in the face of traumatic events so they can do their jobs, and to identify people who require additional mental health intervention. A variety of crisis interventions strategies are used in CISD (Brown et al., 2003). Crisis intervention and critical stress debriefing differ from traditional psychotherapy in that their response occurs immediately after a traumatic event and the goals of such interventions include reducing or preventing impairment from the trauma, thus attempting to prevent psychiatric disorders from developing (Everly & Mitchell, 1999).

As well-meaning as CISD appears to be, it has been met with some criticism and its effectiveness has been questioned recently. Van Emmerik, Kamphuis, Hulsbosch, and Emmelkamp (2002) reported a meta-analysis of studies in which a single-session CISD was done within 1 month of a traumatic event and was compared with non-CISD interventions and no-intervention control participants. They concluded that CISD interventions did not prevent symptoms of posttraumatic stress disorder or other psychological problems from occurring and discouraged clinicians from using traditional CISD for this purpose. Their study only examined the claims of CISD of preventing psychological problems, but the authors do point out that there are still the other goals of CISD: identifying individuals in need of further mental health intervention and reducing the immediate distress of those exposed to the trauma. However, at this point, there is not consensus among clinicians as to either the effectiveness of CISD or whether it should be used.

During the 1970s, still other modalities of therapy began to take form. These briefer therapies emphasized measurement of outcome, demystified the process of therapy for clients, and provided more cost effective procedures. Cognitive therapy, with its emphasis on how our thoughts and assumptions may drive maladaptive behavior and distressing feelings, began to draw attention as a more collaborative and direct therapy. Albert Ellis's publication of *Reason and Emotion in Psychotherapy* in 1962 and then Aaron Beck's publication of a series of articles in 1963 and 1964, *Thinking and Depression,* were both seminal publications in the field that sparked considerable enthusiasm for the cognitive approach (Beck, 1963, 1964; Ellis, 1962). Cognitive therapies shift the focus of treatment to how core beliefs and assumptions impact our mood and behavior. Along with behavior therapy, cognitive therapy was more easily operationalized in terms of specific techniques and outcomes that were measurable than the psychoanalytic or psychodynamic therapies that still dominated the field.

As health care costs surged in the 1970s and 1980s, pressure from the newly established managed care companies to contain health care costs was exerted on all medical practitioners, including mental health professionals. One of the main areas of recommendations and regulations instituted by the managed care industry was for the briefest and most cost efficient treatments available to be used. The reality of practice in the mental health field was that practitioners who wanted to receive payment from medical insurance had to learn to treat patients in briefer time periods and now had to provide rationale to insurance providers for any treatment that was protracted, even for treatment that extended beyond only 10 to 12 sessions. Current practice in mental health treatment has shifted toward providing the most cost effective treatments (in terms of time and money) and away from costly long-term treatments. In the past, patients in psychoanalytic or psychodynamic therapy often remained in therapy for many years and in some cases for their whole lives.

During the same time frame when insurance was undergoing the managed care revolution, research to evaluate the efficacy of various treatment approaches was underway. From the mid-1970s to the 1980s, more systematic empirical examination of various therapies was undertaken. An example of such a study was the Temple University Study conducted by Sloan, Staples, Cristol, Yorkson, and Whipple (1975), which examined in detail the effectiveness of the major schools of therapy of the day (psychodynamic and behavioral) as well as a myriad number of therapist and client variables that might impact the effectiveness of therapy. This classic study found that short-term analytic and behavior therapies were more effective than no treatment. By the 1980s and 1990s an explosion of well-designed, controlled studies of various forms of psychotherapy was taking place. Such research continues into the present century. The results of psychotherapy research in combination with the pressures for accountability by insurance companies greatly influenced both the practices of psychotherapy as well as the policies in the mental health field in the last quarter of the 20th century and now at the beginning of the 21st century.

Mental Health Treatment as a "Health" Treatment

Bornstein (2001) wrote an article titled "The Impending Death of Psychoanalysis" in the 21st century. This ominous prediction for what was once a revolutionary psychological treatment and theory of personality leads to a discussion of the state of mental treatment in the 1990s and the beginning of the 21st century. For those with serious and chronic mental illness, treatment has continued to remain in communities, and many former "asylums" have been converted for other uses or torn down (see http://www.historicasylums.com/). Still, community treatments typically continue to fall short of the needs of mental health consumers, and those with the most serious mental illness are often found among the homeless or prison populations (Levant et al., 2001). Fortunately, increasing numbers of psychotropic medications are being developed, and many more people with serious mental illness are being helped by these medications. However, medication alone is not sufficient to treat those with serious mental illness because of problems with medication compliance, relapse, the high cost of these medications, and their limitations in recovery. Funding for psychosocial rehabilitation that supports medication compliance and assists those with serious mental illness with the everyday tasks of living is insufficient but necessary for community treatment to succeed.

For the majority of mental health consumers with less debilitating disorders who can be treated successfully in the current systems of mental health care, the care itself has continued to focus on brief treatments such as cognitive–behavioral therapy as well as on treatments with data that supported their effectiveness. The 1949 Boulder Conference was a pivotal meeting that discussed and made recommendations for graduate training of clinical psychologists as scientist–practitioners. Its participants forged the way for the integration of research and clinical practice, at least in training. Yet, it hasn't been until recently, as psychotherapy outcome studies have multiplied, that a concurrent emphasis on clinicians paying attention to researchers' findings has truly come to the fore. Empirically validated or supported therapies are those treatments that have been shown in experimental studies to reliably and effectively treat certain psychological disorders. Although some clinicians and researchers have argued that only empirically validated therapies should be practiced, most providers of services and clinical researchers feel that a middle ground should be reached in advocating for empirically validated approaches. Garfield (1998) cautioned psychologists to carefully examine what the effective ingredients really are for empirically validated therapies and also suggested that the term empirically "supported" therapy is more appropriate. He also reminded psychologists of the power of the common factors that are effective across various types of therapy, such as therapist empathy and the client's emotional involvement. In addition, Garfield pointed out what most seasoned clinicians know—that experience gained in treating a wide variety of clients typically improves clinicians' skills and leads to more effective and efficient work. He cautioned against limiting our graduate training to producing specialists rather than generalists.

Kendall (1998) endorsed the phrase "empirically supported psychological therapies" and explained the necessity of empirically evaluating therapies to ensure a high standard of care. In addition, he pointed out the importance of empirical evaluation to ensure that psychological therapy has a valid role in the larger system of health care. However, he did not advocate for such therapies to be mandated by insurance companies, particularly as more research is needed to evaluate therapy conducted in clinical practice outside of research settings. It is clear that, in current day practice, clinicians are being held more accountable by their patients and colleagues (and of course the insurance industry) to show that their treatments are medically necessary and effective. However, they should not lose sight of the importance that common factors have on the effectiveness of therapy across the myriad types of therapy that are available.

Manual-based treatments are an outgrowth of the surge of empirical studies of psychotherapy. Manualized treatments were developed initially by psychotherapy researchers to ensure standardized delivery of the treatments to be evaluated in their studies (Lambert & Ogles, 1988). These types of treatment clearly describe how each session of therapy is to be conducted, including how to implement the therapeutic techniques. Now these treatments have been extended to clinical practice. Examples of manualized treatments include the time-limited psychodynamic therapy of Strupp and Binder (1984) and the behaviorally oriented treatment of Barlow (1992) for anxiety disorders. Clinicians have presented heated arguments both in favor and against this type of treatment. Scaturo (2001) pointed out that even without treatment manuals, clinicians have always struggled to operationalize theories of mental illness or descriptions of therapies for their use in individual cases. He discussed the pros and cons of manualized treatment and concluded that individuals with "circumscribed difficulties" such as "focal anxiety" are more amenable to manualized approaches, whereas those with more complex and varied difficulties will likely respond best to more integrative treatments that may include some of the treatment techniques in the manualized treatment (p. 528). In addition, Scaturo also reminded psychologists that "nonspecific" factors, such as therapist–patient rapport, therapist empathy and compassion, and patient motivation, that were confirmed to be important in the process therapy research of the 1960s and 1970s will continue to be important ingredients in effective therapy. Manualized treatments do not negate the need for these "common" factors to be present.

"Evidence-based" practice is a movement in the field that attempts to bring the knowledge gained from clinical researchers to clinical practitioners. This term has been more traditionally applied in the field of medicine. For example, in 1992, the *Journal of the American Medical Association* (JAMA), published guidelines in teaching the practice of medicine using an "evidence-based medicine" approach (Evidence-Based Medicine Working Group, 1992). There are many citations in the medical literature of evidence-based approaches. The American Academy of Family Physicians published a system of identifying various levels or degrees of evidence-based medicine to assist practitioners in discerning the degree or "level" of scientific basis for published interventions (see http://www.aafp.org/; Wright, 2003). Another example of medicine's attempt to bridge the researcher–clinician gap by disseminating such evidence is an organization called "The Cochrane Collaboration." The organization assembles and distributes systematic reviews of healthcare interventions internationally (see http://www.cochrane.org). Yet, even in the field of medicine, evidence-based practice continues to be critiqued by clinicians as being difficult to always implement in practice.

Currently in the mental health field, there has been increasing focus on how to apply the concept of evidence-based treatment to psychological interventions. Advocates for this approach in clinical practice equally emphasize empirically supported treatments, patient characteristics, as well as therapist factors in deciding which treatments to use, rather than just simply choosing from a list of empirically supported treatments. Westen, Novotny, and Thompson-Brenner's (2004) discussion of evidence-based practice in psychotherapy nicely delineated the complexities that need to be considered when conducting psychotherapy research in the laboratory and then applying such research in practice. They pointed out that simply applying the randomized control trial designs typically used to categorize therapy as "supported" or "unsupported" in the empirically supported therapy literature is not always valid and often not applicable to real world patients. Considering patient and therapist variables is seen as particularly important in research and practice. For example, the importance of patient factors (e.g., their personality and temperament, etiology of their problems, and situational variables) is typically not evaluated in most research on empirically supported therapies. Typically, a *DSM–IV* (*Diagnostic and Statistical Manual of Mental Disorders, Fourth Edition*) Axis I diagnosis determines inclusion in a study. However, nondiagnostic factors have been found to influence therapy outcome, particularly patient personality. Certainly, most patients seen in clinical practice have comorbid conditions (i.e., more than one presenting problem), yet the research on therapies typically only includes patients without comorbidity. Overrelying on *DSM–IV* categories to place patients in treatment studies appears a great source of concern in generalizing results to practice. Westen et al. noted that this is particularly problematic given that in practice about one third to one half of patients are difficult to place in *DSM–IV* categories, presenting, with other complaints, interpersonal problems or low self-esteem.

In addition to patient factors, therapist factors should be considered in whether a therapy will be effective. According to Westen et al. (2004), therapist allegiance to a particular treatment approach has not been adequately accounted for in therapy studies. For example, therapists conducting therapy in the assumed *more* effective condition (e.g., cognitive–behavioral therapy or interpersonal therapy) versus therapists in the assumed *less* effective treatment condition (e.g., minimal contact control or nondirective) may inadvertently produce stronger treatment results that are really more related to therapist effectiveness rather than to the treatment itself.

Ablon and Marci (2004) have also promoted the importance of including therapist and patient factors in consideration of what treatment to use. They have advocated for research and practice to focus on the "transactional process between therapist and patient" (p. 664). These authors and many others have pointed out that the essential ingredients in empirically supported therapies have not often been shown to be the treatment per se and may actually be common factors in the change process, such as the interactions between therapist and patient or patient or therapist personality. In sum, although there are still notable gaps between psychotherapy research and clinical practice, researchers and clinicians are actively elucidating where these gaps are and how to close them. At this time, perhaps Westen at al.'s suggestion for "empirically informed therapies" may be most realistic. As in medicine, several prestigious psychotherapy researchers have begun publications to review and disseminate important clinical research to practitioners in a way that is more usable in the field.

In addition to the current focus on effectiveness, therapy is also becoming less paradigm specific and more integrative. Integrative therapy approaches attempt to use the most effective ideas and techniques from a variety of therapy approaches and integrate them to provide the most effective treatment for a specific individual. One example of integration of psychological treatments described by Scaturo (2001) is psychodynamic and behavioral clinicians' inclusions of the client's family in the individual's treatment rather than just seeing the client as an individual "divorced" from his or her family system. Another example of integration occurred when many behavior therapists moving away from the "radical" behaviorism of the 1950s and 1960s began to include mediational variables, namely cognition, in their treatments in the 1970s and 1980s. Certainly, many treatment providers integrate biological treatment (namely psychotropic medication) and psychotherapy. Integrative therapy today attempts to individualize treatments by combining the best techniques from a variety of therapy approaches to most effectively (and perhaps most efficiently) treat the individual.

Psychiatric Treatment in the 21st Century: For Better or For Worse?

As we enter the 21st century, all professionals who now treat mental illness should pause to reflect on the progress we have made in mental health treatment over the past 200 years and to look forward toward how treatment efforts should be focused in this century. Patrick DeLeon (2002), a very vocal and influential psychologist and attorney who is an expert on APA policy, has predicted that the future of psychology includes continued influence from the health care industry, more integration of treatments, psychologists' acquiring prescription privileges (e.g., New Mexico in 2002 and Louisiana in 2004), and telehealth services providing more access to mental health treatments for consumers. In addition, DeLeon, Brown, and Kupschella (2003) have pointed out that mental health professionals will be subject to more accountability for their services by consumers as a result of consumers' increasing access to medical information on the Internet. Although psychologists may be predicted to have expanded roles in this century, the role of psychiatrists may be more uncertain. Shorter (1997) pointed out that the numbers of medical students choosing psychiatry as their profession has been declining significantly. He noted that in 1984, 3.5% of medical students went into psychiatry, whereas by 1994 only 2.0% of medical students chose psychiatry as their specialty. It may be surprising to learn that by the mid-1900s only 500 medical school graduates were beginning psychiatry residency programs. Interest in pursuing psychiatry as a career has waxed and waned over the years. As many psychological associations lobby legislatures for their members (appropriately trained) to gain prescription privileges, the current distinction of psychiatrists as the experts in the delivery of psychotropic medications is in danger of being lost. However, Shorter (1997) asserted that because of psychiatrists' status as "physicians," he believed that psychiatrists would still be sought by consumers, and furthermore, he asserted that they are more highly regarded than other mental health professionals.

In terms of what theoretical orientations or types of psychological therapies and treatment formats will dominate treatment in this century, Norcross, Hedges, and Prochaska (2002) have conducted a Delphi poll of expert psychotherapists every decade since 1980. In this poll, they ask psychotherapists to rate trends in psychotherapy over the next decade. In their most recent poll, they found that these experts predicted an increase in therapists practicing short-term therapy; this prediction received the highest absolute rating in terms of increase in the next decade. Overall, four themes summarized their findings: evidence, efficiency, evolution, and integration. In regard to "evidence," these experts predicted that evidence-based therapies would be required by health care companies. Evidence-based therapies are those that have been shown to be effective through objective, valid measures of improvement. "Efficiency" is essentially economy; brief therapies and less expensive therapies will be most popular. "Evolution" refers to their predictions that old and current theories and techniques of therapies may evolve into newer ones but that no new revolutionary psychotherapy techniques will be born. Finally, "integration" of therapies will emphasize more cohesion rather than division among therapy approaches. As noted above, integrative therapies will use the best from a variety of theoretical approaches and individualize the treatment according to the patient's particular personality, life circumstance, and problems.

As for the role of psychiatric treatment in medical treatment or health care as whole, many mental health professionals predict that mental health treatment will become more integrated into medical treatment. In a recent article in APA's *Monitor on Psychology* (Daw, 2002) entitled "Psychology as a 'Comprehensive Health Profession,'" the author quoted the APA 2001 President, Norine G. Johnson, PhD, as stating that as psychologists "we need to erase the line between health and mental health" (Daw, p. 82). One piece of evidence for this type of integration is the new medical reimbursement procedure codes (current procedural terminology [CPT] codes) that allow patient's medical conditions to be treated with psychological interventions even without the existence of a separate psychiatric diagnosis. For example, psychological treatment for individuals with cancer has been shown in many studies to extend patients' survival time (e.g., Fawzy et al., 1993). Daw (2002) also noted the emphasis of many research studies over the past several decades on showing the benefits of psychological interventions on other aspects of consumers' physical health. There is also more behavioral science research in the public health arena. Finally, Daw noted that many states' licensure bodies are providing certification of psychologists as "health service providers" in addition to their more traditional titles of "licensed psychologists."

In addition to this emphasis on health rather than just mental health, a policy statement by the APA Public Interest Directorate is emphasizing the need to provide "equitable and just treatment of all segments of society" (APA Public Interest Directorate, 2003). Current policy emphasizes the need to consider the diversity of the consumers we treat and to alter our treatment methods to accommodate the diverse needs of our clientele. Bingham, Porch-Burke, James, Sue, and Vasquez (2002) noted the move toward a multicultural awareness that includes respect and competence in understanding differences in race and ethnicity but also includes areas of "gender, sexual orientation, and disability" (p. 77). This focus on cultural diversity seems particularly important for minorities given that there is a large discrepancy between the low number of ethnic minority members in APA relative to the ethnic minority population in the United States. DeLeon et al. (2003) pointed out that the adoption of *Guidelines for Multicultural Education, Training, Research, Practice, and Organizational Change for Psychologists* in August 2002 as APA policy clearly reflects the current and future commitment of APA to address multicultural issues in this field (APA Council of Representatives, 2002).

As the population of older adults has steadily increased in our society, the psychological needs of our aging population have also been receiving more attention. Several pieces of legislation have been introduced in the U.S. Congress to improve older adults' access to mental health care (e.g., The Positive Aging Act; see http://www.seniorjournal.com/NEWS/Politics/5-05-31PositiveAgingAct.htm and http://capwiz.com/aagp/mail/oneclick_compose/?alertid=7655301). The APA has disseminated a variety of publications to promote improved understanding of the mental health needs of older adults (see http://www.apa.org/). The APA's "Graduate Geropsychology Education" initiative provides graduate training funds to support education and training in geropsychology.

In addition to the recognition of diversity on policy and treatment, changes in technology and communication at the end of the 20th century and the beginning of the 21st century are predicted to affect both policy and treatment in this field. With increased access to information in this field, consumers and elected officials will more readily have the information needed to advocate more fully for mental health care that is equal to other types of medical care. Although mental health parity laws exist now, most only provide limited parity for mental health treatment. If the future health care systems really do integrate mental health systems of care into physical health systems of care, differences in insurance reimbursement for mental versus medical treatment should no longer exist.

Finally, quality of care will continue to be an issue in the 21st century as it has been for centuries. In the current and future health care system, health care providers will continue to be pressed for objective evidence that their treatments are efficacious and safe. DeLeon et al. (2003) have stated that the basic safety of patients will be the first step in ensuring quality of care. Safety will continue to be of paramount concern in the prescription of psychotropic medication, particularly given that adverse effects of such medications have increased more than 44% from 1993 to 2000.

Summary

As we enter the 21st century, mental health professionals have been called by their various professional groups to become more active in contributing their knowledge and views to their legislators, in developing health care policy alongside providers of physical medical care, in providing accurate, research-based information to the media, and even in running for political offices themselves. Although only a minority of mental health providers will move outside direct practice to pursue these activities, these tasks will be increasingly important in the future to ensure that providers are able to provide quality and effective care to their patients.

FOR BETTER OR FOR WORSE?

I suspect that as we begin the 21st century both mental health providers and consumers of mental health care would agree that we are largely "better" than "worse." We still have a long way to go in our treatment of individuals with serious mental illness in our communities—prison health care is not a solution. Certainly, there continue to be many dedicated mental health professionals working in the community to treat individuals with serious and persistent mental illness despite the low pay. We have certainly come a long way over the course of the 20th century in terms of our ability to treat both serious and less serious psychiatric problems. My hope is that with the progress that is being made in fields like neuroscience and behavioral genetics and the realization that there must be a role for psychological interventions along with biological treatments that by the end of the 21st century we will see more "cures" for and "prevention" of mental illness rather than just "treatments."

References

Ablon, J. S., & Marci, C. (2004). Psychotherapy process: The missing link: Comment on Westen, Novotny, and Thompson-Brenner (2004). *Psychological Bulletin, 130,* 664–668.

American Academy of Family Physicians. (n.d.). Retrieved June 8, 2005, from http://www.aafp.org/

The American Association for Geriatric Psychiatry. (2005, May 26). *Positive Aging Act reintroduced in Congress.* Retrieved June 24, 2005, from http://capwiz.com/aagp/mail/oneclick_compose/?alert id=7655301

American Psychological Association, Council of Representatives. (2002, August). *Guidelines for multicultural education, training, research, practice, and organizational change for psychologists.* Retrieved from http://www.apa.org/pi/multiculturalguidelines.pdf

American Psychological Association, Public Interest Directorate. (2003). *The APA public interest directorate's mission statement.* Washington, DC: Author.

Baer, L., Rauch, S. L., Ballantine, H. T., Jr., Martuza, R., Cosgrove, E., Cassem, E., et al. (1995). Cingulotomy for intractable obsessive–

compulsive disorder: Prospective long-term follow-up of 18 patients. *Archives of General Psychiatry, 52,* 384–392.

Barlow, D. (1992). The development of an anxiety research clinic. In D. K. Fridheim (Ed.), *History of psychotherapy: A century of change.* Washington, DC: American Psychological Association.

Beck, A. T. (1963). Thinking and depression. I. Idiosyncratic content and cognitive distortions. *Archives of General Psychiatry, 9,* 324–444.

Beck, A. T. (1964). Thinking and depression. II. Theory and therapy. *Archives of General Psychiatry, 10,* 561–571.

Bingham, R. P., Porch-Burke, L., James, S., Sue, S. W., & Vasquez, M. J. T. (2002). Introduction: A report on the National Multicultural Summit II. *Cultural and Ethnic Minority Psychology, 8,* 75–87.

Bornstein, R. F. (2001). The impending death of psychoanalysis. *Psychoanalytic Psychology, 18,* 3–20.

Brown, L. M., Shiang, J., & Bongar, B. (2003). Crisis intervention. In G. Stricker & T. A. Widiger (Eds.), *Handbook of psychology: Clinical psychology* (pp. 431–451). New York: Wiley.

Daw, J. (2002, June). Psychology as a 'comprehensive health profession.' *Monitor on Psychology, 33,* 82–83.

DeLeon, P. H. (2002). Presidential reflections past and future. *American Psychologist, 57,* 425–430.

DeLeon, P. H., Brown, K. S., & Kupschella, D. L. (2003). Editorial: What will the 21st century bring? *International Journal of Stress Management, 10,* 5–15.

Ellis, A. (1962). *Reason and emotion in psychotherapy.* New York: Lyle Stuart.

Everly, G. S., & Mitchell, J. T. (1999). *Critical incident stress management (CISM): A new era and standard of care in crisis intervention* (2nd ed.). Ellicott City, MD: Chevron.

Evidence-Based Medicine Working Group. (1992). Evidence-based medicine. A new approach to teaching the practice of medicine. *Journal of the American Medical Association, 268,* 2420–2425.

Fawzy, F. I., Fawzy, N. W., Hyum, C. S., Gutherie, D., Fahey, J. L., & Morton, D. (1993). Malignant melanoma: Effects of an early structured psychiatric intervention, coping, and affective state on recurrence and survival six years later. *Archives of General Psychiatry, 50,* 681–689.

Garfield, S. L. (1998). Some comments on empirically supported treatments, *Journal of Consulting and Clinical Psychology, 66,* 121–124.

Grob, G. N. (1994). *The mad among us: A history of the care of America's mentally ill.* New York: Free Press.

Kendall, P. C. (1998). Empirically supported therapies. *Journal of Consulting and Clinical Psychology, 66,* 3–6.

Lambert, M. J., & Ogles, B. M. (1988). Treatment manuals: Problems and promise. *Journal of Integrative and Eclectic Psychotherapy, 7,* 187–204.

Levant, R. F., Reed, G. M., Ragusea, S. A., DiCowden, M., Murphy, M. J., Sullivan, F., et al. (2001). Envisioning and accessing new roles for professional psychology. *Professional Psychology: Research and Practice, 32,* 79–87.

Norcross, J. C., Hedges, M., & Prochaska, J. O. (2002). The face of 2010: A Delphi poll on the future of psychotherapy. *Professional Psychology: Research and Practice, 33,* 316–322.

Rogers, C. (1951). *Client-centered therapy.* Boston: Houghton Mifflin.

Satel, S. (2003, November 1). Out of the asylum, into the cell. *The New York Times,* p. A15.

Scaturo, D. J. (2001). The evolution of psychotherapy and the concept of manualization: An integrative perspective. *Professional Psychology: Research and Practice, 32,* 522–530.

Senior Journal. (2005, May 31). *Positive Aging Act reintroduced for 2005 by same four legislators.* Retrieved June 24, 2005, from http://www.seniorjournal.com/NEWS/Politics/5-05-31PositiveAgingAct.htm

Shorter, E. (1997). *A history of psychiatry: From the era of the asylum to the age of Prozac.* New York: Wiley.

Sloan, R. B., Staples, F. R., Cristol, A. H., Yorkson, N. J., & Whipple, K. (1975). Short-term analytically oriented psychotherapy versus behavior therapy. *American Journal of Psychiatry, 132,* 373–377.

Strupp, H. H., & Binder, J. L. (1984). *Psychotherapy in a new key: A guide to time-limited dynamic psychotherapy.* New York: Basic Books.

Van Emmerik, A. A. P., Kamphuis, J. H., Hulsbosch, A. M., & Emmelkamp, P. M. G. (2002). Single-session debriefing after psychological trauma: A meta-analysis. *The Lancet, 360,* 766–771.

Westen, D., Novotny, C. M., & Thompson-Brenner, H. (2004). The empirical status of empirically supported psychotherapies: Assumptions, findings, and reporting in controlled clinical trials. *Psychological Bulletin, 130,* 631–663.

Wright, J. (September 1, 2003). New AFP feature provides guides for use at the point of care. *American Family Physician.* American Academy of Family Physicians.

Zacks, R. (1997). *An underground education: The unauthorized and outrageous supplement to everything you thought you knew about art, sex, business, crime, science, medicine, and other fields of human knowledge.* New York: Doubleday.

Leonard S. Milling, Phuong M. Chau, and Mary Alice Mills-Baxter

A Review of Psychopathology

6

Introduction

Psychologists' understanding of psychopathology has been fundamentally shaped by the diagnostic systems that we use to organize abnormal behaviors into mental disorders. During the middle of the 20th century, two important diagnostic systems were introduced that have continued to the present day. The *Diagnostic and Statistical Manual* (*DSM*) published by the American Psychiatric Association (APA) is currently the most widely used system in the United States and Canada (APA, 2000). The *Manual of the International Statistical Classification of Diseases, Injuries, and Causes of Death* (ICD) published by the World Health Organization (WHO, 1998) now in its 10th edition, is the most popular diagnostic system used outside of North America. Some clinicians reject the categorical approach underlying these formal diagnostic systems, preferring instead to take a more dimensional approach in which abnormal behaviors (e.g., anxiety, depression, and neurosis) are described along a quantitative dimension (e.g., a 1 to 100 on which 1 is low and 100 is high).

The current version of the *DSM* identifies 16 general groupings of major mental disorders, such as anxiety, depression, and schizophrenia, plus two groupings of chronic or lifelong mental disorders (i.e., personality disorders and mental retardation). In this chapter, we summarize the essential features of the mental disorders contained in *DSM–IV–TR* (APA, 2000) focusing on the primary symptoms, course, and current theories of etiology of each set of disorders that you are most likely to encounter in a practicum setting. For more information about the mental disorders, you should see *DSM–IV–TR*.

In *DSM–IV–TR*, abnormal behaviors are described on five dimensions known as *axes*. The 16 acute mental disorders involving such problems as anxiety, depression, and schizophrenia are diagnosed on Axis I. In contrast, the presence of the two chronic, lifelong disorders, mental retardation and personality disorders, are diagnosed on Axis II. Any general medical conditions thought to be related to the mental disorder(s) in question are noted on Axis III. Psychosocial and environmental problems relevant to the diagnosed mental disorder(s) are indicated on Axis IV. Finally, Axis V is reserved for a numerical rating indicating the individual's overall level of adjustment, known as the global assessment of functioning.

Anxiety Disorders

These disorders comprise a broad spectrum of problems, each with distinct features, but bound by the subjective experience of intense dread and worry. Although occasional anxiety is a normal part of life, anxiety disorders are diagnosed when the anxious state is persistent, debilitating, and interferes with an individual's everyday functioning.

Panic disorder is characterized by sudden and repeated *panic attacks* in which the individual experiences extreme terror and feelings of impending doom. During these episodes, the individual may experience accelerated heart rate, sweating, dizziness or lightheadedness, chills, trembling, chest discomfort, and fears of losing control or going crazy. The panic attacks must be accompanied by persistent concern over the occurrence of future attacks and worry about their implications (e.g., losing one's mind or dying). Some individuals with panic disorder also develop *agoraphobia*, in which excessive anxiety over future episodes leads to avoidance of places and situations where escape may be difficult or embarrassing should a panic attack occur. Panic disorder usually has an onset between late adolescence and mid-30s. Although the course of the disorder can be highly variable, the usual course is chronic with periods of remission.

Phobias are defined as persistent and irrational fears related to particular objects or situations. Individuals with a phobia generally recognize their concerns to be excessive and unreasonable, but are unable to control them. The phobic situation is either endured with great distress or avoided altogether, as exposure often provokes an immediate anxiety response. *Specific phobia* refers to an unwarranted fear of a specific object or situation. Some common examples include fear of animals, enclosed spaces, heights, or injection needles. On the other hand, *social phobia* is generally linked to the presence of other people and social or performance situations, in which the person has an intense fear of publicly behaving in an embarrassing manner and being negatively evaluated by others. Public speaking, social gatherings, and other social activities can cause extreme distress for individuals with social phobia. The onset of both specific phobia and social phobia is typically in late childhood or early adolescence. The course of these disorders is often continuous, although the extent of impairment may fluctuate according to life's demands. For instance, a person whose intense phobia of airplanes led him to avoid flying his entire life might find that he is able to cope with flying once a year for work-related activities. Similarly, a job promotion involving frequent meetings and presentations may force a person to overcome her social anxiety.

Obsessive–compulsive disorder (OCD) is characterized by recurrent obsessions and/or compulsions that cause marked distress and significantly interfere with an individual's everyday activities. *Obsessions* refer to intrusive and recurrent thoughts, such as repeated doubts (e.g., doubts about locking the front door), fears of dirt and contamination, or concerns about orderliness. *Compulsions* refer to repetitive behaviors or mental acts that the individual feels must be performed to prevent the distress that accompanies the obsessions or to avoid some catastrophic event, although the compulsive behavior is not realistically related to its intended purpose. For example, a person with an excessive fear of germs may chew each mouthful of food at least one hundred times to decontaminate the food. Other common compulsions include cleaning, checking (e.g., checking if all doors are locked), and hoarding useless items. Usually, OCD begins in adolescence or early adulthood, with onset typically earlier for males (childhood and early adolescence) than females (early 20s). Onset is usually associated with some stressful life event, and the majority of cases exhibit a chronic course that waxes and wanes depending on the amount of stress in the individual's life.

Posttraumatic stress disorder (PTSD) and *acute stress disorder* are diagnosed when an individual develops an extreme stress response following a traumatic experience. These disorders were first brought to public attention by war veterans, but they are also common in victims of rape, torture, kidnap, child abuse, car accidents, or even natural disasters such as earthquakes. The traumatic event must have been directly experienced or witnessed and caused feelings of horror, fear, and a sense of helplessness. Individuals continually re-experience the event (through thoughts, images, dreams, or flashbacks), avoid stimuli associated with the trauma, and exhibit increased physiological arousal (e.g., insomnia, increased irritability, hypervigilance, or exaggerated startle response). All ages can be affected, with symptoms typically beginning within three months of the trauma, although for others, onset may occur months or years after the event. The principal difference between PTSD and acute stress disorder concerns the duration of symptoms. Individuals with acute stress disorder develop symptoms and recover within a month of the trauma and for the most part are able to return to their normal lives, whereas individuals with PTSD continue to experience extreme symptoms of posttraumatic stress for many months and sometimes even years after the traumatic experience.

The essential feature of *generalized anxiety disorder* (GAD) is chronic and excessive worry about almost all aspects of life. This "free-floating anxiety" can entail agonizing over meeting work expectations, general apprehension about the future, irrational fears that accidents will befall loved ones, or constant rumination over other possible catastrophes. The anxiety is difficult to control and physical manifestations include restlessness, fatigue, irritability, concentration difficulties, sweating, muscle tension, and sleep disturbances. Although most individuals report that they have had symptoms since childhood or adolescence, adult onset is not uncommon. The course is chronic, but fluctuating, with stressful life events playing a large role in the severity of symptoms.

The etiology of the anxiety disorders is complex and often involves the interplay between genetic factors, brain chemistry, personality, and life events. Almost all of the anxiety disorders occur more often among biological relatives, suggesting a possible genetic diathesis (i.e., predisposition). In addition, research studies have linked some of these disorders with chemical imbalances in the brain or overstimulation of specific brain regions. Specifically, OCD is related to low levels of serotonin in the brain, and individuals with panic disorder often have autonomic systems that are easily aroused by a wide range of stimuli. On the other hand, cognitive–behavioral models emphasize the role of cognitions and behavior in the anxiety disorders. An individual with a phobia of airplanes may associate heights with danger after a bad fall during childhood, or social phobia can be caused partly by negative self-views or a lack of social skills. Stressful life events, especially in cases of PTSD and acute stress disorder, also play a significant role in the etiology of anxiety disorders.

Eating Disorders

These disorders are characterized by a profound disturbance in both eating behavior and thoughts about body shape and size. Anorexia nervosa and bulimia nervosa are the two most commonly diagnosed eating disorders and have many clinical features in common. The distinguishing feature between the two diagnoses involves body weight. Individuals with anorexia nervosa lose a large percentage of total body weight, whereas individuals with bulimia nervosa maintain weight within or slightly above the expected weight range.

Anorexia nervosa is characterized by maladaptive eating behaviors among lower than normal body weight individuals. The disorder is identified by four primary clusters of symptoms. First, the hallmark symptom of anorexia nervosa is the refusal to maintain body weight at or above the minimally normal level expected for age and height (i.e., body weight less than 85% of the guidelines set in the Metropolitan Life Insurance charts). If the onset of the disorder occurs in childhood or adolescence, this symptom may manifest as a failure to achieve expected weight gain. Second, individuals with anorexia nervosa display an overriding fear of becoming fat—a fear that does not diminish in the face of weight loss and even severe emaciation. Third, people suffering from anorexia nervosa experience severe body image distortion (i.e., a disturbance in how one's body and size are perceived). This self evaluation of shape and weight generally has an overarching influence on self-esteem and mood. Finally, amenorrhea (i.e., the absence of menses for 3 consecutive months) occurs in postmenarchal women with anorexia nervosa due to abnormally low levels of estrogen secretion. Prepubescent girls who develop anorexia nervosa often will not have a first period until weight restoration and gain have been achieved.

Anorexia nervosa has two subtypes. The *restricting type* is diagnosed in individuals who achieve weight loss mainly through dieting or excessive exercise. The *binge-eating/purging type*, on the other hand, specifies that the individual has regularly engaged in binge eating (i.e., consumption of larger than normal amounts of food in a limited time period) or purging behavior (e.g., self-induced vomiting).

The average age of onset for anorexia nervosa is 17 years and is often associated with a significant life stressor. The course of the disorder varies widely. Eventually, 70% of individuals do recover, but long-term mortality from anorexia nervosa (as a result of physiological complications and suicide) is over 10%, the highest of any psychiatric disorder (APA, 2000). Etiology is likely multifaceted. There is a much higher prevalence of anorexia nervosa in industrialized societies and particularly in those that value the thin-body ideal.

Bulimia nervosa is distinguished by maladaptive eating behaviors among normal weight or above normal weight individuals. The most distinctive features of this disorder are the presence of recurrent episodes of binge eating (i.e., eating a volume of food within a 2-hour time period that is significantly larger than most people would consider normal, and feeling that the eating behavior is out of control) as well as the recurrent use of compensatory behaviors to avoid resulting weight gain (e.g., vomiting, laxative abuse, diuretic abuse, fasting, or excessive exercise). The self-worth of individuals with this disorder tends to be unduly influenced by feelings about body size and shape. Bulimia nervosa should not be diagnosed if the binge–purge episodes occur only in the context of anorexia nervosa. Like anorexia nervosa, bulimia nervosa also has two subtypes. If the individual vomits or uses laxatives, diuretics, or enemas, the disorder is considered to be of the *purging type*. If compulsive exercise or fasting is the compensatory calorie-shedding behavior, the label *nonpurging type* is given.

The onset of bulimia nervosa usually occurs in late adolescence or early adulthood and is often precipitated by a period of dieting. The course may be chronic, but is most often intermittent, with relapses occurring in periods of stress. As is the case with anorexia nervosa, cultural and media influences projecting an unrealistically thin ideal are implicated in the development of the disorder.

Mood Disorders

The prominent feature of these disorders is a disturbance in mood. Mood disorders are typically categorized as either *unipolar* (the presence of depressed mood only) or *bipolar* (the presence of two alternating extremes in mood, depressed mood and elevated mood). The unipolar disorders include major depressive disorder and dysthymic disorder, and the bipolar disorders include Bipolar I disorder, Bipolar II disorder, and cyclothymic disorder.

Major depressive disorder is one of the most prevalent disorders in the *DSM*. It is diagnosed when an individual experiences depressed mood or a loss of interest or pleasure for a period of two or more consecutive weeks, in addition to at least four of the additional symptoms: feelings of worthlessness, guilt, or hopelessness; decreased interest in previously pleasurable activities; sleep disturbances; changes in appetite; significant weight loss or gain; loss of energy; difficulty concentrating; and recurrent thoughts of death or suicide. However, depression affects people differently. Most people experience the usual symptoms of extreme sadness, exhaustion, and social withdrawal, whereas the predominant symptoms for others may be agitation, restlessness, and somatic complaints such as headaches and stomach pains. Major depressive disorder affects people of all ages in life, but typical onset is in the mid-20s. Onset may also be associated with the postpartum period (postpartum depression) or seasonal patterns. For individuals with seasonal affective disorder, depressive symptoms accompany the shortening days of the fall and winter months and subside in the spring and summer months. Approximately 60% of individuals who experience a depressive episode will experience a second episode, with risk increasing for each subsequent episode.

Dysthymic disorder is a mild to moderate form of depression that persists for a minimum of two years. Although symptoms are less severe than those for major depressive disorder, dysthymic disorder is often more resistant to treatment because the condition is more chronic. Dysthymic disorder usually has an early onset (childhood, adolescence, or early adulthood), with many who experience dysthymic disorder developing major depressive disorder at some point in their lives.

The bipolar disorders require the presence of at least one manic episode. During a *manic episode*, symptoms may include elevated or irritable mood, racing thoughts, increased self-esteem, feelings of grandiosity, increased talkativeness, decreased need for sleep, and involvement in pleasurable, but potentially destructive behaviors (e.g., making rash and unnecessary purchases and reckless driving). *Bipolar I disorder* is diagnosed when an individual experiences at least one manic episode, which for some individuals may alternate with episodes of depression. In *Bipolar II disorder*, depressive episodes alternate with periods of hypomania. Symptoms of *hypomania* are identical to those of manic episodes, but are not sufficiently severe to impair functioning or require hospitalization. In *cyclothymic disorder*, there is frequent cycling of depressive and manic symptoms, but they are not severe enough to meet criteria for any of the other mood disorders. The bipolar disorders typically have an early onset (late adolescence to early adulthood) and poor prognosis. The majority of individuals who experience a manic episode continue to have future episodes.

The bipolar disorders are essentially a biological disorder with a strong genetic etiology. The unipolar depressions are strongly influenced by both biological and environmental factors. Genetics are an important diathesis in some cases of unipolar depression. Cognitive diatheses include low self-esteem and pessimistic views of the world and future. Despite these predispositions, the development of a unipolar depression may require further precipitating factors such as death of a loved one, illness, job loss, lack of a social network, or marital difficulties. The exact etiology is different for every individual and often embedded in a network of causes that contribute to the development of the disorder.

Schizophrenia and the Psychotic Disorders

Psychosis refers to a serious mental condition involving gross misperceptions of reality, as well as seeing and hearing things that are not there. *Schizophrenia* is a form of psychosis that lasts for an extended period of time. The symptoms of schizophrenia are of two kinds. *Positive symptoms* are distinguished by the presence of distorted and abnormal behaviors, whereas *negative symptoms* are characterized by the absence or loss of normal behaviors.

There are four main kinds of positive symptoms. A *delusion* is a grossly distorted belief based on a misunderstanding of reality. An individual suffering from a delusion experiences events in the same way that others do, but arrives at an incorrect understanding of the meaning of those events. There are many different kinds of delusions. For example, in a *delusion of persecution*, the person incorrectly believes that he or she is being harassed, attacked, or tormented by an individual or group, such as a foreign government. In a *delusion of reference*, the individual incorrectly believes that sounds or other common stimuli are intended only for him or her. For example, such a person might think that static on the radio was an attempt by the CIA to contact him or her. In a *somatic delusion*, the individual incorrectly believes that there is something wrong with his or her body. For example, he or she may believe that aliens have surgically removed all of their internal organs and replaced them with those of other people.

Hallucinations are another positive symptom, in which the affected individual experiences events that are not there. The most common kind of hallucination in schizophrenia is auditory, in which the person hears voices in his or her head or out of thin air. Tactile hallucinations are the second most common, in which the individual feels something touching or moving underneath his or her skin (e.g., bugs moving under the skin). Another common kind of hallucination is visual, in which the individual sees visions of people or faces.

Disorganized speech and thinking is characterized by disturbances in the structure of thought. For example, a person may evidence *loose associations*, in which there is a very weak connection between each of the sentences in their verbalizations. Also, affected individuals may evidence *neologisms*, or made-up words whose meaning is known only to them. Additionally, in a *perseveration*, the person may repeat the same word or idea over and over.

In *disorganized and catatonic behavior*, an individual with schizophrenia may display grossly disorganized and inappropriate behavior. Catatonic behavior is characterized by odd motor movements, postures, or gestures. More specifically, in a *catatonic stupor*, the individual may become immobile and hold the same posture for an extended period of time. Alternatively, the person may exhibit *catatonic excitement*, in which the activity level is wild and restless.

Whereas the positive symptoms of schizophrenia are characterized by the presence of abnormal behaviors, the negative symptoms involve the absence of normal and adaptive behaviors. Individuals with schizophrenia may evidence *flat affect*, in which there is a reduction in the expression of affect or feelings. Such individuals may stare straight ahead with a glazed expression. In *alogia*, there is a reduction in the amount of speech. Sometimes alogia is characterized by a reduction in the total amount of speech, known as *poverty of speech*, and other times it is characterized by a normal amount of speech, but with a reduction in the amount of information conveyed, known as *poverty of content*. Finally, *avolition* refers to an inability to initiate or complete any type of goal-directed behavior. Affected individuals may sit for hours at a time, making no attempt to do anything at all.

There are five subtypes of schizophrenia in *DSM–IV–TR*. In the *paranoid type*, the patient typically has elaborate delusions and auditory hallucinations. The *disorganized type* is distinguished by disorganized and inappropriate affect, speech, and behavior. In the *catatonic type*, the person displays motor disturbance involving catatonic behavior. The *undifferentiated type* is reserved for individuals who display positive and negative symptoms, but do not meet the criteria for the previous three subtypes. Finally, the *residual type* is diagnosed when the person had a previous episode of schizophrenia, but no longer displays positive symptoms.

Schizophrenia typically has its onset in the 20s. The course of the disorder tends to be predictable. During the *prodromal phase*, symptoms develop gradually and insidiously. The longer the prodromal phase, the worse the prognosis. During the *active phase*, the symptoms are flagrant and obvious to others. Finally, during the *residual phase*, the psychotic symptoms subside in frequency or intensity.

Contemporary theories of etiology emphasize biological causative factors. Family, adoption, and twin studies clearly point to a genetic basis for the disorder. Also, neurotransmitter studies support a *dopamine theory of schizophrenia* in which affected individuals are said to have a large number of dopamine receptors or very sensitive dopamine receptors. Interestingly, research has shown that high levels of the neurotransmitter dopamine do not seem to be associated with schizophrenia, but the presence of excessive or overly sensitive dopamine receptors do seem to be related to the occurrence of the positive symptoms of schizophrenia. Schizophrenia has also been found to be associated with excessive levels of serotonin and low levels of glutamate. Additionally, brain imaging studies have shown that individuals with schizophrenia often suffer from enlarged ventricles (i.e., the fluid-filled cavities in the brain), as well as frontal and temporal lobe abnormalities. Most environmental theories of schizophrenia have not been supported by research, except for the theory of *expressed emotion*, which contends that individuals with schizophrenia tend to come from families in which there is a lot of criticism, hostility, and emotional overinvolvement. These family interactions may serve to worsen the functioning of individuals who are biologically disposed to developing schizophrenia.

In addition to schizophrenia, there are a number of other psychotic disorders in the *DSM*. A *brief psychotic disorder* involves the sudden occurrence of positive psychotic symptoms (e.g., delusions and hallucinations) that last less than a month. In a *schizophreniform disorder*, the person evidences symptoms of schizophrenia, but the symptoms are not severe enough to interfere with social or occupational functioning. Individuals with a *schizoaffective disorder* suffer from the symptoms of both schizophrenia and a mood disorder. In a *delusional disorder*, the person evidences no impairment except for one semiplausible delusion. Finally, in a *shared psychotic disorder*, two people share the same delusions. In this disorder, an *inducer* develops certain delusions and causes another person, the *receiver*, to adopt the same incorrect beliefs.

Substance-Related Disorders

These disorders are related to the use of a drug of abuse (e.g., illegal drugs or alcohol), toxin exposure (e.g., lead, pesticides, and carbon monoxide), or the side effects of a medication (over-the-counter or prescribed). The term *substance*, then, refers to drugs of abuse, toxins, and medications. In *DSM–IV–TR*, the *substance-related disorders* are divided into two groups: (a) substance use disorders and (b) substance-induced disorders.

The *substance use disorders* involve impairments in personal, occupational, or social functioning resulting from prolonged use of a substance. These disorders include both substance abuse and substance dependence. A diagnosis of *substance abuse* is concerned with the interpersonal and legal consequences of prolonged substance use. Here, the focus is on the social problems associated with repeated substance use. Individuals diagnosed with substance abuse may fail to fulfill major role obligations (e.g., absences at work or school and neglect of child or household) or use their preferred substance in situations in which it poses a physical risk (e.g., driving and swimming). They may be arrested or suffer other legal problems as a result of using a substance. Among individuals who have just started to use a substance on a regular basis, a diagnosis of substance abuse is more likely than a diagnosis of substance dependence.

A diagnosis of *substance dependence* is concerned with impairments in physiological, cognitive, and behavioral functioning that result from prolonged substance use. Here, the focus is on the biology and psychology of the affected person. Individuals diagnosed with substance dependence typically demonstrate symptoms of *tolerance* (i.e., need for increased amount of substance to achieve intoxication) and *withdrawal* (i.e., negative physical and psychological effects that result when a regular substance user abruptly discontinues or decreases use). Such individuals may use their preferred substance in greater quantities or for longer periods than was planned and often fail in attempts to decrease substance use. A great deal of time is often devoted to procuring the substance, using it, or recovering from its effects. People diagnosed with substance dependence may show a decline in work and social activities as a result of the substance use. These individuals will continue to use the substance despite knowledge of physical or psychological problems caused by or exacerbated by the substance. A person may be diagnosed with substance abuse or substance dependence, but not both. If the person meets the criteria for both diagnoses, substance dependence is given rather than substance abuse.

The course for substance dependence and substance abuse disorders is dependant on several factors, such as the substance involved and the frequency and duration of use. The etiology of substance dependence and substance abuse also varies based on the substances involved. A genetic component has been discovered in alcohol dependence, and other substance abuse problems often follow a familial pattern. Parental modeling and familial attitudes toward substance use play a role as well, as does positive or negative peer pressure. Personality traits of high level of negative affect and an enduring desire for arousal are often associated with substance use as well.

In contrast to the substance use disorders in which the focus is on the long-term consequences of prolonged substance use, the *substance-induced disorders* are concerned with the immediate biological and psychological effects of using, reducing, or discontinuing a substance. A diagnosis of *substance intoxication* is concerned with the immediate consequences of exposure to a substance (e.g., intoxication following consumption of large amounts of alcohol). A diagnosis of *substance withdrawal* involves the immediate biological and psychological consequences of reducing or stopping a substance (e.g., craving for heroin and physiological distress during an attempt to stop its use). An individual may be diagnosed with a substance-induced disorder and simultaneously diagnosed with one of the substance use disorders.

Cognitive Disorders

Cognition generally refers to higher mental functions such as thought, memory, learning, problem solving, decision making, and related processes. Cognitive disorders, then, result in the deterioration of one's usual cognitive abilities and significantly impair daily functioning.

Delirium involves a disturbance in consciousness such that awareness becomes impaired and there is difficulty in shifting, focusing, or sustaining attention. As a result, the individual usually experiences confusion, disorientation, and perceptual disturbances. In addition to impaired awareness, the individual must exhibit another change in cognition, which can include memory impairment, disorganized thinking, changes in psychomotor activity, or language deficits. Individuals may also experience sleep disturbances and emotional bouts of anxiety, depression, anger, or euphoria. Delirium has an acute onset that is often temporary in duration, although intensity levels may fluctuate rapidly during the course of the disorder. The causes of delirium usually have a physiological basis and can result from drug effects, fever, head injury, metabolic disturbances such as malnutrition, or medical conditions. In most instances, the condition subsides or disappears after the underlying cause is successfully treated.

Unlike delirium, *dementia* is a chronic condition that is often irreversible in its course and gradually worsens with time. Dementia is defined by the presence of multiple cognitive difficulties, including severe memory impairments and at least one of the following additional symptoms: aphasia (deterioration of language ability), apraxia (impaired motor skills), agnosia (difficulty recognizing or identifying previously familiar objects), or other disturbances in higher mental functioning. The frequency of dementia increases in late adult-hood, and symptoms signaling onset are often subtle at first because they may be difficult to differentiate from the normal signs of aging. However, symptoms become more noticeable to others as mental abilities continue to diminish and are accompanied by drastic personality changes and a loss of initiative in normal tasks and activities. As the disorder progresses, individuals gradually lose their ability to engage in even the most basic daily living activities and eventually require long-term care. Many neurological diseases can result in dementia, the most common type being *Alzheimer's disease,* a degenerative brain disorder in which abnormal particles form and gradually destroy healthy nerve cells in the brain. Some other common disorders that result in dementia include Huntington's disease, Parkinson's disease, or vascular dementia (which can be caused by a single stroke or the cumulative effects of repeated strokes).

Amnestic disorders are characterized by severe memory impairments in the absence of any other significant cognitive deficits. Memory disturbances can involve the inability to remember past events (*retrograde amnesia*) or difficulty in learning and recalling new memories (*antero-grade amnesia*). Amnestic disorder can result from drug intoxication effects or general medical conditions such as head injury, stroke, or vitamin deficiency. Depending on its underlying cause, the course of the disorder is variable. For instance, carbon monoxide poisoning may lead to an acute onset with symptoms gradually subsiding with time, whereas a traumatic head injury may cause persisting and irreversible memory problems.

Mental Retardation

Mental retardation is characterized by subaverage intellectual function-ing with coexisting deficits in adaptive abilities (e.g., self-care) that begins before the age of 18 years. Intellectual functioning is determined to be subaverage when intelligence quotient (IQ) test scores fall below the 70 to 75 range. (The average score in the general population on an IQ test is 100, and the majority of people achieve scores falling between 85 and 115.) Although some early intervention programs such as Head Start have had significant success with disadvantaged young children, IQ tends to be a stable trait and is therefore largely unaffected by attempts to improve it. Adaptive functioning refers to the ability of individuals to perform basic self-care tasks, function in their particular environment, and achieve an age-appropriate level of independence.

A deficit in adaptive behavior is often the presenting symptom in children with mental retardation, as such deficits frequently appear before a low IQ is evident. Unlike IQ deficits, adaptive problems are responsive to remedial education and usually improve with the proper support. A diagnosis of mental retardation must be established before age 18 years to prevent individuals who experience a change in intellectual functioning or adaptive abilities as a result of accident or illness from being incorrectly classified as mentally retarded.

Four degrees of mental retardation are specified in *DSM–IV–TR*, on the basis of the level of intellectual impairment. *Mild* mental retardation (IQ level 50–55 to 70) accounts for approximately 85% of individuals with the disorder. As children, these individuals have minimal sensorimotor impairment, develop social and communication skills throughout the preschool years, and are often indistinguishable from their peers. By the late teens, most individuals with mild retardation will acquire academic skills up to a sixth-grade level and as adults usually achieve the social and vocational skills necessary to be self-supporting. Some supervision and guidance is usually necessary. *Moderate* mental retardation (IQ level 35–40 to 50–55) accounts for 10% of the population with mental retardation. Brain damage and neurological dysfunctions that hinder fine motor skills are more common in this group; however, these individuals do usually acquire communication skills in early childhood and benefit significantly from vocational training. Although rarely progressing beyond a second-grade level academically, most adults with moderate mental retardation are capable of performing semiskilled or unskilled work in a supervised setting and adapt well to life in a family or group home environment. *Severe* mental retardation (IQ level 20–25 to 35–40) encompasses 3% to 4% of all people with mental retardation. These individuals acquire little to no speech during childhood and do not significantly profit from instruction. As adults, they can master simple tasks with close supervision. Physical abnormalities are common. Another 1% to 2% of individuals with mental retardation are considered to have *profound* mental retardation (IQ level below 20 or 25). This group often requires total supervision and nursing care throughout the entire lifespan, and the childhood mortality rate is very high. Individuals with profound retardation generally have a diagnosed neurological condition that accounts for their impairments.

Currently, only 25% of cases of mental retardation have an identifiable biological etiology. Down Syndrome and fragile X syndrome are the two leading chromosomal causes of mental retardation, but there are many recessive-gene diseases such as phenylketonuria (PKU) that can also cause the disorder. Maternal infectious diseases (e.g., rubella, herpes simplex, and HIV/AIDS) can cause retardation in the developing fetus, particularly during the first trimester. Childhood head injuries from falls or car accidents, and exposure to environmental toxins such as lead-based paint or mercury can also result in mental retardation. Although the 25% of individuals with mental retardation owing to an identifiable biological cause are distributed evenly across socioeconomic lines, cases of mild and moderate mental retardation are overrepresented in lower socioeconomic groups. This discrepancy in the distribution suggests that deprivation and lack of access to resources also play a role in the retardation of development.

Somatoform Disorders

These disorders are diagnosed when bodily symptoms are reported that cannot be explained by any medical conditions. In contrast to cases of malingering or factitious disorders in which the illness is either entirely fabricated or intentionally produced because doing so would lead to some benefit (i.e., primary gain), individuals with somatoform disorders genuinely experience physical symptoms, but the symptoms appear in the absence of any organic or medical cause.

Physical pain is the primary complaint in *pain disorder* and one of the many physical symptoms necessary to diagnose *somatization disorder*. *Conversion disorder* involves sensory and motor symptoms (e.g., paralysis of limbs or loss of vision) for which no physiological basis can be found. *Body dysmorphic disorder* refers to an excessive preoccupation with an imagined or exaggerated defect in one's physical appearance. Last, *hypochondriasis* is characterized by persistent and unrealistic concerns over developing a disease, despite frequent medical evaluations and reassurances.

Factitious Disorders

These disorders are characterized by the intentional production of physical or psychological symptoms in an individual's effort to assume the sick role. Symptoms and signs may be made up or self-inflicted. Unlike cases of *malingering* in which there is an external incentive to assume an illness (e.g., financial gain or time off from work), in factitious disorders there is no external motivator other than the person's desire to take on the role of the patient. Some individuals may spend large portions of their lives getting admitted to different hospitals and undergoing unnecessary medical procedures, as is the case in *Munchausen's syndrome*. In *Munchausen's by proxy*, a parent or caretaker deliberately fabricates or induces illness in his or her charge to gain attention and sympathy. Onset of factitious disorders is usually in early adulthood, and although it can be confined to one or two episodes, the course tends to be chronic. Predisposing factors may include the presence of other mental disorders, particularly a severe personality disorder or the history of a medical condition that required extensive contact with physicians in childhood.

Dissociative Disorders

These disorders are characterized by extreme changes in sense of identity, memory, perception, or consciousness. Individuals with *dissociative amnesia* display significant memory gaps that are often related to painful events and are too extreme to be explained by normal forgetfulness. In *dissociative fugue*, the individual moves away from home and assumes a new identity, with a complete loss of past memories. *Dissociative identity disorder* (formerly known as multiple personality disorder) involves the presence of two or more distinct personality states or identities that take control of the individual's behavior at different times. *Depersonalization disorder* is defined by episodes in which there are feelings of unreality or detachment from the self.

Onset of dissociative disorders is often related to trauma or extreme stress. The occurrence of dissociative amnesia and dissociative identity disorder is highest for individuals who suffered physical or sexual abuse in childhood, whereas depersonalization disorder and dissociative fugue are most often associated with life-threatening situations such as military combat or natural disasters. The course can be highly variable, with cases of dissociative identity disorder and depersonalization disorder generally being the most chronic and recurrent.

Sexual and Gender Identity Disorders

Three sets of disorders are incorporated in this group of problems: sexual dysfunctions, paraphilias, and gender identity disorders. A *sexual dysfunction* is diagnosed when there exists a persistent disturbance in an individual's sexual desire or the psychophysiological changes that normally characterize the sexual response cycle. This set of diagnoses includes problems with sexual interest (i.e., *sexual desire disorders* such as *sexual aversion disorder*), sexual arousal and excitement (i.e., *sexual arousal disorders* such as *male erectile disorder*), ability to achieve orgasm (i.e., *orgasmic disorders* such as *female orgasmic disorder* and *premature ejaculation*), and pain during intercourse (i.e., *sexual pain disorders* such as *vaginismus*). The courses of these disorders are highly variable and are dependant on the etiology.

Paraphilias are characterized by persistent and intense sexual urges or behaviors focusing on unusual objects or situations. For the diagnosis of paraphilia to be made, these fantasies or behaviors must result in significant distress or impairment in some important area of functioning. Paraphilias include *exhibitionism* (exposure of one's genitals to a stranger), *fetishism* (reliance on nonliving objects, such as females' undergarments, for arousal), *frotteurism* (rubbing against a nonconsenting partner, usually in a crowded place), *pedophilia* (sexual activity with a child), *sexual masochism* (having one's primary focus of sexual arousal be the fantasy or act of being beaten, humiliated, or otherwise made to suffer), *sexual sadism* (having one's primary focus of sexual arousal be the fantasy or act of causing suffering to another living being), *transvestic fetishism* (heterosexual male engagement in cross-dressing fantasies or behavior), and *voyeurism* (viewing unsuspecting persons who are naked or engaged in sexual activity). The paraphilias have variable courses, but they tend to be intermittent and chronic, intensifying in times of stress.

Gender identity disorder is characterized by a persistent cross-gender identification (the desire to be the opposite sex or an insistence that one is in fact the opposite sex trapped in the wrong body). For this diagnosis to be made, the individual must feel ongoing discomfort with his or her own assigned sex, and there must be no physical intersex condition present. Onset usually occurs in childhood or early adolescence, and the course is variable. Some individuals seek sex-reassignment surgery.

Sleep Disorders

These disorders encompass a range of sleep difficulties and are organized into *dyssomnias* (disturbances in the amount, quality, or timing of sleep) or *parasomnias* (unusual behavior or physiological events related to sleep periods).

Insomnia refers to difficulties in initiating or maintaining sleep, whereas *hypersomnia* refers to excessive sleepiness (indicated by long sleep periods, sleep episodes during the day, or extreme difficulties with awakening). *Circadian rhythm sleep disorder* involves sleep disruptions that result from a mismatch between a person's circadian rhythm and the sleep–wake schedule required by his or her environment. *Breathing-related sleep disorder* is characterized by sleep disruptions caused by respiratory abnormalities such as apnea (the temporary cessation of breathing during sleep). The most uncommon of the dyssomnias is *narcolepsy*, involving brief periods of "sleep attacks" during which the individual unintentionally falls into varying degrees of sleepiness.

The parasomnias include sleepwalking disorder, nightmare disorder, and sleep terror disorder. *Sleepwalking disorder* is characterized by episodes of unusual physical movement during sleep, such as rising out of bed or walking. *Nightmare disorder* and *sleep terror disorder* involve abrupt awakenings from sleep that are usually accompanied by intense fear.

Sleep disorders can result from general medical conditions, substance use, or another mental disorder. The course is highly variable depending on the underlying cause.

Impulse Control Disorders

These disorders are characterized by the repeated failure to resist a temptation or drive to do something that causes harm to the person or others. The individual usually feels mounting tension before performing the act, and relief immediately after commission of the act, and may or may not feel ensuing guilt. Impulse control disorders include: *intermittent explosive disorder* (episodes of aggressive outbursts leading to assaults or property destruction), *kleptomania* (repeated theft of objects that are not needed for monetary value or personal use), *pyromania* (fire setting for pleasure or tension relief), *pathological gambling*, and *trichotillomania* (recurrent pulling of one's hair, resulting in noticeable hair loss). Courses are variable and disorder-specific.

Adjustment Disorders

These disorders are diagnosed when an individual develops emotional or behavioral symptoms in response to an identifiable stressor or stressors. Stressors are not limited to, but may include, interpersonal problems (divorce or abuse), transitional periods (beginning college or job loss), or natural disasters. Symptoms must develop within 3 months of the stressful event and by definition last less than 6 months. If symptoms persist beyond 6 months, other disorders (e.g., major depressive disorder or anxiety disorder) are considered.

Adjustment disorders are organized into one of six subtypes depending on the predominant symptoms. The most common subtypes include *adjustment disorder with depressed mood* (predominant manifestations are depressed mood, sadness, and feelings of hopelessness) and *adjustment disorder with anxiety* (in which nervousness, worry, and fear are the most striking symptoms). In some cases, individuals develop atypical symptoms in reaction to a stressor. For example, a child may become socially withdrawn and bury herself in schoolwork rather than mourn following the death of a parent. For these instances, a diagnosis of *adjustment disorder unspecified subtype* is made.

Personality Disorders

These disorders are stable, inflexible patterns of inner experience and behavior that deviate from social norms, cause personal distress, or negatively impact social or occupational functioning. The diagnosis of a personality disorder should only be made when the maladaptive pattern can be traced back to adolescence or early adulthood and is not the symptom of another mental disorder (e.g., substance-related disorders). These disorders are grounded in personality traits, but in a personality disorder, the behavior patterns are extreme and maladaptive. The *DSM–IV* recognizes 11 personality disorders, including *antisocial personality disorder* (i.e., disregard and violation of other people's rights), *histrionic personality disorder* (i.e., attention seeking and dramatic emotional display), *narcissistic personality disorder* (i.e., admiration seeking, self-centered, grandiosity, and a lack of empathy), and *borderline personality disorder* (i.e., unstable interpersonal relationships, weak self-image, and significant impulsivity). Personality disorders are coded on

Axis II in the *DSM* so that they are not overshadowed by the more flagrant clinical disorders (e.g., mood disorders) that are coded on Axis I.

Disorders Usually First Diagnosed in Infancy, Childhood, or Adolescence

Many of the disorders diagnosed in adults are also commonly diagnosed in children and adolescents. Some disorders appear exactly the same way in youngsters (e.g., simple phobia), whereas others are distinguished by a slightly different presentation in children and adolescents compared with adults (e.g., major depressive disorder). However, there is a special category of disorders that tend to have their onset during childhood. It is to these disorders that we now turn.

Perhaps the most common reason why youngsters are referred to mental health services involves the three attention deficit and disruptive behavior disorders. *Attention-deficit/hyperactivty disorder* (ADHD) is characterized by an inability to sustain attention (especially to tasks that are not intrinsically interesting), elevated motor activity (e.g., running and climbing in situations in which it is not appropriate, and talking excessively), and poor impulse control (e.g., acting without thinking, difficulty waiting one's turn, and blurting out answers). ADHD is thought to be a lifelong disorder in which the affected individual typically shows some improvement in poor impulse control and elevated motor activity during adulthood. Contemporary theories of etiology emphasize biological factors. Family, adoption, and twin studies suggest there is a genetic predisposition to the disorder. Neuroimaging studies indicate that the frontal lobes (i.e., the part of the brain responsible for impulse control and regulation of behavior) of these children are smaller and less responsive to stimulation. Environmental toxins such as maternal smoking during pregnancy appear to play a role. Theories of etiology involving food additives and refined sugar have not been supported nor have psychological theories of etiology.

Oppositional defiant disorder involves a pattern of negativistic, defiant, and disobedient behavior. Typically, these behaviors are directed at authority figures such as parents or teachers. These youngsters deliberately do things that that will annoy other people. The usual age of onset of this disorder is before age 8 and characteristically no later than early adolescence. In contrast, *conduct disorder* is characterized by a pattern of behavior in which the basic rights of others are violated or major social norms are broken. Typical behaviors include aggression, property damage, deceitfulness or theft, and violation of major rules. Although both disorders involve externalizing problems, conduct disorder goes beyond defiant behavior to major violations of the rights of others and social rules (e.g., bullying, fighting, cruelty to animals, and fire setting). Conduct disorder is usually first diagnosed in late preadolescence or early adolescence. An earlier onset (i.e., before puberty) predicts a worse prognosis. Evidence of genetic etiology to oppositional defiant disorder and conduct disorder is mixed. Youngsters diagnosed with these disorders tend to come from families in which discipline is lax and inconsistent. Modeling of aggressive behavior by parents and peers may also be an important etiological factor.

Another set of disorders usually first diagnosed early in life that are commonly encountered by practicum students are the pervasive developmental disorders. These disorders are characterized by very poor or nonexistent language ability, very poor or nonexistent social relationships, and stereotyped behavior (i.e., odd or unusual behaviors that are adhered to inflexibly). There are four pervasive developmental disorders. *Autistic disorder* is characterized by severe deficits in interpersonal and language skills that begin by age 3. *Asperger's disorder* is distinguished by social deficits, in combination with normal or near normal language skills and has a later age of onset than autistic disorder. Youngsters diagnosed with *childhood disintegrative disorder* display normal development for at least the first two years of life, but by age 10, they develop autistic symptoms. This disorder is more common among males. Finally, *Rett's disorder* is characterized by normal development until age 6 to 18 months. A deceleration in head growth is observed at this point, as well as the loss of previously acquired motor skills and social interaction skills. This disorder is seen only in girls.

The etiology of these disorders appears to be biological in nature. Family and twin studies suggest there is strong genetic basis for autistic disorder. Furthermore, neurological factors such as abnormal brain wave patterns, brain enlargement, cerebellum and frontal lobe underdevelopment, cerebellum damage, and elevated levels of serotonin have been implicated in the etiology of the pervasive developmental disorders. There has been no support for the psychoanalytic notion that the parents of autistic children are cold and rejecting.

We should briefly touch on some of the other disorders that are typically first diagnosed during childhood. The learning disorders, motor skills disorders, and communications disorders refer to problems in academic functioning, motor functioning, and language ability that are substantially below what would be expected on the basis of the youngster's age and IQ. The feeding and eating disorders of infancy and early childhood are diagnosed when there are persistent feeding and eating problems, such as *pica* (i.e., eating of nonnutritive substances). The tic disorders involve vocal and motor tics in which the youngster makes sudden, recurrent motor movements (e.g., eye blinking) or vocalizations (e.g., throat clearing). The elimination disorders, *enuresis* and *encopresis*, involve urination and defecation in inappropriate places beyond the age that such episodes would be expected. *Separation anxiety disorder* involves developmentally inappropriate anxiety about separation from home or major attachment figures (e.g., parents). Finally, *selective mutism* is diagnosed in youngsters who have the ability to speak, but choose not to do so in certain situations (e.g., school).

Summary

We believe *DSM–IV–TR* represents a significant advance over the early versions of the *DSM* in that it clearly describes the diagnostic symptoms associated with each of the mental disorders. However, some of the limitations of the *DSM* should be noted. First, the *DSM* relies on a categorical or "all or none" approach to diagnosis that may obscure differences among individuals with the same diagnosis. Second, applying a diagnosis to somebody creates the risk of causing a *stigma* (i.e., a negative social halo) that can influence how that person is later perceived by others. Third, psychologists' knowledge of the causes of the various mental disorders is not developed to the point at which etiology can be used to help establish a *DSM* diagnosis for a patient or client. Finally, *DSM–IV–TR* may not adequately integrate culture into how symptoms are clustered in various disorders. Typical combinations of symptoms in North America may not be typical in Asia or Africa, for example. Similarly, the clustering of symptoms may be different for North Americans who strongly identify with a culture from outside of North America.

Nevertheless, the *DSM* is a very useful tool for mental health clinicians. The *DSM* facilitates communication among psychologists, psychiatrists, and social workers in clinical situations and in research. Furthermore, the etiologies of the various mental disorders eventually may be identified by research in which the *DSM* is used as the basis of classification. Finally, diagnosis of the mental disorders using the *DSM* helps to specify appropriate treatments for patients and clients.

References

American Psychiatric Association. (2000). *Diagnostic and statistical manual of mental disorders* (4th ed., text rev.). Washington, DC: Author.

World Health Organization. (1998). *The manual of the world international statistical classification of diseases and related health problems: ICD–10–Revised.* Geneva, Switzerland: Author.

Lee H. Matthews

Psychological Assessment | 7

Psychological assessment may include a wide range of observational and testing procedures. It is not possible within one chapter to cover all the material that is usually covered in an undergraduate course in tests and measurements. In this chapter, I provide basic information about reliability and validity, interviewing, mental status assessments, screening instruments, and full battery assessments. The most significant change in assessment has been the shift from full battery to screening approaches, mainly as a result of reimbursement policies of insurance companies. Screenings may be used for testing in a variety of areas such as intellectual, personality, cognitive and neuropsychological functioning. Screenings usually have few items and may assess only a single area of functioning, For example, the Shipley Institute of Living Scale, a screen for intellectual functioning, has only 2 scales that provide an estimate of verbal intelligence. In contrast, full battery assessments usually consist of multiple scales, measuring several different functions. For example, the Wechsler Adult Intelligence Scale—III not only has six scales to assess verbal intelligence, but it also has five scales to assess performance (visual) intelligence and three additional scales which allow calculations of working memory and processing speed scores. You should note that the distinction between a screening and complete assessment might be somewhat arbitrary, especially when discussing visual–motor, attention, and personality assessments. I present reimbursement and other factors influencing assessment practices at the end of the chapter.

Psychological testing has a long and consistent history. In a recent review of the psychological tests most commonly used in clinical practice, Camara, Nathan, and Puente (2000) noted that although newer versions of many of these tests are on the current list, many are the same as those from the 1960s (see Table 7.1). Depending on your field placement site, you may find the tests used may be different or more specialized.

Many different types of psychological assessments exist, and the following is only a brief overview of some of the various areas in which testing may occur. *Interviewing* is used to obtain historical information and determine the individual's capacity to handle other testing. An interview is a conversation with a purpose or goal. A *mental status examination* may be given to obtain organized behavioral observations

Table 7.1

Rank-Order List of the Top 12 Clinical Psychology Tests

Rank	Test	Current version
1	Wechsler Adult Intelligence Test—Revised (WAIS–R)	WAIS–III
2	Minnesota Multiphasic Personality Inventory (1 and 2)	MMPI–2
3	Wechsler Intelligence Scale for Children—Revised and III	WISC–IV
4	Rorschach Inkblot Technique	Same
5	Bender Visual–Motor Gestalt Test (BG)	Same
6	Thematic Apperception Test (TAT)	Same
7	Wide Range Achievement Test—3 (WRAT–3)	Same
8	House—Tree—Person (H–T–P)	Same
9	Wechsler Memory Scale—Revised (WMS–R)	WMS–III
10[a]	Beck Depression Inventory (BDI)	BDI–II
10[a]	Millon Clinical Multiaxial Inventory (MCMI)	MCMI–III
12	Trail-Making Test, Parts A and B (Trails)	Same

Note. From "Psychological Test Usage: Implications in Professional Psychology," by W. J. Camara, J. S. Nathan, and A. E. Puente, 2000, *Professional Psychology: Research and Practice, 31*, pp. 141–154. Copyright 2000 by the American Psychological Association.
[a] These two tests were tied in rank.

and basic orientation. *Attention and concentration* tasks such as immediate recall of numbers (Digit Span) to assess attention, more complex tasks such as recall of numbers in reverse order (Digits Backward), or concentration tasks such as attending to verbal material in a visual presentation and identifying a predetermined target (Continuous Performance Test—Second Edition) are used to assess distractibility and impaired ability to maintain purposeful focus. Deficits in these areas may represent a global disability or involve one or more expressive or receptive modality, such as reaction time, vigilance, visual search, and matching tasks. *Intelligence or cognitive* tasks such as the Wechsler Abbreviated Scale of Intelligence (WASI); the Wechsler Adult Intelligence Scale—III (WAIS–III); Wechsler Intelligence Scale for Children—IV (WISC–IV); the Wechsler Preschool and Primary Scale of Intelligence—III (WPPSI–III); and the Stanford-Binet Intelligence Scale—Fifth Edition (SB–5) are generally reported on the basis of the concept of *intelligence quotient* (IQ). Although no one definition of intelligence is likely to satisfy all psychologists, many experts say it is the overall ability to excel at a variety of tasks, usually involving both verbal and performance tasks and related to success in schoolwork or life. The concept of IQ provides a method of comparing a person's score to the performance of the average individual of the same age. An IQ or standard score (a newer term is *index*) with a mean of 100 indicates that the person performed similarly to the average performance of other people the same age. *Achievement* tests such as the Wide Range Achievement Test—3 (WRAT–3) are used to assess past training, usually academic in nature, and evaluate general areas such as reading, spelling, and arithmetic or more specific areas such as knowledge of psychology, history, or social studies. Tests of *mood* or *personality* status may involve either *objective personality* or *projective personality* testing. *Objective* tests are self-report instruments, such as the Beck Depression Inventory—II (BDI–II) or the Minnesota Multiphasic Personality Inventory—2 (MMPI–2). *Projective* measures such as the Rorschach Inkblot Technique ("What does the inkblot look like?") and the Thematic Apperception Test ("Tell me a story that goes with this picture") use ambiguous stimuli to obtain a dynamic view of the personality. *Visual spatial* testing such as the Bender Visual–Motor Gestalt Test may assess skills such as copying or construction of drawings, reproduction of block designs, or integration of visual information. *Language* assessment measures such as the Peabody Picture Vocabulary Test—3 (PPVT–3) may involve reception, expression, or comprehension of language. *Memory* tests, such as the Wechsler Memory Scale—III, (WMS–III) assess immediate, delayed, and working memory. Many memory screenings assess only one area, such as learning a list of words, recalling sentences, or repeating stories. Memory assessment may involve auditory, visual, tactile, or other types of input.

Neuropsychological tests such as the Luria–Nebraska Neuropsycho-logical Battery (LNNB) assess brain–behavior relationships and are used to determine the effects of head trauma, strokes, brain tumors, and toxic or degenerative disorders on daily functioning. Two approaches to testing are used, *fixed batteries* (same group of tests administered in a standardized way to every person) and *flexible batteries* (results of one test are used to determine if another test is to be administered so the number of tests given varies across people or problems). *Behavioral* measures may assess developmental levels (Vineland Adaptive Behavior Scales), social adjustment, or behavioral excesses/deficits (Conners' Rating Scale—Revised).

At least two psychometric properties are important when considering the use of a test and interpreting the results. These are reliability and validity. *Reliability* refers to the consistency and stability of test scores across situations (Anastasi & Urbina, 1997). When making important decisions about a person on the basis of the results of the testing, you want to have confidence that if a different psychologist had given the test on a different day or in a different place, the results would have been the same. Psychological tests, like many forms of measurement, do not have absolute reliability. Suppose you have someone measure your height with a ruler and about three hours later have another person repeat the measurement. If one said you were 5 feet, 8 3/4 inches and the other said you were 5 feet, 8 5/8 inches, you would probably not feel that your ruler was broken and that you needed a new one. Most of us would accept that this small difference might be a personal change or within an acceptable range of error for the instrument. This same concept relates to psychological tests. Test manuals provide information about the statistical evaluation of the reliability of the test, usually reported as a *reliability coefficient*. Psychologists use several different methods for evaluating the reliability of test scores. One common approach (the example above) is known as test–retest reliability. In this case, you correlate pairs of scores obtained by the same person on two different administrations of the same test. Another type of reliability, alternate form or parallel form, requires that two or more versions of the test be developed. The person is tested with both forms and the scores are correlated. Split-half reliability involves comparing one half of the test with the other half. For example, you might compare the odd-numbered items with the even-numbered ones. Of course, for all these methods, you evaluate a large number of people's scores in this way before you have a good idea about the consistency of the scores. For most psychological tests to be considered to be reliable, the test–retest correlation should be in the .80 to .90 range.

The *validity* of a test is the degree to which the test measures what it purports to (says it) measure (Messick, 1995). Although there are numerous types of or ways to calculate validity, there are at least four widely used important types of validity. These are *face validity, content validity, predictive validity*, and *construct validity*. *Face validity* is based on the surface content of the test and relates to what the test seems to measure to the person being examined, rather than to what the test actually measures, which may not be directly related to the topic in which the test designer is interested. Thus questions like "How sad do you feel?" "How often do you feel sad?" on a test labeled *The Sadness Test* may be face valid and simply ask for specific information on sadness rather than on some underlying concept such as level or number of symptoms of depression that the test designer actually wants to know. Unfortunately, face validity does not guarantee that the test is valid. There are numerous reasons for this, but one is that individuals may not always either see themselves accurately or describe accurately how they are feeling. *Content validity* measures the extent to which a test samples information adequately from a particular concept. For example, if a test designer defines depression as a theoretical concept involving the three elements of feelings (e.g., sadness or fatigue), physical signs (e.g., sleep disturbance and changes in appetite), and changes in thought patterns (e.g., negative view of self and the world), then the test should have questions that access all three types of information. A test with adequate content validity might have questions not only about "How often do you feel sad?" but also "Do you have problems with falling asleep?" and "Are you hopeless about the future?" *Predictive validity* (also known as criterion validity) indicates the degree to which a test score predicts some criterion, such as a specific diagnosis, a specific pattern of behavior, or as a somewhat silly example, having a test score which predicts a person's ability to juggle bean bags. Predictive validity is based on comparing scores from one test with the same person's score to another test or a real world measure of performance that is related to what the test measures. For example, if a preadmission test is designed to predict levels of success in undergraduate school, then grades in undergraduate school might be an accurate criterion. To test for predictive validity, you would administer the preadmission test to all students and later compare their scores with their grade-point averages at the time of graduation. *Construct validity* is the degree to which a test measures some theory, on the basis of a scientific or an informed idea (construct) used to explain or describe some behavior. For example, you might have a theory about personality patterns that are important to the construct of "creativity." You could then generate hypotheses about differences between low scorers and high scorers on a test of creativity. If the test is a valid measure of creativity, then the low and high scorers will have personality patterns as predicted by the theory. A test that has construct validity will correlate positively with other valid measures of the construct. For example, a new test for creativity has construct validity if it is highly correlated with other valid measures that define the construct of creativity. For more details on this topic, consult a general tests and measurements textbook (Gregory, 2004).

Related to reliability and validity are the concepts of *normative sample (norms)* and *cut scores (cutoff scores)*. For many psychological tests, that is the average (or arbitrarily set) score of some more (or less) well-defined population or group. As an example not related to psychology, think about the concept of 20–20 vision. That is an arbitrary standard of visual acuity that is used to place a person in relation to that "ideal" score. Depending on the type and use of any test, comparisons may be made between a person's performance and a large sample of a specific age, such as comparing a 6-year-old child to 6-year-old norms. However, norms are important primarily to the extent that they are based on large, heterogeneous, culturally diverse samples or apply to the individual you are testing. A cut score (sometimes referred to as a cutoff or cutoff score) is often a numerical score used to indicate a reference point that is based on research or judgment. Cut scores are used to divide test scores into two or more categories. For example, a simple "pass–fail" cut score might be based on obtaining a test score of 60 points. Score above 60 points and you pass the test; score below 60 points and you fail the test. A test may have multiple cut scores to indicate different categories such as mild, moderate, or severe levels of anxiety.

Psychological Screening

Screenings can aid in the referral, diagnosis, treatment, or termination of therapy for a client (outpatient) or patient (inpatient). Screenings, in contrast to more comprehensive evaluations, have a more limited point of focus. In the mood and personality section, many measurements are single scales with the emphasis on depression, often described as the "common cold of mental health," and anxiety measures, as these are among the most frequent disorders seen in general clinical practice. Appendix 7.1 lists some commonly used screening procedures. These are arranged by type of assessment and include age ranges (Franzen & Berg, 1998) and a brief description of the instrument.

Full Battery Assessments

A "full battery" or comprehensive assessment may be limited to a certain area such as personality assessment but more often involves evaluation of an individual's level of functioning across a variety of cognitive, achievement, personality, and other areas of assessment. The aim is to sample behavior across situations that vary from structured to semistructured to unstructured. Appendix 7.2 lists some commonly used full battery assessments. This appendix provides age ranges and a brief description of these instruments, which are arranged by type of assessment.

Summary

In recent years, some significant trends have developed within the areas of psychological assessment. The major developments in psychological interviewing have been on structured and semistructured interviews. This trend can be traced to several sources, including the increased reliance on diagnostic procedures using operationally defined criteria for making psychiatric diagnoses.

Although mental status examinations were primarily developed for older populations, they have been increasingly used for individuals presenting with a variety of symptoms and diagnoses, including cognitive disorganization, confusional states, and dementia as well as those patients with a physical disorder showing acute mental disturbances and with psychiatric patients.

Screenings have grown in popularity with changes in the mental health care delivery system in this country. Some risks are inherent in any screening instrument, such as reliability errors based on a small number of test items being administered, which may be partially overcome by focusing on highly specific referral questions. With cognitive screening measures, questions of validity need to be considered, as there is a tendency to overestimate the actual level of intellectual functioning with some of these instruments. In a similar manner, too brief a personality or neuropsychological screening may underestimate the degree of psychopathology. Careful selection of tests can greatly decrease these types of errors, as can the trend for increased emphasis on reliability and validity data.

Managed care has become a dominant force producing major changes in the mental health care delivery system in this country, influencing both the practice and training of psychologists. The effects of managed care in the past 10 years have had a profound impact on the delivery of psychological assessment, for example, the markedly shorter lengths of psychiatric inpatient hospital stays (down from an average of 21 days to 5 days). When the effects of managed care are combined with decreased funds available for psychological assessments and the need for precertification of evaluations (which potentially shortens the length of time in which a psychological evaluation can be accomplished), the result is a significant shift in delivery of inpatient assessment services to screening measures. In community mental health centers, increasing patient load along with decreasing numbers of staff members also calls for more rapid assessment and the shift to screenings.

At the same time, many of the comprehensive instruments in most common use in clinical practice (see Table 7.1) are newer editions of the tests used for the past 40 years. Several trends have emerged in full battery assessment. One of these trends is the development of different types of tests that are conormed on the same sample and have the same structure for scoring, such as the same type of standard and index scores across the Wechsler series of achievement, intellectual, and memory tests. The advantages are in making interpretations, detecting deficits, and strengths across testing areas much easier.

Historically most "traditional" screenings were based on methods such as *selected subtests*, using a few of the subtests from a complete test, or *selected items*, using only the odd numbered items from all of the subtests. More recently, another trend is shorter versions or adaptations of comprehensive tests, which are conormed with multiple comprehensive batteries but have equivalent rather than the same test items.

The emphasis on shorter, more focused outpatient treatment is another trend, often on the basis of a predetermined, limited number of sessions. The use of screening tests to assess severity of mental health concerns and as a way to evaluate progress is an area that is gaining more attention.

As to the future of psychological assessment, there is increased interest in outcome studies to determine the effectiveness of various treatment modalities and techniques. Thus, there is likely to be a greater demand for short, repeatable instruments (perhaps in multiple parallel forms) to assess therapeutic progress.

The use of screening and comprehensive psychological evaluation has always had a place within clinical psychology, and although faced with multiple issues, appears to have a vital future in the field.

Appendix 7.1
Psychological Screening

Mental Status Exams

1. *Mini-Mental Status Examination* (MMSE; Folstein, Folstein, & McHugh, 2001). Application: Ages 18 and older. The MMSE, perhaps the most widely used structured mental status exam, has 30 items, is administered in 10 minutes, and assesses orientation, registration, attention, calculation, serial subtractions, recall, short-term memory, naming, and language repetition. Separate norms for clients who are illiterate, over age 80, and have less than a ninth-grade education are provided.

2. *The Mental Status Examination in Neurology* (Strub & Black, 2000). Application: Ages 16–adult. Administration time is 50 minutes. Areas assessed include language skills, identification of clothing and objects that are commonly found in clinic or hospital rooms, reading, writing, and spelling. Memory functions, simple and complex copying of drawings, and higher cortical functions are assessed as well as geographic orientation and visual neglect and frontal lobe dysfunction.

3. The *COGNISTAT* (Kiernan, Mueller, & Langston, 1995). Application: Ages 20–94. It assesses cognitive and intellectual functioning in five basic areas: Language (Spontaneous Speech, Comprehension, Repetition, and Naming subtests); Construction; Memory; Calculations; and Reasoning (Similarities

and Judgment subtests). Measures of Attention, Level of Consciousness, and Orientation are assessed independently. Norms are based on two standardization age groups (20–39 and 40–66 years), a geriatric group (70–92 years), and a neurosurgical group (25–88 years) with documented brain lesions (e.g., stroke and brain tumor).

4. *Dementia Rating Scale—2* (DRS–2; Jurica, Leitten, & Mattis, 2001). Application: Ages 55–89. The DRS–2 can be administered in about 20 minutes. Originally developed to quantify the mental status of elderly persons even with profound cognitive impairment, that is, patients already identified as having some level of dementia. Items are similar to a neurologist's bedside mental status exam. Subtests include Attention, Initiation/Perseveration, Construction, Conceptualization, and Memory. There are age and education-corrected norms and percentile comparisons with patients with Alzheimer's disease.

5. *Repeatable Battery for the Assessment of Neuropsychological Status* (RBANS; Randolph, 1998). Application: Ages 20–89. The RBANS takes 30 minutes and has two parallel forms, permitting retesting. There are 12 subtests measuring the five domains of Immediate Memory, Visuospatial/Constructional, Attention, Language, and Delayed Memory. Standard scores can be obtained.

Attention and Concentration Tests

1. *Digit Span Subtest of the Wechsler Adult Intelligence Scale—III* (WAIS–III; Wechsler, 1997a). Application: Ages 16–89. Perhaps the most widely used method for the assessment of immediate auditory attention and working memory. Includes both Digits Forward (repeating longer series of numbers) and Digits Backward, (reversing longer sequences of numbers) so it assesses mental control. One of the most sensitive WAIS–III subtests to the effect of brain dysfunction (WISC–III subtest is the same for children). Standard scores can be obtained.

2. *Digit Symbol Subtest of the WAIS—III* (Wechsler, 1997a). Application: Ages 16–89. A symbol–number substitution task, requiring matching numbers with symbols. It is a motor performance test that requires sustained attention, motor speed,

visual–motor coordination, and persistence. WISC–III Coding Subtest is similar.

3. *Stroop Color and Word Test* (Golden & Freshwater, 2002). Application: Ages 15–adult. The Stroop measures cognitive processing, flexibility, and resistance to interference. It consists of three tasks, reading a list of repeating printed words (Word), verbalizing the color of ink (Color), and an interference task (Word–Color). The latter requires naming the color in which words are printed disregarding the verbal content (a word *red* could be printed in blue ink with the correct response naming the color of the ink. New norms based on T-scores and interpretations are provided.

Intellectual and Cognitive Tests

1. *Wechsler Abbreviated Scale of Intelligence* (WASI; Wechsler, 1999). Application: Ages 6–89. The WASI is a screening measure that can be administered in a two-subtest (15 minutes) or four-subtest (30 minutes) format (Vocabulary, Block Design, Similarities, and Matrix Reasoning are the subtests). Although similar in format, all test items are new and parallel to the WAIS–III and WISC–III and have conormative links to both for estimating IQ. The two subtests yield a full scale intelligence quotient (FSIQ), whereas the four-subtests give FSIQ, verbal intelligence quotient (VIQ), and performance intelligence quotient (PIQ). Reliability on FSIQ range from .92 to .98. Validity correlations are in the .81 to .92 range.

2. *Kaufman Brief Intelligence Test* (K–BIT; Kaufman & Kaufman, 1990). Application: Ages 4–90. The K–BIT administration time is 30 minutes. There are two subtests, Vocabulary and Matrices, however, the Vocabulary includes both Expressive Vocabulary (name a pictured object) and Definitions (over the age of 7) in which the person has to produce the word that best fits two clues, a phrase description and a partial spelling of the word. Matrices involves visual organization and abstract reasoning. A score for Vocabulary, Matrices, and Composite IQ can be calculated.

3. *Shipley Institute of Living Scale* (SIL; Shipley, 1994). Application: Ages 14 and older. The SIL requires 10 to 20 minutes to administer. There is a 40-item Vocabulary test and a 20-item Abstract thinking task. Scores for Vocabulary, Abstraction,

and a total are calculated. It is also possible to calculate a conceptual quotient (CQ), which is an index of impairment, based on a comparison of the vocabulary to abstraction scores, and an abstraction quotient, which is the CQ score adjusted for age. Estimates of IQ can be obtained for both the WAIS and WAIS–R.

4. *Slosson Intelligence Test—3* (SIT–3; Slosson, Nicholson, & Hibpshman, 2000). Application: Ages 4–65. The SIT–3 was recently nationally restandardized. The six domains of General Information, Comprehension, Quantitative, Similarities and Differences, Vocabulary, and Auditory Memory can be assessed in about 20 minutes. Deviation IQ scores, standard scores, and percentiles can be obtained.

Achievement Tests

1. *Wide Range Achievement Test—Third Edition* (WRAT–3; Wilkinson, 1993). Application: Ages 5–75. The WRAT–3 assesses single-word reading, spelling, and arithmetic skills in about 30 minutes. The most often cited achievement test (ranking seventh in Table 7.1), it has two alternative test forms (Blue and Tan) and provides test–retest capacity. Age-corrected norms, based on a stratified sample of the 1990 U.S. census, provide standard scores, grade equivalents, and percentiles. Validity correlations are in the .60 to .80 range.

Mood and Personality Tests

1. *Beck Depression Inventory—II* (BDI–II; Beck, Steer, & Brown, 1996). Application: Ages 13 years and older. The BDI–II is the most widely used test for depression (tied for 10th place in the list of most commonly used tests, see Table 7.1) and has 21 groups of statements, each item having a four-point scale. It measures intensity of depression on the basis of cognitive, affective, somatic, and performance symptoms and requires about 5 minutes to complete. Cut scores ranging from minimal to severe are provided.

2. *Beck Anxiety Inventory* (BAI; Beck, 1993). Application: Ages 17–80. The *BAI* consists of 21 items (having a 4-point

scale), each descriptive of some anxiety feature such as subjective distress and somatic or panic-related symptoms. Norms include a variety of anxiety and panic disorders.

3. *Reynolds Adolescent Depression Scales—Second Edition* (RADS–2; Reynolds, 2000). Application: Ages 11–20. The RADS–2 is a 30-item, self-report measure of depression assessing the four dimensions of Dysphoric Mood, Anhedonia/Negative Affect, Negative Self-Evaluation, and Somatic Complaints.

4. *Reynolds Child Depression Scale* (RCDS; Reynolds, 1989). Application: Ages 8–12. The RCDS is a 30-item screening test using a 4-point response format in a self-report measure of depression similar to the RADS–2.

5. *Revised Children's Manifest Anxiety Scale* (RCMAS; Reynolds & Richmond, 1985). Application: Ages 6–19. A self-report measure of anxiety in children, the RCMAS has four scales: Physiological Anxiety, Worry/Oversensitivity, Social Concerns/Concentration, and Lie. *T*-scores are provided.

6. *Hamilton Depression Inventory* (HDI; Reynolds & Kobak, 1995). Application: Ages 18 and older. The HDI has 23 items, is written at a fifth-grade level, and takes approximately 15 minutes to administer and score. Cut scores are provided.

7. *Suicide Probability Scale* (SPS; Cull & Gill, 1988). Application: Ages 13 and older. The SPS has 36 items, each rated on a 4-point scale that generates a normalized *T*-score, a total score that can be compared with low-, moderate-, or high-risk populations drawn from both inpatient and outpatient settings to calculate a Suicide Probability Risk score. Four subtests measure Hopelessness, Suicide Ideation, Negative Self-Evaluation, and Hostility.

8. *The State–Trait Anxiety Inventory* (STAI; Spielberger, 1983). Application: Ages are high school to adult. The STAI has two separate 20-item (4-point rating) self-report scales for assessing State (temporary) and Trait (more long standing) Anxiety. Norms are available for working adults, students, and military recruits, with specialized norms available for African-American and Latino populations. Percentiles and *T*-scores are obtained.

Visual Spatial Tests

1. *Bender Visual–Motor Gestalt Test* (BG; Bender, 1938). Application: Ages 5–adult. The *BG* is one of the oldest and most

widely used (fifth most often used in Table 7.1) paper-and-pencil tests of visuoperceptual and visuomotor functioning. It consists of nine figures each on a separate card, which are copied by the client. Although sensitive in representing complex spatial functions in both cerebral hemispheres, the test's clinical sensitivity as a general index of brain dysfunction is often overestimated. Unfortunately, the *BG* is frequently misused as the sole indicator for the presence or absence of brain damage, making it the most misused test for assessment of organicity. Norms are available for children (both to assess visual–motor development and deficits) and for adults.

2. *Test of Visual Perceptual Skills (Non-Motor)—Revised* (TVPS (n-m)–R; Gardner, 1996). Application: Ages 4–13. The TVPS (n-m)–R measures seven visual spatial perception areas, requires very little motor response, and can be administered in 20 minutes. Directions can be by gesture or reportedly given in any language. Perceptual ages, standard scores, and percentiles can be calculated for each area.

Language Tests

1. *Peabody Picture Vocabulary Test—Version 3* (PPVT–3; Dunn & Dunn, 1997). Application: Ages 2.5–40. The PPVT–3 is a test of receptive one-word picture vocabulary. It uses a multiple-choice design and correlates significantly with more comprehensive measures of reading, language, and general achievement. Standard scores, percentiles, and age equivalent scores can be calculated.

2. *Expressive One-Word Picture Vocabulary Test* (EOWPVT–2000; Brownell, 2000a). Application: Ages 2–18. The EOWPVT–2000 is a test of speaking vocabulary involving picture naming. Norms are based on a 1999 sample. Standard scores and percentiles are obtained.

Memory Tests

1. Memory scale of the *Luria–Nebraska Neuropsychological Battery (Form I)* (LNNB Form I; Golden, Hammeke, & Purisch, 1980). Application: Ages 14–adult. The LNNB Form I can be hand

scored, thus allowing administration of only the Memory subtest, which measures verbal and nonverbal short-term memory under both interference and noninterference conditions. Memory tasks include paired-associate learning to both words and to pictures as well as recall of the gist of a paragraph using this relatively brief scale. An age and education *T*-score is obtained.

2. *California Verbal Learning Test—Second Edition* (CVLT–2; Delis, Kramer, Kaplan, & Ober, 2000). Application: Ages 16–89. The CVLT–2 is a list-learning task that measures immediate memory span, learning curve, and effects of retroactive and proactive interference. This edition also has a short form (a nine-word list) and an alternative form for retesting. A total of at least 19 different scores can be obtained.

3. *Wechsler Memory Scale—III Abbreviated* (WMS–III–A; Wechsler, 2003a). Application: Ages 16–89. Administered in 15–30 minutes, the WMS–III–A contains four subtests measuring auditory and visual immediate and delayed memory. Composite standard scores are obtained.

Neuropsychological Tests

1. *Screening Test for the Luria–Nebraska Neuropsychological Battery* (Golden, 1987). Application: Ages 8–12 (Children's Form) and 13 years and older (Adult Form). Each form has 15 items. Designed only to identify clients who need further neuropsychological evaluation, the test is discontinued once eight errors are made, which should prompt either a referral or further testing. Administration time is less than 10 minutes.

2. *Kaufman Short Neuropsychological Assessment Procedure* (K–SNAP; Kaufman & Kaufman, 1994). Application: Ages 11–65. The K–SNAP has four subtests: Mental Status, Number Recall (Digit Span), Gestalt Closure, and Four-Letter Word. Administration time is approximately 25 minutes, and the norms include individuals with a variety of neurological deficits, reading disabilities, clinical depression, and mental retardation. Scale scores, percentile ranks, a standard acore, and an impairment index can be calculated.

Behavioral Tests

1. *Adolescent Anger Rating Scale* (AARS; Burney, 2001). Application: Ages 11–19. The AARS measures the frequency and intensity of four types of anger expression on the basis of *DSM–IV* criteria.

2. *Independent Living Scales* (ILS; Loeb, 1996). Application: Ages 17–65. The ILS assesses the ability to handle daily tasks in those with cognitive decline. It has five scales: Memory/ Orientation, Managing Money, Managing Home and Transportation, Health and Safety, and Social Adjustment. Norms are provided for impaired patients over 17 years of age and over 65 years for those in varied levels of independent living.

Appendix 7.2
Psychological Assessments

Attention and Concentration Tests

1. *Trail-Making Test, Parts A and Part B* (Reitan & Wolfson, 1993). Application: Ages 9–14 (older child) and above 15 years (adult). Trail making (ranked 12th in Table 7.1) has two versions of different lengths, each consisting of two parts. It measures attention, visual search, mental flexibility, and motor skills. Part A, a visual search task, requires numbers that are randomly scattered over a page to be connected in order. Part B includes circled numbers and letters randomly placed on a page, and the task involves alternating sequentially between numbers and letters in a serial order ("connect 1 to A, A to 2, 2 to B"). Norms are available based on age and level of education.

2. *Continuous Performance Test—Second Edition* (The CPT–II; Conners, 2000). Application: Ages: 4– adult. The CPT–II is a computer test requiring attending to verbal material in a visual presentation and identifying a predetermined target. Norms are based on age and gender. Commission and omission errors, percent of target hits and reaction times are scored.

Intellectual and Cognitive Tests

1. *Wechsler Adult Intelligence Scale—Third Edition* (WAIS–III; Wechsler, 1997a). Application: Ages 16–89. The WAIS–III, a measure of general intellectual functioning, is both the most commonly used test by clinicians (see Table 7.1) and the most widely used of all intelligence tests when the patient is an adult (older than 16 years 11 months 31 days). Administration time is 60 to 90 minutes. The test is divided into verbal (seven subtests) and performance (seven subtests) tasks. Scores are calculated for verbal IQ, performance IQ, FSIQ, Verbal Comprehension, Perceptual Organization, Working Memory, and Processing Speed indexes.

2. *Wechsler Intelligence Scale for Children—Fourth Edition* (WISC–IV; Wechsler, 2003b). Application: Ages 6–16 years 11 months 30 days. The WISC–IV (an earlier edition was the third most used test listed in Table 7.1) has norms based on current U.S. census data. Test results can be linked to other intellectual and achievement measures in the Wechsler series. Calculations of IQ scores and index scores are similar to the WAIS–III.

3. *Wechsler Preschool and Primary Scales of Intelligence—Third Edition* (WPPSI–III; Wechsler, 2002). Application: Ages 2 years 6 months–7 years 3 months. The WPPSI–III is divided into two distinct age groups: those children between the ages of 2 years 6 months and 3 years 11 months and those who are between 4 years and 7 years 3 months of age. Within each age group, specific (but different) core subtests are used to calculate IQ and index scores similar to the WAIS–III.

4. *Stanford-Binet Intelligence Scale—Fifth Edition* (SB–5; Thorndike, Hagen, & Sattler, 2003). Applications: Ages 2–85. The SB–5 assesses five factors of Fluid Reasoning, Knowledge, Quantitative Reasoning, Visual Spatial Processing, and Working Memory. A FSIQ, verbal and nonverbal IQ and composite indexes for the five domains as well as subtest scale scores can be calculated.

5. *Woodcock–Johnson III: Tests of Cognitive Ability* (Woodcock, McGrew, & Mather, 2001). Application: Ages 2–adult. There are 10 standard tests and 10 supplemental tests, which are grouped into three broad categories: verbal ability, visual ability, and cognitive efficiency. Standard scores,

percentiles, age and grade equivalents, and developmental levels can be computed.

6. *Kaufman Assessment Battery for Children—Second Edition* (KABC–II; Kaufman & Kaufman, 2004) Applications: Ages 3–19. The KABC–II has five primary scores: Sequential Processing, Simultaneous Processing, Planning, Learning, and Knowledge. Percentiles, age equivalents, and several Composite (IQ) scores can be derived.

7. *Leiter International Performance Scale—Revised* (Leiter–R; Roid & Miller, 1997). Application: Ages 2–20. The Leiter–R is a nonverbal measure of general cognitive ability that requires no verbal instructions. It consists of a revision of the original visualization and reasoning domains for measuring IQ and new attention and memory domains. On this instrument, IQ scores, scaled scores for each subtest, and age-equivalent scores can be obtained.

8. *Bayley Scales of Infant Development—Second Edition* (BSID–II; Bayley, 1993). Application: Ages 1–42 months. The BSID–II assesses cognitive and motor development. It has a Mental scale, a Motor scale, and a Behavioral Rating scale. Norms are provided for infants who are premature, developmentally delayed, autistic, drug exposed, or infected with HIV/AIDS. Index scores are provided.

Achievement Tests

1. *Woodcock–Johnson III: Tests of Achievement* (Woodcock, McGrew, & Mather, 2001). Application: Ages 2–90. There are two parallel forms (A and B) each divided into a standard battery (12 tests) and extended battery (10 tests). Standard scores, percentiles, and age or grade equivalents can be calculated.

2. *Wechsler Individual Achievement Test—II* (WIAT–II; Wechsler, 2001). Application: Ages 5–adult. The WIAT–II also includes college student norms across four areas: Reading, Mathematics, Language, and Writing. Standard scores, percentiles, and age and grade equivalents can be obtained.

3. *Peabody Individual Achievement Test—Revised/Normative Update* (PIAT–R/NU; Markwardt, 1997). Application: Ages: 5–18. The PIAT–R/NU measures academic achievement in the areas of Mathematics, Reading, Recognition, Reading Comprehension, Spelling, Written Expression, and General Information.

Standard scores, grade equivalents and percentiles are calculated.

Mood and Personality Tests

OBJECTIVE PSYCHOPATHOLOGY

1. *Minnesota Multiphasic Personality Inventory—2* (MMPI–2; Butcher, Dahlstrom, Graham, Tellegen, & Kaemmer, 1989). Application: Ages 18 and older. The MMPI–2 is the most widely used comprehensive self-report measure of psychopathology. The second most frequently used test (see Table 7.1), it has 567 questions, 10 primary clinical scales and multiple-validity scales to detect a number of inconsistent or bias response styles to the test, and specialized-content scales. The most widely researched self-report measure in the world, interpretations across a range of diagnostic categories and problem areas are based on *T*-score comparisons.

2. *Minnesota Multiphasic Personality Inventory—Adolescent* (MMPI–A; Butcher et al., 1992). Application: Ages 14–18. The MMPI–A is a 487-item self-report measure of personality that includes the same primary clinical and validity scales as the MMPI–2.

3. *Millon Clinical Multiaxial Inventory—III* (MCMI–III; Millon, 1994). Application: Ages 18 and older. The MCMI–III is the 10th most often used test (see Table 7.1) and is especially useful to assess Axis II personality disorders. It has 11 Clinical Personality Pattern scales, 3 Severe Personality Pathology scales, 7 Clinical Syndrome scales, 3 Severe Syndrome scales, 3 Modifying indexes (for response style) and 1 Validity index. Norms are based on inpatient and outpatient clinical and inmate correctional samples.

4. *Symptom Checklist—90—Revised* (SCL–90–R; Derogatis, 1992). Application: Ages 13 and older. The SCL–90–R is a 90-item (5-point rating scale) self-report inventory that measures nine primary symptom dimensions and provides three global indexes of distress. It takes approximately 15 minutes to complete and has both outpatient and inpatient norms.

PROJECTIVE PERSONALITY

1. *Rorschach Inkblot Technique* (Exner, 1993). Application: Ages 5–adult. A projective technique, it is the fourth most used test (see Table 7.1). There are 10 cards, each with a symmetrical "inkblot." The task is to respond to ambiguous stimuli, as the responses reflect unconscious aspects of personality. The cards are administered in a free association and then inquiry mode. Scoring is based on many different aspects of the responses, with the most widely used scoring system that of Exner (1993).

2. *Thematic Apperception Test* (TAT; Murray & Bellak, 1973). Application: Ages include children and adults. The TAT (the sixth most used test in Table 7.1) consists of 31 pictures to which the individual must make up stories. Interpretation may be based on primary themes, basic needs, social or interpersonal problems, conflicts, or emotions expressed.

3. *House–Tree–Person Technique* (H-T-P; Buck, 1948). Application: Ages include children and adults. The H-T-P (the eighth most used test in Table 7.1) involves drawing these objects, which are then interpreted on the basis of psychodynamic theory.

Visual Spatial Tests

1. *Beery–Buktenica Developmental Test of Visual Motor Integration— Fourth Edition* (VMI; Beery & Buktenica, 1997). Application: 2–18 years. The VMI is a paper-and-pencil test of visual–motor integration. It requires the reproduction of 27 geometric designs within a structured format. There are also two supplemental tests, a Visual Perception task, requiring selecting one form from among others that exactly match a standard, and Motor Coordination, requiring tracing a design within a double-lined path. Standard scores, percentiles, and age equivalents can be obtained.

2. *Rey Complex Figure Test and Recognition Trial* (RCFT; Meyers & Meyers, 1995). Application: Ages 6–17 (children) and 18–69 (adults). The RCFT is a complex visual figure composed of 18 scoring elements to assess visual spatial construction and visual memory. There are four separate administration tasks: Copying, Immediate Recall, 30-Minute Delayed Recall, and Recognition. An accuracy score can be computed for each

task. Normative information is available on a large cross-section of population including geriatric ages.

Language Tests

1. *Test of Adolescent and Adult Language—Third Edition* (TOAL–3; Hammill, Brown, Larsen, & Wiederbolt, 1994). Application: Ages 12–25. The TOAL–3 provides 10 measures of receptive and expressive language skills. An Overall Language Ability score and composite quotients are based on a mean score of 100. Norms are based on over 3,000 people. Standard scores are calculated.
2. *Receptive One-Word Picture Vocabulary Test* (ROWPVT–2000; Brownell, 2000b). Application: Ages: 2–18. The ROWPVT–2000 is a test of hearing vocabulary involving correctly identifying one of four illustrations of an orally spoken word. Standard scores and percentiles can be obtained.

Memory Tests

1. *Wechsler Memory Scale—Third Edition* (WMS–III; Wechsler, 1997b). Application: Ages: 20–89 years. The WMS–III is a comprehensive memory battery with eight Primary Index scores in the areas of auditory and visual memory (both immediate and delayed), working memory, as well as a General Memory index. An earlier edition was the ninth most often used test (see Table 7.1). It is conormed with the WAIS–III, allowing comparisons between memory and intellectual functioning. Percentile ranks as well as age-corrected index scores can be obtained.
2. *Test of Memory and Learning* (Reynolds & Bigler, 1994). Application: Ages: 5–19. The TOMAL is a comprehensive battery for the assessment of immediate and delayed verbal and nonverbal memory, with Verbal, Nonverbal, Composite Memory and Delayed Recall Indexes.
3. *Wide Range Assessment of Memory and Learning—Second Edition* (WRAML–2; Adams & Sheslow, 2003). Application: Ages 5–90 years. The WRAML–2 is a battery yielding Verbal Memory, Visual Memory, Attention–Concentration, Working Memory, and general index scores. Norms and scores are

based on standard scores, percentiles, and scale scores. Age equivalents are available for children.

Neuropsychological Tests

1. *Short Category Test, Booklet Format* (Wetzel & Boll, 1987). Application: Ages 20–79. Assessment of complex concept formation, abstract reasoning, and ability to learn. Normative and standardization samples included a wide range of socioeconomic and educational levels that encompass individuals with both psychiatric and neurological diagnoses in the clinical sample. *T*-scores and percentile ranks are calculated.

2. *Luria Nebraska Neuropsychological Battery* (LNNB; Golden, Purisch, & Hammeke, 1985). Application: Ages 15 and older (There is also a children's battery, ages 8–12). The LNNB Forms I and II are 269-item batteries that require about 2 hours to administer. The test is standardized on the basis of the approach used by the Russian neurologist A. R. Luria. The *LLNB* has 11 Clinical scales, 8 Localization scales, 5 Summary scales, and 28 Factor scales. An updated handbook with norms and interpretative methods was published in 2000.

3. *Halstead–Reitan Neuropsychological Test Composite Battery* (Reitan & Wolfson, 1993). Application: Ages include children (5–8), older children (9–14), and adults (15 and older). The composite is three separate batteries of individual tests. Testing time for each is 5 to 8 hours. Tables of norms by Reitan and other authors permit calculations of level of performance and an impairment index.

Behavioral Tests

1. *Vineland Adaptive Behavior Scales* (Sparrow, Balla, & Cicchetti, 1984) Applications: Ages for the Interview Edition, Survey Form, and Expanded Form are birth–18 years, 11 months and low-functioning adults and for the Classroom Edition are 3 years–12 years, 11 months. Semistructured interview and questionnaire formats with three versions. Each assesses domains such as Communication, Daily Living Skills, Socialization, and Motor Skills. Standard scores, percentile ranks,

stanines, adaptive levels, and age equivalents can be calculated.

2. *Conners Rating Scales—Revised* (CRS–R; Conners, 1997). Applications: Ages 3–17. The CRS–R has multidimensional scales that assess ADHD and comorbid disorders. There are separate long- and short-length checklist forms for Parent Rating, Teacher Rating, and Adolescent Self-Report (ages 12–17) to identify disruptive behavior at home and in the classroom. The long forms provide a comprehensive rating across several subscales and include *DSM–IV* Symptom subscales. The short forms yield scores on four subscales that are identical on all three versions, allowing a direct comparison of results by each informant. Norms allow the calculation of standard scores.

3. *Child Behavior Checklist* (CBCL/6–18; Achenbach & Edelbrock, 2001). Application: Ages 6–18. The CBCL includes checklists completed by parents and teachers to identify disruptive behavior at home and in the classroom. It has been updated to incorporate new normative data, including new *DSM*-oriented scales, and to complement new preschool age forms (CBCL/1.5–5). Parents provide information for 20 competence items covering their child's activities, social relations, and school performance. The CBCL/6–18 has 118 items that describe specific behavioral and emotional problems plus two open-ended items for reporting additional problems. The CBCL/6–18 scoring profile provides raw scores, *T*-scores, and percentiles for three Competence scales (Activities, Social, and School), Total Competence, eight cross-informant syndromes, and Internalizing, Externalizing, and Total Problems.

4. *College ADHD Response Evaluation* (CARE; Glutting, Sheslow, & Adams, 2002). Application: College age students. The CARE measures ADHD symptoms and has two scales, a Student Response Inventory (SRI) and a Parent Response Inventory (PRI). Norms include average college students and a sample of adults diagnosed with ADHD. Cut scores are provided.

References

Achenbach, T. M., & Edelbrock, C. S. (2001). *Child Behavior Checklist (CBCL/6–18)*. Burlington: University of Vermont.

Adams, W., & Sheslow, D. (2003). *Wide Range Assessment of Memory and Learning* (2nd ed.). Wilmington, DE: Wide Range.

Anastasi, A., & Urbina, S. (1997). *Psychological testing* (7th ed.). New York: Macmillan.

Bayley, N. (1993). *Bayley Scales of Infant Development* (2nd ed.). San Antonio, TX: Psychological Corporation.

Beck, A. T. (1993). *Beck Anxiety Inventory*. San Antonio, TX: Psychological Corporation.

Beck, A. T., Steer, R. A., & Brown, G. K. (1996). *Beck Depression Inventory—II Manual*. San Antonio, TX: Psychological Corporation.

Beery, K. E., & Buktenica, N. A. (1997). *The Beery–Buktenica developmental test of visual–motor integration* (4th ed., rev.). Parsippany, NJ: Modern Curriculum Press.

Bender, L. (1938). A visual–motor Gestalt test and its clinical use. *American Orthopsychiatric Association Research Monographs, 3*.

Brownell, R. (2000a). *Expressive One-Word Picture Vocabulary Test*. Novato, CA: Academic Therapy Publications.

Brownell, R. (2000b). *Receptive One-Word Picture Vocabulary Test*. Novato, CA: Academic Therapy Publications.

Buck, J. N. (1948). The H–T–P technique, a qualitative and quantitative scoring manual. *Journal of Clinical Psychology, 4*, 317–396.

Burney, D. M. (2001). *Adolescent Anger Rating Scale*. San Antonio, TX: Psychological Corporation.

Butcher, J. N., Dahlstrom, W. G., Graham, J. R., Tellegen, A., & Kaemmer, B. (1989). *Minnesota Multiphasic Personality Inventory—2 (MMPI–2): Manual for administration*. Minneapolis: University of Minnesota Press.

Butcher, J. N., Williams, C. L., Graham, J. R., Archer, R., Tellegen, A., Ben-Porath, Y. S., & Kaemmer, B. (1992). *Minnesota Multiphasic Personality Inventory—Adolescent: A manual for administration, scoring, and interpretation*. Minneapolis: University of Minnesota Press.

Camara, W. J., Nathan, J. S., & Puente, A. E. (2000). Psychological test usage: Implications in professional psychology. *Professional Psychology: Research and Practice, 31*, 141–154.

Conners, C. K. (1997). *Conners Rating Scales* (Rev. ed.). North Tonawanda, NY: Multi-Health Systems.

Conners, C. K. (2000). *Continuous Performance Test* (2nd ed.). North Tonawanda, NY: Multi-Health Systems.

Cull, J. G., & Gill, W. S. (1988). *Suicide Probability Scale (SPS) manual.* Los Angeles: Western Psychological Services.

Delis, D. C., Kramer, J. H., Kaplan, E., & Ober, B. A. (2000). *California Verbal Learning Test* (2nd ed.). San Antonio, TX: Psychological Corporation.

Derogatis, L. R. (1992). *Symptom Checklist—90—Revised manual.* Minneapolis, MN: Pearson Assessments.

Dunn, L. M., & Dunn, L. M. (1997). *Peabody Picture Vocabulary Test—third edition manual.* Circle Pines, MN: American Guidance Service.

Exner, J. E. (1993). *The Rorschach: A comprehensive system: Vol. 1. Basic foundations* (3rd ed.). New York: Wiley.

Folstein, M. F., Folstein, S. E., & McHugh, P. R. (2001). *Mini-Mental State Examination.* Lutz, FL: Psychological Assessment Resources.

Franzen, M., & Berg, R. (1998). *Screening children for brain impairment* (2nd ed.). New York: Springer Publishing Company.

Gardner, M. F. (1996). *Test of Visual–Perceptual Skills (Non-Motor)* (Rev. ed.). Lutz, FL: Psychological Assessment Resources.

Glutting, J., Sheslow, D., & Adams, W. (2002). *College ADHD Response Evaluation.* Wilmington, DE: Wide Range.

Golden, C. J. (1987). *Screening test for the Luria–Nebraska neuropsychological battery: Adult and children's forms.* Los Angeles: Western Psychological Services.

Golden, C. J., & Freshwater, S. M. (2002). *Stroop Color and Word Test.* Chicago: Stoelting Co.

Golden, C. J., Hammeke, T. A., & Purisch, A. D. (1980). *Manual for the Luria–Nebraska neuropsychological battery.* Los Angeles: Western Psychological Services.

Golden, C. J., Purisch, A. D., & Hammeke, T. A. (1985). *Luria-Nebraska neuropsychological battery: Forms I and II manual.* Los Angeles: Western Psychological Services.

Gregory, R. J. (2004). *Psychological testing* (4th ed.). Boston: Pearson.

Hammill, D. A., Brown, V. L., Larsen, S. C., & Wiederbolt, J. L. (1994). *Test of Adolescent and Adult Language* (3rd ed.). Los Angeles: Western Psychological Services.

Jurica, P. J., Leitten, C., & Mattis, S. (2001). *Dementia Rating Scale—2: Professional manual.* Lutz, FL: Psychological Assessment Resources.

Kaufman, A. S., & Kaufman, N. L. (1990). *Kaufman Brief Intelligence Test.* Circle Pines, MN: American Guidance Service.

Kaufman, A. S., & Kaufman, N. L. (1994). *Kaufman Short Neuropsychological Assessment Procedure.* Circle Pines, MN: American Guidance Service.

Kaufman, A. S., & Kaufman, N. L. (2004). *Kaufman Assessment Battery for Children* (2nd ed.). Circle Pines, MN: American Guidance Service.

Kiernan, R. J., Mueller, J., & Langston, J. W. (1995). *Manual for COGNISTAT (Neurobehavioral Cognitive Status Examination)* Fairfax: Northern California Neurobehavioral Group.

Loeb, P. A. (1996). *Independent Living Scales*. San Antonio, TX: Psychological Corporation.

Markwardt, F. C., Jr. (1997). *Peabody Individual Achievement Test— Revised-Normative Update*. Circle Pines, MN: American Guidance Service.

Messick, S. (1995). Validity of psychological assessment: Validation of inferences from persons' responses and performance as scientific inquiry into score meaning. *American Psychologist, 50*, 741–749.

Meyers, J. E., & Meyers, K. R. (1995). *Rey Complex Figure Test and Recognition Trial*. Lutz, FL: Psychological Assessment Resources.

Millon, T. (1994). *Millon Clinical Multiaxial Inventory— III*. Minneapolis, MN: Pearson Assessments.

Murray, H. A., & Bellak, L. (1973). *Thematic Apperception Test*. Cambridge, MA: Harvard University Press.

Randolph, C. (1998). *Repeatable Battery for the Assessment of Neuropsychological Status*. San Antonio, TX: Psychological Corporation.

Reitan, R. M., & Wolfson, D. (1993). *The Halstead–Reitan Neuropsychological Test Battery: Theory and clinical interpretation*. (2nd ed.). Tucson, AZ: Neuropsychology Press.

Reynolds, C. R., & Bigler, E. D. (1994). *Test of Memory and Learning*. Austin, TX: Pro-Ed.

Reynolds, C. R., & Richmond, B.O. (1985). *Revised Children's Manifest Anxiety Scale manual*. Los Angeles: Western Psychological Services.

Reynolds, W. M. (1989). *Reynolds Child Depression Scale*. Lutz, FL: Psychological Assessment Resources.

Reynolds, W. M. (2000). *Reynolds Adolescent Depression Scales* (2nd ed.). Lutz, FL: Psychological Assessment Resources.

Reynolds, W. M., & Kobak, K. A. (1995). *Hamilton Depression Inventory professional manual*. Lutz, FL: Psychological Assessment Resources.

Roid, G., & Miller, L. (1997). *Leiter International Performance scale* (Rev. ed.). Chicago: Stoelting Co.

Shipley, W. C. (1994). *Manual: Shipley Institute of Living Scale*. Los Angeles: Western Psychological Services.

Slosson, R. L., Nicholson, C. L., & Hibpshman, T. H. (2000). *Slosson Intelligence Test—3*. Los Angeles: Western Psychological Services.

Sparrow, S. S., Balla, D. A., & Cicchetti, D. V. (1984). *Vineland Adaptive Behavior Scales*. Circle Pines, MN: American Guidance Service.

Spielberger, C. D. (1983). *Manual for the State–Trait Anxiety Inventory (Form Y)*. Palo Alto, CA: Consulting Psychologists Press.

Strub, R. L., & Black, F. W. (2000). *The mental status exam in neurology*. (5th ed.). Philadelphia: F. A. Davis.

Thorndike, R. L., Hagen, E. P., & Sattler, J. M. (2003). *Stanford-Binet Intelligence Scale* (5th ed.). Chicago: Riverside.

Wechsler, D. A. (1997a). *Wechsler Adult Intelligence Scale* (3rd ed.). San Antonio, TX: Psychological Corporation.

Wechsler, D. (1997b). *Wechsler Memory Scale* (3rd ed.). San Antonio, TX: Psychological Corporation.

Wechsler, D. (1999). *Wechsler Abbreviated Scale of Intelligence*. San Antonio, TX: Psychological Corporation.

Wechsler, D. (2001). *Wechsler Individual Achievement Test* (2nd ed.). San Antonio, TX: Psychological Corporation.

Wechsler, D. (2002). *Wechsler Preschool and Primary Scale of Intelligence* (3rd ed.). San Antonio, TX: Psychological Corporation.

Wechsler, D. (2003a). *Abbreviated Wechsler Memory Scale* (3rd ed.). San Antonio, TX: Psychological Corporation.

Wechsler, D. (2003b). *Wechsler Intelligence Scale for Children* (4th ed.). San Antonio, TX: Psychological Corporation.

Wetzel, L., & Boll, T. J. (1987). *Short Category Test, Booklet Format manual*. Los Angeles: Western Psychological Services.

Wilkinson, G. S. (1993). *Wide Range Achievement Test Administration manual*. Wilmington, DE: Wide Range.

Woodcock, R. W., McGrew, K. S., & Mather, N. (2001). *Woodcock–Johnson III: Tests of Achievement and Tests of Cognitive Ability*. Allen, TX: DLM Teaching Resources.

Morgan T. Sammons and Peter E. Nathan

Interventions: Empirically Supported Treatments

8

Empirically Supported Treatments for Mental Disorders

WHAT TREATMENTS FOR WHAT DISORDERS?

We had two important decisions to make in writing this chapter. We had to decide which psychosocial and somatic treatments to feature from among the countless mental health treatments that have been developed over the years. We also had to determine which disorders and conditions, from the more than 300 listed in the American Psychiatric Association's (APA's) *Diagnostic and Statistical Manual of Mental Disorders, Fourth Edition* (*DSM–IV*; APA, 1994a), would be the focus of our discussion.

This chapter was authored or coauthored by an employee of the United States government as part of official duty and is considered to be in the public domain. Any views expressed herein do not necessarily represent the views of the United States government, and the author's participation in the work is not meant to serve as an official endorsement.

We decided to limit our coverage of psychopathological disorders to four of the most common: the mood disorders, the anxiety disorders, alcohol abuse and dependence, and schizophrenia. We chose these conditions for two reasons: either because they are among the most prevalent *DSM–IV* disorders, so they are almost certain to be encountered during a practicum assignment, or because they are of such a degree of severity that all students should have some familiarity with them. Because empirically supported psychosocial and somatic treatments have been developed for all of these disorders, clinicians and practicum students can have confidence that they can offer some degree of assistance to patients experiencing these disorders.

A number of recent reviews (e.g., Nathan & Gorman, 2002; Nathan, Skinstad, & Dolan, 2000; Wilson, 1995) have documented the marked advances that have been made over the past two or three decades in both the methodological quality of research on psychotherapy outcomes and the effectiveness of a growing number of psychosocial treatments. In turn, as more effective treatments have been developed and evaluated, pressures have increased on psychologists and other mental health professionals to use them rather than untested but possibly time-honored treatments. These pressures reflect a growing emphasis in American society on increased professional accountability (Barlow, 1996). Providers of psychological services are now expected to show proof that their methods actually work. A variety of practice guidelines that identify preferred treatments based on empirical evidence of effectiveness have been proposed over the past decade. Nathan, Stuart, and Dolan (2000), and Chambless and Ollendick (2001) have provided extensive discussions of the scientific, conceptual, and political issues associated with the development of guidelines to identify empirically supported mental health treatments.

It is important to acknowledge, at the same time, that not all psychologists agree that evidence-based treatments should be the treatment of choice. For those readers interested in the continuing controversy over empirically supported treatments, we refer you to an article discussing unresolved questions that have sustained this controversy (Nathan, 2004). These questions include (a) whether the efficacy model (the traditional laboratory test of psychotherapy outcomes) or the effectiveness model (treatment in the community) provides the most valid picture of which treatments work best; (b) whether common factors (therapist attributes like empathy and warmth and patient characteristics like age and personality) or treatment factors (like which treatment is used) contribute the most to psychotherapy outcomes; (c) whether most psychosocial treatments are equally effective, as some researchers claim, or some treatments are more effective than others, as those who champion empirically supported treatments believe; and (d) whether psychosocial treatment should be considered an art, in which case empirical data on outcomes are relatively unimportant, or psychosocial treatment should be science based, in which case empirical data are very important.

Besides these unresolved controversies, an additional factor has interfered with widespread support from psychologists for empirically supported treatments. A number of treatments with a lengthy history of use, including psychodynamic psychotherapy, group therapy, and family therapy, have generally not been included on lists of empirically supported psychosocial treatments because they do not lend themselves to the efficacy research paradigm used for this approach. All of these treatments continue to be used in typical practicum and internship placements. Descriptions of these approaches are found in many other sources.

In our description of selected empirically supported psychosocial treatments that follows, we refer to both the quality and quantity of research that supports claims of effectiveness. Research quality refers to generally agreed-upon standards that reflect superior research methodology. The effectiveness of the psychosocial treatments included in this chapter has been supported by a substantial number of studies that meet these quality standards. For somatic treatments, the level of empirical support tends to be less robust. This is because most somatic treatments, aside from pharmacotherapy (the subject of a different chapter in this volume), tend to have little staying power in the treatment armamentarium for mental disorders. Also, because the effects of many somatic treatments are nonspecific, they have tended to be given to patients with a range of diagnoses, muddying the water in terms of our ability to gauge their efficacy with specific disorders. For example, electroconvulsive therapy (ECT) has been used to treat both psychosis and severe depression, although most empirical evidence supports its use only in the latter condition.

Although we discuss both somatic and psychosocial interventions for the four common mental disorders we selected, we have somewhat arbitrarily divided this chapter into two sections, each dealing with one or the other type of treatment. This framework is both easier to follow conceptually and reflective of the profound philosophical differences that underlie the development and intervention of medically oriented and psychosocial treatments.

Empirically Supported Psychological Treatments for Mood Disorders

BIPOLAR DISORDER

The lifetime prevalence of Bipolar I and Bipolar II disorder is between 1% and 2% (APA, 2000). Pharmacological treatments (including lithium and the newer mood-stabilizing drugs as well as antidepressant medications, primarily the Selective Serotonin Reuptake Inhibitors [SSRIs]) have been established as treatments of choice for bipolar disorder. However, psychosocial treatments have been shown repeatedly to increase medication adherence, improve quality of life, and help patients cope with stress when they are combined with pharmacological treatments. As is the case with schizophrenia, we have moved from a position in which pharmacotherapy was relied on as the only effective treatment for bipolar disorder to one in which the application of psychological treatments is seen as a vital component of long-term management (Spaulding, Sullivan, & Poland, 2003). Extensive data suggest that the combination of medication and psychosocial treatment reduces bipolar patients' risk of relapse and rehospitalization (Craighead, Miklowitz, Frank, & Vajk, 2002).

Nonadherence to medication, which markedly increases the risk of relapse in bipolar disorder, is a major problem: Up to 59% of patients on long-term lithium maintenance do not adhere to their prescribed medication (Strakowski et al., 1998). Several moderately strong studies have shown that *psychoeducation* designed to inform patients about their disorder and its pharmacological management, including drug side effects, increases medication adherence significantly (Harvey & Peet, 1991).

At least three randomized clinical trials (Cochran, 1984; Lam, Bright, & Jones, 2000; Perry, Tarrier, Morriss, McCarthy, & Limb, 1999) have shown that *cognitive–behavioral therapy* (CBT), combined with psychopharmacological treatment, significantly increases medication adherence, decreases rehospitalizations, and improves social and occupational functioning in patients with bipolar disorder. The rationale for using CBT to treat bipolar patients presumes that the mood swings of bipolar disorder stem partly from negative thought patterns that can be reduced or eliminated by a combination of behavioral redirection and cognitive restructuring. The ultimate aim of both techniques is to increase the patient's reintegration into his or her environment and assist in more effective control of dysfunctional behavior.

Several other studies (discussed in Miklowitz & Goldstein, 1997; Miller, Keitner, Ryan, & Solomon, 2000) suggest that *marital and family therapy*, in combination with pharmacotherapy, reduce relapse and improve occupational and social functioning in bipolar disorder. Family therapists assume that bipolar disorder, like all other psychopathologic conditions, is maintained within the family context. For this reason, the patient's family needs to learn about the disorder. Doing so will enable family members to deal better with the disorder's disruptive effects on the family relationship. Accordingly, patients and family members are taught about the symptoms, course, and treatment of bipolar disorder, with a special emphasis on strategies for presenting relapse.

MAJOR DEPRESSIVE DISORDER

Major depressive disorder (MDD) is one of the most common mental disorders among U.S. adults, with lifetime prevalence rates of 20% to 25% for women and 9% to 12% for men (Kessler et al., 1994). At least two randomized clinical trials each as well as four meta-analyses have shown that CBT and interpersonal psychotherapy are effective psychosocial interventions for patients with MDD (Craighead, Hart, Craighead, & Ilardi, 2002). Most studies directly comparing the outcomes of psychosocial and pharmacological treatments for MDD have concluded that they are comparable in efficacy. However, at least one major study has suggested that the two treatments together may yield more positive outcomes for MDD than either one alone (Craighead et al., 2002).

At present, CBT has been more thoroughly studied than any other psychological treatment for depression. It typically extends for 16 to 20 treatment sessions over 12 to 16 weeks. Its primary goal is to induce patients to change their typically negative world view thought to be both reflective of and responsible for their depression. Patients are initially taught to increase active behavioral performance (behavioral activation). Doing so allows them more successfully to begin to self-monitor behavior and associated thoughts and feelings. In turn, this self-monitoring will, it is hoped, permit depressed patients gradually learn to identify logical errors in their thinking as well as the principal *schemas* that underlie their negative thoughts and logical errors. Beck and his colleagues defined schemas as basic beliefs about oneself and the world that filter, color, and organize experiences (Beck, Rush, Shaw, & Emery, 1979). Persons with depression often experience negative schemas that Beck and his colleagues believe are largely responsible for their depression. The focus of CBT for depression is to identify and then successfully challenge these negative schemas and the logical errors that accompany them. Toward the end of CBT for depression, patient and therapist together work on identifying cognitive strategies (like thought stopping or mindfulness exercises) that might help prevent relapse to an episode of depression.

The role of both biological and psychosocial factors in depression is strongly emphasized in *interpersonal therapy for depression* (IPT). IPT is time limited (12–16 sessions) and emphasizes the reciprocal relationship between biological and psychosocial factors in depression. IPT assumes that interpersonal relationships, interacting with biological predisposition, play preeminent roles in MDD (Klerman, Weissman, Rounsaville, & Chevron, 1984). As a consequence, the goals of IPT for depression include resolution of problems and difficulties in interpersonal functioning, specifically including unresolved grief at the loss of an important relationship; interpersonal disputes, often between spouses or otherwise in the family context; role transitions that affect significant relationships, like job loss or retirement; and social isolation. Besides its well-documented role in the treatment of acute MDD, IPT also apparently helps decrease the likelihood of recurrence of MDD once it has abated (Frank et al., 1990).

Empirically Supported Psychological Treatments for Anxiety Disorders

A great amount of empirical data has been gathered on outcomes of behavioral and cognitive–behavioral treatments for the anxiety disorders. Largely derived from high-quality studies, these data strongly encourage the view that empirically supported treatments exist for panic disorder, agoraphobia with panic attacks, specific and social phobic disorder, obsessive–compulsive disorder, and posttraumatic stress disorder (Barlow, Raffa, & Cohen, 2002; Foa, Davidson, & Frances, 1999; Franklin & Foa, 2002). Despite these disorders' behavioral differences, all appear to respond favorably to the very similar behavioral interventions described below.

PANIC DISORDER WITH OR WITHOUT AGORAPHOBIA

Numerous studies have demonstrated the effectiveness of *situational in vivo exposure* for persons with panic disorder with or without agoraphobia (agoraphobia is an extreme fear of situations from which escape might be difficult or places in which help might not be available should an embarrassing or incapacitating event occur). Situational in vivo exposure for panic disorder (Barlow & Craske, 2000) initially involves identifying the feared situations or activities in a hierarchy of their capacity to cause fearfulness and/or panic. Patients are then taught *behavioral coping strategies,* which often involve attempts to eliminate or modify unjustified or irrational fearful thoughts, to enable the patient to visualize the fear-inducing activities and situations without experiencing crippling fear and panic. Armed with these and other effective coping strategies, most patients can learn to imagine actual exposure to the feared situations in the list. Patients are sometimes accompanied by the therapist or family members or friends during the subsequent in vivo desensitization phase of treatment when they actually expose themselves to the real fear-inducing activity or situation. Although few patients completely lose their symptoms by the end of exposure treatment, most achieve substantial and lasting clinical gains (e.g., Fava, Zielezny, Savron, & Grandi, 1995). Most studies have reported lifetime prevalence rates for panic disorder between 1% and 2% (APA, 2000).

SPECIFIC AND SOCIAL PHOBIA

In vivo exposure has also been shown to be effective in treating both specific and social phobias (Barlow, Esler, & Vitali, 1998). Several CBTs have been developed and tested for social phobia, which is the most common of all the anxiety disorders. Although these treatments incorporate such well-known elements as *social skills training, relaxation training, exposure-based procedures,* and *multicomponent cognitive–behavioral treatment,* Heimberg and Juster (1995) reported that only the exposure-based procedures that actually expose patients to feared social situations in the real world seem to yield positive changes in social phobia greater than those associated with control or comparison treatments. Phobias are quite common: Lifetime prevalence rates have been reported between 7% and 11% (APA, 2000).

GENERALIZED-ANXIETY DISORDER

Generalized-anxiety disorder (GAD) is among the most common of the anxiety disorders and may be amenable to treatment with either psychological treatments alone or such treatments in combination with pharmacotherapy. In particular, CBT for GAD may be targeted at helping the patient identify issues such as selective attention to negative events or the maladaptive nature of persistent worrying. Also, CBT is effective in reducing symptoms of GAD, and some patients may experience longer term remission after being exposed to CBT (Gorman, 2002). Four meta-analyses have supported the utility of CBT in managing GAD (Lang, 2004).

OBSESSIVE–COMPULSIVE DISORDER

Exposure and ritual/response prevention (EX/RP), a set of procedures closely related to situational in vivo exposure, has been shown repeatedly to be effective in reducing obsessive–compulsive symptoms in a number of comprehensive literature reviews and a large number of randomized clinical trials (Franklin & Foa, 2002). Specifically, EX/RP involves convincing patients to undergo repeated exposure to obsessional and ruminative cues, which are the setting events, circumstances, or places that bring on obsessions, ruminations, and ultimately, compulsive behavior. Repeated exposure ideally lasts for 90 minutes or longer, once a week for 15 to 20 weeks. The cues to which the patient may be exposed may include seeing a person (or the picture of a person) with whom the patient has previously had a relationship, revisiting a place (in vivo or in one's imagination) where a traumatic event took place, or reading about a situation the patient associates with a significant event in his or her life. In the presence of these cues, patients are strictly prevented from engaging in the compulsive rituals that usually follow the experience of obsessions and ruminations. Lifetime prevalence for obsessive–compulsive disorder has been estimated to be 2.5% (APA, 2000).

POSTTRAUMATIC STRESS DISORDER

Posttraumatic stress disorder (PTSD) is a disorder of increasing interest in modern society. Its effective treatment is somewhat controversial, with proponents of various therapies often in significant disagreement with each other. Eye Movement Desensitization Response (EMDR) is one example of a controversial treatment for PTSD.

Exposure-based treatments have been found to be effective psychosocial treatments for PTSD (Barlow, 1988). Typically, patient and therapist first create a hierarchy of the anxiety-provoking stimuli associated with the traumatic events that initially induced the PTSD. The patient is then gradually exposed to these stimuli in his or her imagination in the expectation that the anxiety and other feelings associated with them will decrease in intensity during prolonged exposure sessions, especially if those strong feelings are recognized, experienced, and thoroughly discussed. In general, CBT-focused treatments involving exposure or other components have been found to be the most effective interventions, although much investigation remains to be done in this area (Foa, 2000; Robertson, Humphreys, & Ray, 2004). The lifetime prevalence of PTSD in the U.S. adult population is approximately 8% (APA, 2000).

Empirically Supported Psychological Treatments for Alcohol Abuse and Dependence

The lifetime risk of alcohol dependence is approximately 15% in the U.S. adult population (APA, 2000); current (1-year) risk is about 5% (APA, 2000). Alcohol dependence is the most common of the substance use disorders and one of the most common *DSM–IV* conditions.

Finney and Moos (2002) examined the efficacy of 15 psychosocial treatments for alcohol abuse and dependence that had each been evaluated in three or more very well-designed studies. All three of the most effective treatments turned out to be cognitive–behavioral interventions designed to help patients adapt to the difficult life circumstances of the alcoholic. Although a number of new treatments for alcohol dependence are now available, such as acamprosate (Campral) or the opiate receptor blocker naltrexone (ReVia), these play a purely adjunctive role in the management of this difficult spectrum of disorders.

- *Social skills training* (Smith & McCrady, 1991) aims to help patients assert their wishes and needs more appropriately and generally to communicate more effectively; social skills training assumes that social skills deficits contribute to the development and maintenance of depression and lowered self-esteem, both of which are common precursors to abusive drinking.
- *Community reinforcement* (Azrin, Sisson, Meyers, & Godley, 1982) provides patients access to interpersonal, vocational, and financial reinforcements in the community setting contingent on their continued sobriety, retention in treatment, or both. For example, patients who maintain sobriety or are making satisfactory progress toward sobriety are given access to a social club, a job in a sheltered setting, food items, and housing.

■ *Behavioral marital therapy* (O'Farrell, Choquette, Cutter, Brown, & McCourt, 1993) addresses both the alcoholic spouse's abusive drinking and the dysfunctional marriage or partnership it contributes to by promoting development of behavioral contracts between the partners designed to provide the alcoholic spouse access to a range of reinforcers in the relationship (including spousal behaviors like physical affection, emotional concerns, and understanding) contingent on agreed-upon behavioral changes (like a reduction in drinking, threats of violence, or emotional abuse).

Project MATCH and the Veterans Affairs Treatment Studies are two large-scale clinical trials of alcoholism treatments. The National Institute on Alcohol Abuse and Alcoholism's Project MATCH (Project MATCH Research Group, 1993, 1997a, 1997b, 1998) was a randomized clinical trial of more than 1,700 patients, and the Department of Veterans Affairs' Cooperative Study (Ouimette, Finney, & Moos, 1997) was a study of more than 3,000 patients that, although not a randomized clinical trial, was nonetheless well controlled.

Project MATCH was a large national multisite randomized clinical trial designed primarily to evaluate a set of patient–treatment matching hypotheses that anticipated that significant therapeutic gains would be found when patients with specific demographic, diagnostic, and personality characteristics were matched with specific treatments. A second-order Project MATCH goal was to compare the therapeutic outcomes associated with the following three individual, manualized psychosocial treatments.

■ *Cognitive–behavioral coping-skills therapy* (CBT; Kadden et al., 1992), a 12-session treatment derived from social learning theory, was developed on the assumption that abusive drinking is functionally related to major problems in the abuser's life. Accordingly, CBCST provided training to correct patients' diverse skills deficits (e.g., assertive behavior, anger management, social skills, and marital functioning) to increase their ability to cope with situations that commonly lead to relapse.

■ *Motivational enhancement therapy* (MET; Miller, Zweben, DiClemente, & Rychtarik, 1992), a four-session brief intervention, was based on principles of motivational psychology and focused on facilitating abusers' recognition of their alcohol problems and enhancing their motivation to work actively to deal with them by providing them feedback on the likely negative consequences if they continue to drink as they have been drinking. MET therapists are trained to provide feedback in an empathetic and concerned manner so they don't cause patients to become defensive.

The stages-of-change model (Prochaska & DiClemente, 1986) informs MET therapists' assessments of patients' initial motivation to change their behavior.

▪ *Twelve-step facilitation therapy* (TSF; Nowinski, Baker, & Carroll, 1992), a 12-session treatment heavily influenced by the philosophy and methods of Alcoholics Anonymous (AA), was based on the view that alcoholism is a spiritual and medical disease. Accordingly, TSF strove to foster acceptance of the disease of alcoholism and worked toward helping the abuser develop a commitment to AA and its 12 steps. By means of role-playing and behavioral rehearsal, for example, patients learn to anticipate the stressors they would experience when attending AA meetings as newly recovering alcoholics.

Two independent, parallel matching studies were conducted within Project MATCH, one with 952 patients treated exclusively as outpatients (of whom 72% were men), the other with 774 aftercare patients (of whom 80% were men) who had completed a period of inpatient treatment. Patients in both groups were randomly assigned to one of the three treatments. Follow-up contacts with patients began 3 months after treatment ended or the patient withdrew from treatment and continued every 3 months for a year, then at the 2- and 3-year marks.

At the end of the first year, 92% of the outpatients and 93% of the aftercare patients were located: Overall, they demonstrated "significant and sustained improvements in drinking outcomes from baseline to one-year post-treatment. . . . There was little difference in outcomes by type of treatment" (Project MATCH Research Group, 1997a, p. 7). Although most of the patients continued to drink, their consumption levels had dropped by 80% or more. The 24- and 39-month follow-ups (Project MATCH Research Group, 1998) revealed that, for the most part, patients continued to drink at much more moderate levels than before treatment began.

The effectiveness of 12-step, cognitive–behavioral, and combined cognitive–behavioral and 12-step treatments for alcoholism was compared in a study of 3,018 detoxified inpatients already assigned with substance-abuse treatment programs at 15 Department of Veterans Affairs Medical Centers around the United States (Ouimette, Finney, & Moos, 1997). The treatment programs were chosen because they met quite specific quality standards. All programs offered both individual and group therapy. Expected length of stay ranged from 21 to 28 days. A 1-year follow-up of these programs revealed that, as in Project MATCH, the three comparison treatments were associated with equivalent reductions in substance use and comparable improvements in other important areas of functioning, even though most of patients continued to drink and use drugs.

Empirically Supported Psychological Treatments for Schizophrenia

The lifetime prevalence of schizophrenia is generally reported to be between 0.5% and 1.5% (APA, 2000). Antipsychotic drugs, especially the new "atypical," or second-generation, antipsychotics that may offer certain treatment advantages over older agents[1], have become the treatments of choice for schizophrenia on the basis of results from numerous methodologically superior studies over the last two decades (e.g., Bradford, Stroup, & Lieberman, 2002; Ceskova & Svestka, 1993). At the same time, a number of randomized clinical trials along with several hundred less well-designed studies have confirmed the value of *behavior modification programs* for persons with schizophrenia. These programs help reduce the frequency and intensity of psychotic or otherwise disruptive behaviors and increase the frequency of appropriate behaviors by systematically reinforcing desired behaviors and punishing or ignoring unwanted behaviors.

The best known of the behavior modification approaches to schizophrenia is the *token economy* in which inpatients with schizophrenia receive tokens or other tangible reinforcers when they emit wanted behaviors like keeping a bedroom clean or engaging in social interactions (e.g., Menditto, Valdes, & Beck, 1994; Paul & Lentz, 1977). Although these programs do not cure schizophrenia, they enable patients with schizophrenia to lead higher quality lives in institutional settings while making their management far easier as well.

---

[1] As you will see in chapter 9, which addresses medication, the advantages of the second-generation antipsychotics over the older agents (largely of the butyrophenone and phenothiazine classes) are decidedly mixed. Each class possesses a variety of short- and long-term side effects. Each patient's ability to tolerate the side effects of any antipsychotic drug must be carefully assessed at the beginning of treatment, and the patient should be carefully monitored throughout the treatment course for the development of emerging side effects. As with bipolar disorder, the integration of effective psychosocial treatments with pharmacotherapy is positively associated with better long-term management of the disorder.

Structured family programs have also been developed to engage the families of patients with schizophrenia in their treatment. These behavioral methods are generally designed to educate family members about the disease of schizophrenia, on how to cope with it in the family member, and on how to access available community resources for the family member. Some of these programs also teach family members stress management techniques. The programs may also seek to enhance communication skills so that family members can communicate more effectively among themselves about their family member as well as with the family member him- or herself. Several excellent studies have shown that structured educational family interventions provided as adjuncts to antipsychotic drugs and case management for patients with schizophrenia yield better outcomes than drugs and case management alone (Kopelowicz, Liberman, & Zarate, 2002).

Finally, a number of excellent and very good studies (e.g., Eckman, Wirshing, Marder, & Liberman, 1992; Mueser, Wallace, & Liberman, 1995) have shown that persons with chronic schizophrenia living in community settings benefit from social skills training designed to help patients improve assertive behavior and communication skills so they can experience more success in getting what they want and need from their environments.

Somatic Treatments for Psychological Disorders

Somatic interventions for psychological disorders have existed since antiquity. A variety of early somatic therapeutic interventions for madness or melancholia existed, but because mental distress was either presumed to be a component of a physical illness or of spiritual origin, many of these were performed in the context of religious rites. In Western cultures, penitence, exorcism, or death in religious rituals (auto da fe[2] or drowning) of the sufferer to expunge evil or impure influences believed causal of madness were used. In non-Western cultures, shamanistic rituals involving fasting, other forms of prolonged physical deprivation, or administration of potent psychotropic substances were used not only as paths to individual enlightenment but also as treatment for those experiencing emotional distress.

---

[2] Literally, an "act of faith" that often involved burning at the stake.

In Western cultures, one of the best early examples of a somatic intervention aimed at ameliorating psychological (as well as physical) conditions was the séance of Anton Mesmer. Mesmer, an 18th-century entrepreneur of sorts, purported to cure sufferers of nervous conditions by the application of *animal magnetism*. Patients were gathered together in groups, generally around a central object such as a tree or a tub that was believed to be the repository of an electric or magnetic force. Individuals were linked to this object and to each other by grasping chains or cords thought to transmit the curative force. Mesmer played mysterious music on a glass harmonica while he suggested to patients the source of their ills. Although his treatment enjoyed a period of great popularity in Europe, particularly among the privileged classes in Paris, within a few years it was debunked by scientists of the day who could not replicate the effects of animal magnetism. Mesmer was forced to flee from Paris and died in relative obscurity (Gallo & Finger, 2000). His legacy is left in the term mesmerism, which reflects the state of heightened suggestibility that led his patients to report the curative power of the séance. Mesmerism is considered to be the forerunner of modern clinical hypnotherapy.[3]

MODERN SOMATIC TREATMENTS

In more recent times, a number of somatic therapies have captured the attention of the psychiatric field. As you shall see, few of these have withstood the test of empirical scrutiny and most have been consigned to a highly dubious position in the history of mental health treatment.

Psychosurgery: Prefrontal Leucotomy (Lobotomy)

The most notorious form of somatic treatment used in modern psychiatry was the procedure known as leucotomy, commonly called lobotomy. This technique was developed by a Portuguese psychiatrist, Egas Moniz, but achieved worldwide use through the aggressive promotion of a Washington, DC, psychiatrist, Walter Freeman (see Valenstein, 1986, for the definitive review of lobotomy and other somatic procedures used during midcentury). Despite its known debilitating after-effects (including mental dulling and a state of psychological and physical apathy), lobotomy became, for a period in the 1940s and 1950s, one of the most widely used treatments for severe mental disease.

---

[3] Students interested in the history of mesmerism and other forms of psychotherapy will do no better than to find a copy of Henri Ellenberger's treatise, *The Discovery of the Unconscious*, Basic Books, 1981.

Working under the assumption that the prefrontal cortex was both a nonessential element of the central nervous system and the origin of most nervous disorders, Freeman devised a procedure to sever white matter tracts between the prefrontal cortex (PFC) and other areas of brain.

Psychosurgery: Anterior Cingulotomy

Psychosurgery was largely abandoned in the aftermath of Freeman's overzealous attempts to popularize lobotomy. In the past decade, however, a limited form of psychosurgery has been used much more selectively to treat cases of severe obsessive–compulsive disorder that are unresponsive to medications or behavioral treatment. In this procedure, known as anterior cingulotomy, the anterior cingulate gyrus is selectively lesioned, using high-frequency radio beams (the "gamma knife"). Because these lesions are selective, and the procedure does not involve craniotomy, side effects, although still present, are less pronounced than with more indiscriminant lesioning. Some patients report improvement in severe obsessive–compulsive disorder following the procedure, and indeed, for those with extremely severe and persistent symptomatology, it is possible (but not proved) that cingulotomy may be of benefit. Complete symptom resolution is rare, and different individuals respond at different rates. Long-term neuropsychological deficits, primarily in cognitive sequencing, image comparison, and deficits in attention, have been demonstrated (Cohen et al., 1999; Ochsner et al., 2001). Because of limited efficacy and concerns about the production of permanent neurological damage, anterior cingulotomy is rarely used.

Electroconvulsive Therapy

At present, ECT is a common, albeit still controversial, psychiatric procedure involving the application of electrical current of varying amplitude and frequency to induce a seizure. Electrodes are placed either unilaterally or bilaterally on the scalp of an anesthetized patient, and sufficient current is administered to induce a generalized seizure. It is hypothesized that the induction of a seizure represents the therapeutic component of ECT. This remains unproved, but ECT is linked to a number of now obsolete maneuvers, such as the administration of camphor or other epileptogenic drugs that were undertaken by Meduna and others beginning in the 1930s on the basis of the observation that psychiatric symptoms improved after patients experienced seizures. (See Isenberg & Zorumski, 1999, for a comprehensive review of ECT.) Unlike earlier treatments based on seizure induction, modern ECT is performed under general anesthesia using a rapidly acting paralytic agent that prevents contraction of skeletal muscle (seizures induced without paralytic agents often resulted in broken teeth, fractured vertebrae, long bone fractures, and separation of muscle and tendon tissue from bone). An initial course of treatment for ECT is generally 2 to 3 procedures a week administered for 2 to 3 weeks, with follow-up, or maintenance, treatments given 1 to 2 times monthly for an indefinite period. ECT is often combined with antidepressant medication.

Although a widespread clinical practice, this combination has not been extensively scrutinized in the literature. As with antidepressants, patients do not respond immediately to ECT, and a time lag of several weeks is common before full antidepressant effects are seen. ECT is commonly used to manage "treatment resistant" depression (i.e., depression that has not responded to at least two trials of different classes of medication or other therapies; Trivedi, 2003), although most experts point out that it is equally effective for other forms of depression. Treatment with ECT generally results in improvement on most objective measures of depression, but its effects are transient, and as with other forms of treatment for depression, most patients will relapse without further intervention. ECT was originally used to treat the symptoms of schizophrenia, but it was observed to be more effective for patients with depressive symptoms. ECT has been hypothesized to be of particular benefit for patients with delusional depression or those with late life depression, although evidence for its preferential use in late life depression is unclear (van der Wurff, Stek, Hoogendijk, & Beekman, 2005).

The mechanism of action of ECT remains unknown. Those opposed to the use of ECT have argued that the procedure often results in brain damage as manifest by sometimes persistent memory impairment. Others claim that the procedure itself is not therapeutic but that the memory impairment associated with it represents the therapeutic element, in that depressed patients cannot remember those events or cognitions that caused them to become depressed. It seems unlikely that either of these explanations is valid. In at least one study, the degree of clinical improvement was not correlated with the degree of memory impairment (McElhiney, Moody, Steif, & Prudic, 1995). ECT affects the function of numerous neurotransmitters, and like antidepressants (for which the exact mechanism of action is equally unknown), it seems that modulation of neurotransmitter function, possibly resulting in the synthesis of brain hormones such as brain-derived neurotrophic hormone, is likely responsible for its therapeutic effects.

ECT is generally considered to be safe; the risk of death as a result of the procedure appears to be related to the risks of undergoing general anesthesia (Isenberg & Zorumski, 1999). Nevertheless, the procedure is not without risk and is relatively contraindicated in those with brain tumors or other lesions, seizure disorders, and significant cardiovascular illness.

ECT is associated with a variety of side effects, mostly transitory and mostly related to the administration of anesthesia. Nausea and vomiting, joint and muscle pain, and headache are common immediately after the procedure. The risk of producing a persistent seizure disorder is small, but present. The most significant controversy regarding the use of ECT continues to be the degree and duration of neurocognitive deficits (primarily retrograde and anterograde amnesia) that are common following the procedure. Although exact statistics are difficult to obtain, and few long-term studies of neurocognitive deficits in ECT exist, the majority of patients complain of memory loss for events occurring around the time of the course of ECT, and many others complain of retrograde amnesia for events occurring months prior to the procedure. A smaller percentage of patients complain of inability to consolidate new memories for long periods of time after the procedure.

Although the number of patients experiencing memory deficits and the duration of such deficits continues to be contentious, other points are clear. Bilateral electrode placement, more frequent treatment, and higher dose of electrical stimulus are all more associated with both anterograde and retrograde amnesia (bilateral electrode placement has, however, more antidepressant efficacy than unilateral placement). Although it was hoped that modulating the type of electrical current delivered (brief pulse or sine wave) might minimize effects on memory, this does not appear to be the case (UK ECT Review Group, 2003).

The popularity of ECT has fluctuated over the years. Prior to the introduction of effective antidepressants, it was a commonly used procedure—indeed, many lobotomies were performed in the period of unconsciousness that follows administration of ECT. With the surge in the use of medication for depression, the popularity of ECT waned, but it again became prominent when it was clear that some severe forms of depression were resistant to pharmacotherapy. Although its proponents continue to hold that ECT is the most effective treatment for severe depression, its use has been curtailed by legislation and public opinion. Patient advocacy groups continue to lobby against ECT, raising questions about its safety and long-term side effects.

Phototherapy or "Light Box Therapy"

Normal seasonal variations in the quantity of available natural light have been hypothesized to lead to sustained changes in mood, often clinical depression, in susceptible individuals. Although this diagnosis remains rather controversial, the *DSM–IV* (APA, 1994a) notes that a seasonal pattern may be observed in certain forms of depression, characterized by depressive episodes beginning at a particular time of year, usually the fall or winter, and often accompanied by pronounced symptoms of low energy, need for sleep, increased appetite, weight gain, and carbohydrate craving.

Several facts support the association between changes in ambient light and mood disorders. First, changes in circulating hormones (principally cortisol) and neurotransmitters (serotonin) have been found to be different in some patients with and without the disorder (Joseph-Vanderpool et al., 1991; Schwartz et al., 1999), although these findings are by no means definitive. Second, the disorder is speculated to be more prevalent in northern latitudes where changes in the amount of available light differs dramatically between seasons. Finally, seasonal affective disorder is also often associated with sleep disorders, and disruptions of circadian rhythm (sleep disorder) may also be responsive to phototherapy. Circadian rhythm disorders are also common in shift workers and travelers across several time zones (i.e., *jet lag*). It is interesting that, in patients diagnosed with depression, a period of sleep deprivation has been demonstrated to result in at least transient improvement in mood (Berger, van Calker, & Riemann, 2003; Giedke, Klingberg, Schwarzler, & Schweinsberg, 2003).

The treatment of seasonal affective disorder with phototherapy is straightforward: The patient is exposed to bright light, usually generated by a series of fluorescent tubes contained in a portable box. These are available in different sizes and produce light of varying intensities, generally in the range of 2,500 to 10,000 lux, as compared with normal room light of 100 to 150 lux. Whether a specific quantity of light is required to produce a therapeutic change is unknown, as is the mechanism of its effect. Theories relating to the production of the sleep-inducing hormone melatonin do not account for all the effects of phototherapy (Wyatt, 2000), and in general, results of investigations into bright light therapy are decidedly mixed. A systematic review of bright light therapy for the management of insomnia in older adults was inconclusive (Montgomery & Dennis, 2002), but here as in other studies, the authors noted that the general absence of adverse side effects and the potential efficacy in some patients suggest that it may be of potential benefit to some.

Exercise Therapy

There is intriguing, if incomplete, evidence that a structured program of physical exercise is an effective measure against depression. Several meta-analyses of controlled and uncontrolled studies have demonstrated a positive effect derived from aerobic or nonaerobic exercise conducted approximately 2 to 3 times weekly. However, when poorly designed or uncontrolled studies were removed from the analysis, the association, although apparently positive, was weaker (Lawlor & Hopker, 2001). At least one randomized trial has directly compared aerobic exercise, antidepressant medication (the SSRI sertraline or Zoloft), and a combination of exercise and medication in older patients with depression (Blumenthal et al., 1999). This study found that although medication had a somewhat faster onset of action than exercise, at four months patients in all groups reported equivalent improvement on standard measures of depression, and there was some evidence that those who continued with exercise beyond the end of the study period were at lower risk of relapse than those who did not (Babyak et al., 2000). Because exercise has salutary effects on sleep hygiene and physical well-being, it is recommended that exercise be made an integral component of any treatment for patients with depression.

In sum, although the evidence is not yet definitive, there appears to be a growing body of well-conducted studies demonstrating that exercise is of benefit in the management of depression, anxiety, and other nervous disorders. Whether exercise has any specific effect for any particular disorder is unknown. It is equally unknown if there is a dose–response effect to exercise (i.e., does more exercise result in greater psychological improvement?) or the type of exercise that is most beneficial, although a variety of aerobic and nonaerobic protocols have been recommended. We do know, however, that exercise is positively associated with reports of well-being as well as with objective measures of physical health and that body mass index, physical health, and exercise are predictors of "successful" aging after reaching age 60 (Vailliant & Mukamal, 2001). Moreover, levels of physical activity seem to be inversely correlated with depression from as early as childhood (Sallis, Prochascka, & Taylor, 2000).

A commonsense approach will dictate whether assessment of a patient's exercise plan and overall physical health be made a portion of a comprehensive treatment plan for anxiety, depression, and other common forms of mental distress. In designing an intervention, several key points should be kept in mind. The design of exercise regimens, if more than a simple admonition to increase an already established pattern, should probably be left to athletic trainers or others with specific experience and should obviously incorporate any physical limitations the patient may have. The patient's ability to master an exercise regimen and thus avoid further disappointment or loss of feelings of self-efficacy should be carefully assessed prior to recommending a specific program. Finally, programs should be incremental, with numerous proximate goals to enhance a sense of accomplishment.

Exercise programs for those with serious and persistent forms of mental distress, such as schizophrenia, should also not be ignored.

Weight gain and diabetes are two complications resulting from the use of many newer antipsychotic medications, and a well-designed program of exercise, diet, and patient awareness is essential if the health consequences of these conditions are to be avoided.

Transcranial Magnetic Stimulation

In transcranial magnetic stimulation (TMS), an electrode is placed on the scalp, generally over the area of the dorsolateral prefrontal cortex, and a strong magnetic current is subsequently applied. Like ECT, the procedure is repeated, generally daily, for a period of several weeks. Unlike ECT, the aim is generally not to induce a seizure, although if a pulse of sufficient strength is applied, a seizure may result. Patients treated with TMS have been observed to improve without induction of a seizure. This observation casts doubt on the role of seizure as the therapeutic component of ECT. The use of anesthesia is not required, and patients are alert throughout the procedure. It is hoped that TMS will be an effective treatment against depression without causing the memory deficits seen in ECT. Indeed, a recent study found improvements in cognitive functioning after a 3-week course of TMS (Martin et al., 2003). Although most authors believe that ECT is more effective than TMS, a few studies have found little difference in outcome between the two procedures. Others, however, have found no difference between the administration of "sham" TMS and TMS using magnetic stimulation. A recent meta-analysis of TMS did not find any strong evidence to support the use of TMS in depression (Martin et al., 2003).

Magnetic Seizure Therapy

Because of potentially less deleterious neurocognitive effects, magnetic seizure therapy (MST) is also being explored as an alternative to ECT. In this procedure, TMS is administered to an anesthetized patient with sufficient power to induce a generalized seizure. Conclusions about its safety and utility await further trials, but it is an area of some current interest because of the potential safety benefits provided by this procedure over ECT. It must be said, then, that the role of both TMS and MST remains quite unclear in the management of depression (Lisanby et al., 2003).

Vagus Nerve Stimulation

The U.S. Food and Drug Administration has approved the use of cervical vagus nerve stimulation (VNS) in the treatment of refractory epilepsy since 1997. In this procedure, electrodes are implanted on the patient's left vagus nerve in the neck area, and a pulse generator is also implanted under the skin. The device is programmed to deliver regularly timed impulses to the vagus nerve. Additional stimulation can also be delivered by the patient if the onset of a seizure is felt. Electrical stimulation of the vagus nerve results in a reduction in the frequency and severity of seizures for many (but not all) patients and complete elimination of seizures in a few (perhaps 15%). The benefits of the device are cumulative; it typically becomes more efficient with use over time (Andrews, 2003). More recently, this device has been proposed as a treatment for depression on the basis of open-label[4] trials (Kosel & Schlaepfer, 2003). This use, however, has been demonstrated only in small open-label trials, and one trial comparing VNS to a sham procedure failed to show significant results for the active treatment at 10 weeks (Carpenter, Friehs, & Price, 2003). The mechanism by which VNS exerts its antidepressant effects (if any) is unknown, but likely involves ascending stimulation of deep brain structures involved in the regulation of emotion.

Summary

This brief summary of empirically supported treatments for common mental disorders should, we hope, provide the reader with a general overview of techniques that have been or are currently used in clinical practice. Obviously, numerous treatments could not be discussed in one short book chapter, and we refer you to other sources, such as Nathan and Gorman (2002), for more in-depth reviews. We hope that you will keep the following overarching principles in mind when considering these various interventions:

1. Psychosocial and somatic treatments for mental disorders remain frustratingly nonspecific. We often do not know the therapeutic component of either form of treatment, nor do we know if manipulation of individual factors (e.g., a certain neurotransmitter or a certain cognitive or behavioral process) represents the curative element of either a somatic or a psychosocial treatment. There is some cause for optimism, however. We are increasingly able to formulate specific biological

---

[4] Open-label, or unblended, trials refer to studies in which the nature of the intervention is known to the investigator. Hence, an open-label drug trial indicates that the investigator knows that an active drug, and not a placebo, is being administered.

and psychological treatments for specific disorders, and as our knowledge advances, we should be able to further refine our therapeutic options.

2. Although we remain unable, in most instances, to determine the causality of a mental disorder (i.e., we don't really know if behaviors cause pathological changes in brain chemistry, if fundamental abnormalities in brain pathophysiology lead to aberrant behaviors, or if both mechanisms are involved), it is certain that brain and behavior are ineluctably intertwined. In clinical terms, this sometimes, but not always, means that a combination of both somatic (often pharmacologic) and psychological treatments represents the optimum treatment for certain disorders, such as severe depression, mania, or other forms of psychosis. Certain disorders may respond to psychological interventions alone, but it is rare that somatic treatments are indicated as the *sole* intervention for any disorder.

3. In evaluating both somatic and psychological treatments, it is vital to assess both the *strength of the evidence* and the *quality of the research* in determining the potential efficacy of a treatment and its applicability to a specific condition. A few well-designed randomized trials may boost our confidence in a particular treatment, but until these results have been replicated and their effects assessed in general clinical populations, our understanding remains incomplete.

In conclusion, the current literature clearly supports a strong role for psychotherapy, particularly cognitive–behavioral psychotherapy or interpersonal therapy, in the management of depression. Effects of psychotherapy for depression equal or surpass medication treatment, although there is some evidence that the combination of both, at least in some patients, results in greatest improvement. Behavioral and cognitive–behavioral treatments are also effective in managing phobias, obsessive–compulsive disorders, and other anxiety disorders. For some of these, their effects exceed those of medication. Psychoeducation and other supportive therapies are also used to improve adherence to medication regimens, reduce relapse, and improve social functioning in schizophrenia and bipolar disorder.

With the exception of ECT, less evidence exists to support the use of somatic treatments. Earlier treatments such as lobotomy have been decisively repudiated. Some somatic treatments, such as phototherapy or exercise therapy, are likely of some benefit, but their effects are frustratingly nonspecific. ECT is effective in treating depression, but because of ongoing concerns about its neurocognitive side effects, active investigation of transcranial magnetic stimulation and other treatments is ongoing; their future role remains to be determined. In chapter 9, the role of psychopharmacology in the management of mental disorders is discussed.

References

American Psychiatric Association. (1994a). *Diagnostic and statistical manual of mental disorders* (4th ed.). Washington, DC: Author.

American Psychiatric Association. (2000). *Diagnostic and statistical manual of mental disorders* (4th ed., text rev.). Washington, DC: Author.

Andrews, R. J. (2003). Neuroprotection trek—The next generation. *Annals of the New York Academy of Sciences, 993,* 1–13.

Azrin, N. H., Sisson, R. W., Meyers, R., & Godley, M. (1982). Alcoholism treatment by disulfiram and community reinforcement therapy. *Journal of Behavior Therapy and Experimental Psychiatry, 13,* 105–112.

Babyak, M., Blumenthal, J. A., Herman, S., Khatri, P., Doraiswamy, M., Moore, K., et al. (2000). Exercise treatment for major depression: Maintenance of therapeutic benefit at 10 months. *Psychosomatic Medicine, 62,* 633–638.

Barlow, D. H. (1996). Health care policy, psychotherapy research, and the future of psychotherapy. *American Psychologist, 51,* 1050–1058.

Barlow, D. H. (1988). *Anxiety and its disorders: The nature and treatment of anxiety and panic.* New York: Guilford Press.

Barlow, D. H., & Craske, M. G. (2000). *Mastery of your anxiety and panic: Client workbook for anxiety and panic.* San Antonio, TX: Graywind Psychological Corporation.

Barlow, D. H., Esler, J. L., & Vitali, A. E. (1998). Psychosocial treatments for panic disorders, phobias, and generalized anxiety disorder. In P. E. Nathan & J. M. Gorman (Eds.), *A guide to treatments that work* (1st ed., pp. 288–318). New York: Oxford University Press.

Barlow, D. H., Raffa, S. D., & Cohen, E. M. (2002). Psychosocial treatments for panic disorders, phobias, and generalized anxiety disorder. In P. E. Nathan & J. M. Gorman (Eds.), *A guide to treatments that work* (2nd ed., pp. 301–335). New York: Oxford University Press.

Beck, A. T., Rush, A. J., Shaw, B. F., & Emery, G. (1979). *Cognitive therapy of depression: A treatment manual.* New York: Guilford Press.

Berger, M., van Calker, D., & Riemann, D. (2003). Sleep and manipulations of the sleep–wake rhythm in depression. *Acta Psychiatrica Scandinavica, 108*(Suppl. 418.), 83–91.

Blumenthal, J. A., Babyak, M. A., Moore, K. A., Craighead, W. E., Herman, S., Khatri, P., et al. (1999). Effects of exercise training on older patients with major depression. *Archives of Internal Medicine, 159*, 2349–2356.

Bradford, D., Stroup, S., & Lieberman, J. (2002). Pharmacological treatments for schizophrenia. In P. E. Nathan & J. M. Gorman (Eds.), *A guide to treatments that work* (2nd ed., pp. 169–199). New York: Oxford University Press.

Carpenter, L. L., Friehs, G. M., & Price, L. H. (2003). Cervical vagus nerve stimulation for treatment resistant depression. *Neurosurgery Clinics of North America, 14*, 275–282.

Ceskova, E., & Svestka, J. (1993). Double-blind comparison of risperidone and haloperidol in schizophrenic and schizoaffective psychoses. *Pharmacopsychiatry, 26*, 121–124.

Chambless, D. L., & Ollendick, T. H. (2001). Empirically supported psychological interventions: Controversies and evidence. *Annual Review of Psychology, 52*, 685–716.

Cochran, S. D. (1984). Preventing medical noncompliance in the outpatient treatment of bipolar affective disorders. *Journal of Consulting and Clinical Psychology, 52*, 873–878.

Cohen, R. A., Kaplan, R. F., Zuffante, P., Moser, D. J., Jenkins, M. A., Salloway, S., & Wilkinson, H. (1999). Alteration of intention and self-initiated action associated with bilateral anterior cingulotomy. *Journal of Neuropsychiatry & Clinical Neurosciences, 11*, 444–453.

Craighead, W. E., Hart, A. B., Craighead, L. W., & Ilardi, S. S. (2002). Psychosocial treatments for major depressive disorder. In P. E. Nathan & J. M. Gorman (Eds.), *A guide to treatments that work* (2nd ed., pp. 245–261). New York: Oxford University Press.

Craighead, W. E., Miklowitz, D. J., Frank, E., & Vajk, F. C. (2002). Psychosocial treatments for bipolar disorder. In P. E. Nathan & J. M. Gorman (Eds.), *A guide to treatments that work* (2nd ed., pp. 263–275). New York: Oxford University Press.

Eckman, T. A., Wirshing, W. C., Marder, S. R., & Liberman, R. P. (1992). Techniques for training schizophrenic patients in illness self-management: A controlled trial. *American Journal of Psychiatry, 149*, 1549–1555.

Fava, G. A., Zielezny, M., Savron, G., & Grandi, S. (1995). Long-term effects of behavioural treatment for panic disorder with agoraphobia. *British Journal of Psychiatry, 166*, 87–92.

Finney, J. W., & Moos, R. H. (2002). Psychosocial treatments for alcohol use disorders. In P. E. Nathan & J. M. Gorman (Eds.), *A guide to treatments that work* (2nd ed., pp. 157–168). New York: Oxford University Press.

Foa, E. B. (2000). Psychosocial treatment of posttraumatic stress disorder. *Journal of Clinical Psychiatry, 61*(Suppl. 5), 43–48.

Foa, E. B., Davidson, J. R. T., & Frances, A. (Eds.). (1999). The expert consensus guideline series: Treatment of posttraumatic stress disorder. *Journal of Clinical Psychiatry, 60,* 1–76.

Frank, E., Kupfer, D. J., Perel, T. M., Cornes, C. L., Jarrett, D. J., Mallinger, A., et al., (1990). Three-year outcomes for maintenance therapies in recurrent depression. *Archives of General Psychiatry, 47,* 1093–1099.

Franklin, M. E., & Foa, E. B. (2002). Pharmacological treatments for posttraumatic stress disorder. In P. E. Nathan & J. M. Gorman (Eds.), *A guide to treatments that work* (2nd ed., pp. 411–445). New York: Oxford University Press.

Gallo, D. A., & Finger, S. (2000). The power of a musical instrument. Franklin, the Mozarts, Mesmer, and the Glass Harmonica. *History of Psychology, 3,* 326–343.

Giedke, H., Klingberg, S., Schwarzler, F., & Schweinsberg, M. (2003). Direct comparison of total sleep deprivation and late partial sleep deprivation in the treatment of major depression. *Journal of Affective Disorders, 76,* 85–93.

Gorman, J. M. (2002). Treatment of generalized anxiety disorder. *Journal of Clinical Psychiatry, 63*(Suppl. 8), 17–23.

Harvey, N. S., & Peet, M. (1991). Lithium maintenance: II. Effects of personality and attitude on health information acquisition and compliance. *British Journal of Psychiatry, 158,* 200–204.

Heimberg, R. G., & Juster, H. P. (1995). Cognitive behavioral treatments: Literature review. In R. G. Heimberg, M. R. Liebowitz, D. A. Hope, & F. R. Schneier (Eds.), *Social phobia: Diagnosis, assessment, and treatment.* New York: Guilford Press.

Isenberg, K. E., & Zorumski, C. F. (1999). Electroconvulsive therapy. In B. J. Sadock & V. A. Sadock (Eds.), *Comprehensive textbook of psychiatry.* Baltimore: Williams & Wilkins.

Joseph-Vanderpool, J. R., Rosenthal, N. E., Chrousos, G. P., Wehr, T. A., Skwere, R., Kasper, S., & Gold, P. W. (1991). Abnormal pituitary–adrenal responses to corticotropin releasing hormone in patients with seasonal affective disorder: Clinical and pathophysiological implications. *Journal of Clinical Endocrinology and Metabolism, 72,* 1382–1387.

Kadden, R., Carroll, K. M., Donovan, D., Cooney, N., Monti, P., Abrams, D., et al. (1992). *Cognitive–behavioral coping skills therapy manual: A clinical research guide for therapists treating individuals with alcohol abuse and dependence.* (Project MATCH Monograph Series, Vol. 3, DHHS Publication No. ADM 92-1895). Rockville, MD: National Institute on Alcohol Abuse and Alcoholism.

Kessler, R., McGonagle, K., Zhao, S., Nelson, C., Hughes, M., Eshelman, S., et al. (1994). Lifetime and 12-month prevalence of *DSM–III–R* psychiatric disorders in the United States. *Archives of General Psychiatry, 51*, 8–19.

Klerman, G. L., Weissman, M. M., Rounsaville, B. J., & Chevron, E. S. (1984). *Interpersonal psychotherapy of depression.* New York: Basic Books.

Kopelowicz, A., Liberman, R. P., & Zarate, R. (2002). Psychosocial treatments for schizophrenia. In P. E. Nathan & J. M. Gorman (Eds.), *A guide to treatments that work* (2nd ed., pp. 201–228). New York: Oxford University Press.

Kosel, M., & Schlaepfer, T. E. (2003). Beyond the treatment of epilepsy: New applications of vagus nerve stimulation in psychiatry. *CNS Spectrums, 8*, 15–21.

Lam, D. H., Bright, J., & Jones, S. (2000). Cognitive therapy for bipolar illness: Pilot study of relapse prevention. *Cognitive Therapy Research, 24*, 503–520.

Lang, A. (2004). Treating generalized anxiety disorder with cognitive–behavioral therapy. *Journal of Clinical Psychiatry, 65*(Suppl. 13), 14–19.

Lawlor, D. A., & Hopker, S. W. (2001). The effectiveness of exercise as an intervention in the management of depression: Systematic review and meta-regression analysis of randomized controlled trials. *British Medical Journal, 322*, 1–8.

Lisanby, S. H., Morales, O., Payne, N., Kwon, E., Fitzsimons, L., Luber, B., et al. (2003). New developments in electroconvulsive therapy and magnetic seizure therapy. *CNS Spectrums, 8*, 529–536.

Martin, J. L. R., Barbanoj, M. J., Schlaepfer, T. E., Clos, S., Perez, V., Kulisevsky, J., & Gironell, A. (2003). Transcranial magnetic stimulation for treating depression. *Cochrane Database of Systematic Reviews, 3*. Retrieved December 7, 2003, from http://www.cochrane.org

Martis, B., Alam, D., Dowd, S. M., & Hill, S. K. (2003). Neurocognitive effects of repetitive transcranial magnetic stimulation in sever major depression. *Clinical Neurophysiology, 114*, 1125–1132.

McElhiney, M. C., Moody, B. J., Steif, B. L., & Prudic, J. (1995). Autobiographical memory and mood: Effects of electroconvulsive therapy. *Neuropsychology, 9*, 501–517.

Menditto, A. A., Valdes, L. A., & Beck, N. C. (1994). Implementing a comprehensive social-learning program within the forensic psychiatric service of Fulton State Hospital. In P. W. Corrigan & R. P. Liberman (Eds.), *Behavior therapy in psychiatric hospitals* (pp. 61–78). New York: Springer Publishing Company.

Miklowitz, D. J., & Goldstein, M. J. (1997). *Bipolar disorder: A family-focused treatment approach.* New York: Guilford Press.

Miller, I. W., Keitner, G. I., Ryan, C. E., & Solomon, D. S. (2000, June). *Family treatment of bipolar disorder*. Paper presented at the meeting of the Society for Psychotherapy Research, Braaga, Portugal.

Miller, W. R., Zweben, A., DiClemente, C. C., & Rychtarik, R. G. (1992). *Motivational enhancement therapy manual: A clinical tool for therapists treating individuals with alcohol abuse and dependence*. (Project MATCH Monograph Series, Vol. 2, DHHS Publication No. ADM 92-1893). Rockville, MD: National Institute on Alcohol Abuse and Alcoholism.

Montgomery, P., & Dennis, J. (2002). Bright light therapy for sleep problems in adults aged 60+. *Cochrane Database of Systematic Reviews, 2*. Retrieved December 7, 2003, from http://www.cochrane. org

Mueser, K. T., Wallace, C. J., & Liberman, R. P. (1995). New developments in social skills training. *Behaviour Change, 12*, 31–40.

Nathan, P. E. (2004). The evidence base for evidence-based mental health treatments: Four continuing controversies. *Brief Treatment and Crisis Intervention, 4*, 243–254.

Nathan, P. E., & Gorman, J. M. (2002). *A guide to treatments that work* (2nd ed.). New York: Oxford University Press.

Nathan, P. E., Skinstad, A. H., & Dolan, S. L. (2000). Clinical psychology II: Psychological treatments: Research and practice. In K. Pawlik & M. R. Rosenzweig (Eds.), *The international handbook of psychology* (pp. 429–451). London: Sage.

Nathan, P. E., Stuart, S. P., & Dolan, S. L. (2000). Research on psychotherapy efficacy and effectiveness: Between Scylla and Charybdis? *Psychological Bulletin, 126*, 964–981.

Nowinski, J., Baker, S., & Carroll, K. (1992). *Twelve-step facilitation therapy manual: A clinical research guide for therapists treating individuals with alcohol abuse and dependence*. (NIAAA Project MATCH Monograph, Vol. 1, DHHS Publication No. ADM 92-1893). Rockville, MD: National Institute on Alcohol Abuse and Alcoholism.

Ochsner, K. M., Kosslyn, S. M., Cosgrove, G. R., Cassem, E. H., Price, B. H., Nierenberg, A. A., & Rauch, S. L. (2001). Deficits in visual cognition and attention following bilateral anterior cingulotomy. *Neuropsychologia, 39*, 219–230.

O'Farrell, T. J., Choquette, K. A., Cutter, H. S. G., Brown, E. D., & McCourt, W. F. (1993). Behavioral marital therapy with and without additional couples relapse prevention sessions for alcoholics and their wives. *Journal of Studies on Alcohol, 54*, 652–666.

Ouimette, P. C., Finney, J. W., & Moos, R. H. (1997). Twelve-step and cognitive–behavioral treatment for substance abuse: A comparison of treatment effectiveness. *Journal of Consulting and Clinical Psychology, 65*, 230–240.

Paul, G. L., & Lentz, R. J. (1977). *Psychosocial treatment of chronic mental patients: Milieu versus social-learning programs.* Cambridge, MA: Harvard University Press.

Perry, A., Tarrier, N., Morriss, R., McCarthy, E., & Limb, K. (1999). Randomised controlled trial of efficacy of teaching patients with bipolar disorder to identify early symptoms of relapse and obtain treatment. *British Medical Journal, 16,* 149–153.

Prochaska, J. O., & DiClemente, C. C. (1986). Toward a comprehensive model of change. In W. R. Miller & N. Heather (Eds.), *Treating addictive behavior: Processes of change* (pp. 3–27). New York: Plenum Press.

Project MATCH Research Group. (1993). Project MATCH: Rationale and methods for a multisite clinical trial matching patients to alcoholism treatment. *Alcoholism: Clinical and Experimental Research, 17,* 1130–1145.

Project MATCH Research Group. (1997a). Matching alcoholism treatment to client heterogeneity: Project MATCH post-treatment drinking outcomes. *Journal of Studies on Alcohol, 58,* 7–29.

Project MATCH Research Group. (1997b). Project MATCH Secondary *a priori* hypotheses. *Addiction, 92,* 1671–1698.

Project MATCH Research Group. (1998). Matching alcoholism treatments to client heterogeneity: Project MATCH three-year drinking outcomes. *Alcoholism: Clinical and Experimental Research, 22,* 1300–1311.

Robertson, M., Humphreys, L., & Ray, R. (2004). Psychological treatments for posttraumatic stress disorder: Recommendations for the clinician based on a review of the literature. *Journal of Psychiatric Practice, 10,* 106–118.

Sallis, J. F., Prochaska, J. J., & Taylor, W. C. (2000). A review of correlated of physical activity of children and adolescents. *Medicine and Science in Sports and Exercise, 32,* 963–975.

Schwartz, P. J., Turner, E. H., Garcia-Borreguero, D., Sedway, J., Vetticad, R. G., Wehr, T. A., et al. (1999). Serotonin hypothesis of winter depression: Behavioral and neuroendocrine effects of the 5-HT(1A) receptor partial agonist ipsapirone in patients with seasonal affective disorder and healthy control subjects. *Psychiatry Research, 86,* 9–28.

Smith, D. E., & McCrady, B. S. (1991). Cognitive impairment among alcoholics: Impact on drink refusal skills acquisition and treatment outcome. *Addictive Behaviors, 16,* 265–274.

Spaulding, W. D., Sullivan, M. E., & Poland, J. S. (2003). *Treatment and rehabilitation of severe mental illness.* New York: Guilford Press.

Strakowski, S. M., Keck, P. E., McElroy, S. L., West, S. A., Sax, K. W., Hawkins, J. M., et al. (1998). Twelve-month outcome after a first hospitalization for affective psychosis. *Archives of General Psychiatry, 55,* 49–55.

Trivedi, M. (2003). Treatment resistant depression: New therapies on the horizon. *Annals of Clinical Psychiatry, 15,* 59–70.

UK ECT Review Group. (2003). Efficacy and safety of electroconvulsive therapy in depressive disorders: A systematic review and meta-analysis. *The Lancet, 361,* 799–808.

Vailliant, G. E., & Mukamal, K. (2001). Successful aging. *American Journal of Psychiatry, 158,* 839–847.

Valenstein, E. (1986). *Great and desperate cures: The rise and decline of psychosurgery and other radical treatments for mental illness.* New York: Basic Books.

Van der Wurff, F. B., Stek, M. L., Hoogendijk, W. L., & Beekman, A. T. F. (2005). Electroconvulsive therapy for the depressed elderly. *The Cochrane Library, Issue 2.* Retrieved June 12, 2005, from http://www.cochrane.org

Wilson, G. T. (1995). Empirically supported treatments as a basis for clinical practice: Problems and prospects. In S. C. Hayes, V. M. Follette, R. M. Dawes, & K. E. Grady (Eds.), *Scientific standards of psychological practice: Issues and recommendations* (pp. 163–196). Reno, NV: Context Press.

Wyatt, J. K. (2000). Seasonal affective disorder. In A. E. Kazdin (Ed.), *Encyclopedia of psychology* (Vol. 7, pp. 200–201). Washington, DC: American Psychological Association and Oxford University Press.

Bruce K. McCormick

The Use of Medicine in the Treatment of Mental Disorders

9

During the 20th century, two major events strongly influenced the understanding of mental disorders and how they may be treated. The first half of the century saw the work of Sigmund Freud, who suggested that certain types of life experiences may bring about mental disorders. Although today many authorities are critical of some of the specifics of Freud's original ideas, it is almost universally recognized that events in people's lives affect their behavior, and when those events exceed their ability to cope with stress in a healthy manner, disorders of thought and behavior may result. The lasting legacy of Freud and the many others who built on his work is the use of psychotherapy to treat mental disorders. Today many approaches to psychotherapy are used in mental health treatment. An overview of the most prominent of these methods is presented in chapter 8 of this book.

The second half of the 20th century included the discovery that certain bioactive chemical compounds can be of tremendous value in the management of symptoms of disordered thought and behavior. Indeed, in some cases, medicine was found to be so effective that people with disturbances so severe that their survival required around-the-clock supervision in hospitals or institutions experienced a reduction in symptoms so dramatic that they could live in a normal home situation. Others, although still in need of supervision, improved sufficiently to participate in work, recreational activities, and psychotherapy. The discovery that medicine can be a very effective part of treatment brought about the recognition that biology as well as life experiences can contribute to the nature, severity, or perhaps even the cause of mental disorders. Today, the majority of mental health professionals recognize both psychosocial (i.e., environmental) and biological factors as influencing the presence and the specific characteristics of mental disorders. Currently, the use of *psychotropic*[1] medicine is commonly included as a part of many comprehensive plans for mental health treatment.

How Will Knowing About Medicines Be Helpful?

A basic knowledge of medicines used in mental health treatment can be of value to you as a psychology practicum student in several ways. In a comprehensive inpatient program such as a hospital, you may see how medicines and psychotherapy are used together in a treatment plan. You may have opportunities to join meetings with the many professionals involved in treating patients. These meetings are often called *staffings* or meetings of a *multidisciplinary team* or *treatment team*. Among the many things discussed during such staffings will be what medicines a patient is taking and if those medications appear to be producing the desired results. It is common for the mental health care team to provide information about how a patient is sleeping, eating, interacting with others, and if the concerns that brought the patient to treatment are improving. Often the type or dose of medicine a patient is taking will be maintained or changed depending on input from those meetings.

Understanding the basics of medicines is valuable in understanding how such decisions are made. Additionally, knowing the types of medicines a patient is taking may give a clue to the pattern of symptoms or kinds of difficulty that individual was exhibiting before treatment was started. If you have an opportunity to interact with patients during your practicum, you may be able to tell that some of their thoughts

---

[1] Psychotropic literally means "mind altering."

and behaviors are affected by medicines, and you may notice some effects of medicine, such as frequent thirst or sedation that, although not desirable, may also result from the use of medicine.

It is likely that you will have an opportunity to observe one or more treatment settings. Some patients with very serious and difficult to treat chronic mental disorders spend many months or years of long-term care in a hospital. Many others may receive a period of a several days or a few weeks of acute care in a hospital until such time as their condition improves sufficiently so they may return home. Often it is the effectiveness of psychotropic medications that shortens hospital stays and allows individuals to remain or to return home and be treated on what is termed an *outpatient* basis. That is, they live independently but have appointments at a treatment facility one or more times per week. During those appointments, the patients may participate in group or individual psychotherapy. In addition, they may review with their prescriber how the medications they are taking seem to be working and discuss any side effects or other problems they may be experiencing. These medication checkups to review the effectiveness of their medicines (often informally called "med checks") allow examination of a patient's overall physical and mental health and provide time for any adjustments that might be needed in their prescription. Frequent medication checkups are required for many of the more potent psychotropic medications.

How Are Medicines Named?

The names given medicines may sound strange or unusual. Adding to this potential for confusion is that most medicines actually have three different types of names: a chemical name, a generic name, and a brand name.[2] The *chemical name*, which is an actual designation of the chemical composition of the drug, is not commonly used except by chemists involved in the research and development of drugs. The *generic name*—usually a much-shortened version of the chemical name—is a simpler and more easily remembered way to refer to the same substance. When a pharmaceutical company develops a compound, the company usually patents the new medicine and gives it a *brand name* that is exclusively used for the medicine when made by that company. When a patent

---

[2] A brand name is sometimes called a trade name.

expires and other companies can make the same medicine, it can have different brand names depending on the manufacturer. For example, the generic, diphenhydramine, is marketed under the different brand names of Benadryl, Caladryl, and even Simply Sleep.

To illustrate this admittedly complicated system of naming drugs, consider the example of a common medicine, a compound frequently used for relief from pain that has the chemical name N-acetyl-p-amino-phenol. Although that name may not be readily known, you may recognize its generic name, acetaminophen, and almost certainly you know the brand name of Tylenol. The advantage of shortening a chemical name to easier generic and brand names is even more apparent with this example of a common psychotropic medicine that has the imposing chemical name of $(\pm)$-N-methyl-3-phenyl-3-[$(\alpha, \alpha, \alpha,$ -trifluro-p-tolyl)oxy] propylamine hydrochloride and the empirical formula of $C_{17}H_{18}F_3NO \cdot HCl$, the generic name of fluoxetine, and the brand name of Prozac.

WHY THREE NAMES?

The examples above clearly show the advantages of using a name for medicines other than the cumbersome chemical name. Yet why have both generic and brand names? The answer has mainly to do with sales, marketing, and advertising. Any prescription drug for use with humans in the United States must first receive approval from the Food and Drug Administration (FDA). Before receiving FDA approval, the company that plans to market a medicine must conduct extensive research to demonstrate that the product is effective for its intended use and safe for consumers. The research, development, manufacturing, and then testing of possible medicines often take several years and cost many millions of dollars. In order for companies to recoup money spent to bring a medicine to market and then make a profit, new prescription drugs are usually patented. While the patent is in effect (usually 17 years), only the company holding the patent may sell the drug. At the time it has exclusive rights to sell a medicine the pharmaceutical company will copyright a brand name, which unlike the patent, does not expire but rather continues to be legally protected for exclusive use by that company. When a patent does expire, other companies are allowed to manufacture the medicine and to market it (usually at a lower cost) under its generic name but not by its original brand name.[3]

---

[3] Occasionally a company will copyright more than one name for the same medicine. Usually this is done when the drug is marketed for more than one purpose. For example, Prozac, which is marketed for depression, also has the brand name Seraphim when it is marketed for premenstrual distress.

Often, a medicine—known by its brand name—will gain acceptance from prescribers and consumers while the patent is in effect. The manufacturing company hopes that consumers will continue to select the brand name medicine even when the patent runs out. For example, the patent for Tylenol has long since expired, but many consumers still buy the brand name medicine they know and have confidence in, ignoring generic preparations that are equally available and at a lower cost.

What Are Generic Medicines?

The term *generic medicines* refers to medicines that, as explained above, are manufactured by a company other than the one that originally developed and patented those compounds. Many of the newer psychotropic medications only exist as brand name drugs, but several, such as fluoxetine (Prozac) as well as many of the older, established medications, are available in a generic form. Generic medications are virtually always lower in cost than brand name medications. In actual use it is sometimes difficult to know if a particular patient is receiving a brand name or a generic drug, especially if one is unfamiliar with the names of each. Formal writing style requires that brand names be capitalized and that generics begin with lowercase letters. That convention is not always followed in quickly written treatment notes and patient chart entries, however, and capitalization of generics is perhaps the most common error. Moreover, in casual conversation one may refer to a brand name drug even though a generic will be actually used. For example, in treatment team meetings, a prescriber may suggest giving a patient "Prozac," when that facility uses only the generic, fluoxetine.

HOW DO GENERIC MEDICINES COMPARE WITH BRAND NAME MEDICINES?

Most medicines that are taken by mouth (orally) include both active and inactive ingredients. Active ingredients are the actual chemicals that are the medicine; inactive ingredients include fillers, color, sometimes flavor additives, and other substances to hold or contain the active ingredients. The FDA requires that all generic medicines contain roughly the same amount of active ingredients as was in the original brand name medicine; however, the inactive ingredients may be very different. In most cases, generic medicines, whether they are psycho-tropics or other types of prescription drugs, work equally well as the originals. Differences in inactive ingredients sometimes change, within limits,[4] how quickly the medicine actually goes to work in the body or how much of the active ingredient is actually available for use in the body. Typically, any such differences are small and biologically inconsequential; however, occasionally some individuals do respond better to brand name than generic psychotropic medicines. To save money many treatment facilities and many insurance companies insist on the use of generic medications when they are available.

How Do Medicines Work to Treat Mental Disorders?

The human brain is an organ made up of millions and millions of cells, mostly nerve cells, which are called *neurons*. The neurons in the brain send signals throughout the nervous system of the body and to muscles, glands, and organs. Nerve cells typically consist of a cell body with a nucleus; a branching system of structures called *dendrites,* which receive signals from other neurons; and a long fiber called an axon, which sends signals to other parts of the body.

Different areas of the brain and corresponding nerve pathways from the brain through the spinal cord reach all areas of the body and control and regulate all body functions, including breathing and heartbeat, voluntary movement and reflexes, and the functioning of organs and healing of injuries. Nerve signals in the brain also influence and are affected by thoughts, feelings, and emotions. Within the brain there are many billions of connections between neurons through which signals (nerve impulses) are sent and received. Medicines that are used to treat emotional disorders typically work by altering the transmission of signals between neurons in the brain. Most medicines have a long and complicated trip, however, before they can enter the blood stream and move to synapses to produce their desired effect.

---

[4] Generic medicines are required to have 80% to 120% actual availability of the active ingredients as compared to brand name medicines.

How Do Medicines Get to Where They Can Be of Use?

When thinking of medicines for the treatment of mental disorders, most people probably consider pills or capsules—that is, medications that are taken orally (po). Indeed the majority (although certainly not all) of psychotropic medicines are taken by mouth. Most of the digestible things people ingest, including food and drugs, are absorbed into the blood stream through the small intestines. About 80% of the blood from the small intestine then goes directly to the liver. The liver produces a complex system of enzymes that attempt to convert any nonnutritional substance to a form that can be easily eliminated from the body. That function allows the body to rid itself of the minute amounts of toxins and other nonnutrients people may happen to ingest or otherwise absorb throughout their lives. The liver does not, however, distinguish between chemicals people may have unknowingly or accidentally encountered and chemicals that they have taken for the treatment of illness. This means that soon after a person takes an oral medicine, the liver works to break that medicine down chemically so that it can be eliminated from the body. If the liver enzyme system is not able to bring about the complete elimination of a substance, it still transforms it so that later it can be broken down to a more easily eliminated state. Usually the transformation by the liver causes the substance to become ionized—that is, electrically charged, which makes it more easily dissolved in water and therefore eliminated by the kidneys through the urine.[5] The substance that results from being changed (metabolized) by enzymes in the liver is called a *metabolite*.

Because metabolism can destroy medicines when they are taken by mouth, the amount of a medicine taken (the dosage) must be large enough so that a sufficient amount of active ingredients remains in the bloodstream even after passing through the liver. However, some medicines, although effective in themselves, are metabolized by the liver to a form (called an *active metabolite*) that can be as or more effective than the original medicine. For example, two antidepressant medications, imipramine (Tofranil) and fluoxetine (Prozac) have active metabolites[6] that last longer and are more effective than the medicines

---

[5] For this reason, urinanalysis is often used to check for recent drug use.

[6] The active metabolites for Tofranil and Prozac are desimpramine and norfluoxetine, respectively.

before they are changed by the liver enzymes. Just as the dosage of a medicine may need to be increased to overcome metabolism from the liver, in the case of an active metabolite, the dosage may need to be reduced for a patient with liver disease or with impaired kidney function or other problems with elimination.

An alternative to using sufficiently large doses of a medicine to avoid having the medicine destroyed through metabolism is to avoid altogether the initial "first pass" of blood from the small intestine to the liver. This may be accomplished by administration of drugs through routes that do not involve the gastrointestinal tract. Alternatives to oral administration include inhalation (such as might be used for treating asthma or for rapid infusion of nicotine for smoking cessation), rectal absorption (as with suppositories), absorption through the skin (*transdermal*) or through tissue at the underside of the tongue (*sublingual*), as well as injections directly into the blood stream (*intravenous* or IV) or muscle tissue (*intramuscular* or IM). Intramuscular injections of tranquilizing and antipsychotic medications have long been used to produce rapid sedation of highly agitated patients. An additional advantage of intramuscular injections is that many medicines prepared for that route of administration are rather thick (*viscous*) and take time to be completely absorbed in the blood stream, producing a sort of timed-release effect.

Even when a medicine has passed through (or bypassed) the liver, there are other obstacles to overcome before it reaches the neuronal synapses. Proteins in the bloodstream[7] have a strong chemical affinity for many medicines and active metabolites and bind with them, essentially "locking them up" before they reach their site of action. Sometimes as much as 70% or 80% of a medicine can be *protein bound*. Additionally, the brain is protected from being exposed to many foreign elements by what is called the *blood–brain barrier*, an anatomical structuring that allows only very small molecules to pass directly into the blood supply to the brain. Some medicines, such as the class of tranquilizers known as *benzodiazepines*,[8] have a very small molecular size that allows them to cross the blood–brain barrier rapidly and consequently produce their sedating effect quite rapidly. Other medicines with larger molecular structures have to rely on other much slower and less efficient means of passing the blood–brain barrier. Thus, the factors of liver metabolism, protein binding, metabolite activity, kidney function,

---

[7] Albumin, in particular, is one such protein.

[8] Examples of benzodiazepines include diazepam (Valium), alprazolam (Xanax), and lorazepam (Ativan).

and molecular structure all affect the amount of medication and choice or route of administration that might be needed for a given patient.

How Do Medications Affect Nerve Transmissions?

Transmission of a signal through a given nerve cell occurs in one direction only and takes place through a change in electrical charge along the length of that neuron. Typically, a neuron will receive sufficient stimulation of its dendrites to cause the nerve cell to fire (technically, to reach an *action potential*). The signal then travels the length of the neuron to its axon. Beyond the axon is a small space called a *synapse*[9] that must be crossed for the signal to continue. Transmission of a signal across the synapse takes place by release from the axon of a few molecules of particular substances called *neurotransmitters* that cross the synapse and chemically bind to *receptor sites* on the receiving neuron or (other cell) that is to be stimulated. When enough receptor sites are stimulated at the same time, changes take place in the chemistry of the receiving cell that cause it to reach an action potential and transmit a signal (if it is also a nerve cell) or perform some other function (such as expand or contract if it is a muscle cell). This process of *synaptic transmission* involves submicroscopic structures and minute amounts of chemicals and can take place several times per second.

There are many different known neurotransmitters and probably more yet to be discovered. Particularly relevant to brain functions involving what are considered emotional disorders are neurotransmitters such as *dopamine, serotonin,* and *norepinephrine. Acetylcholine* is another neurotransmitter that is often affected by psychotropic medications. A neurotransmitter that works outside the brain where neurons stimulate *end organs* such as the heart, muscles, glands, and blood vessels, acetycholine is responsible for many of the side effects commonly experienced with psychotropic medicines.

After their release from the neuronal axon, neurotransmitters have but a brief opportunity to stimulate receptor sites before they are

---

[9] This space is also called a "synaptic cleft."

destroyed or removed from the synapse. Psychotropic medications usually work by increasing or by reducing a neurotransmitter's ability to stimulate receptor sites.

Normally, some neurotransmitters are chemically destroyed soon after they are released by molecules of an enzyme called *monoamine oxidase* (MAO) that is naturally present in the synapse. A class of antidepressant medications called *monoamine oxidase inhibitors* (MAOI), as the name implies, inhibits the action of monoamine oxidase molecules by chemically changing them so that they can no longer destroy neurotransmitters.

Neurotransmitters can be removed from the synapse by binding with molecules that then transport them back into the axon from which they were released. The process of returning neurotransmitters to the axon is called *reuptake*. Many psychotropic medicines work by chemically blocking the bond between transporter molecules and neurotransmitters, thereby preventing reuptake of the neurotransmitters and allowing them to remain in the synapse, increasing the chance for stimulation of the receptor sites of the receiving cell. Medicines that function in this way are called *reuptake inhibitors* and are sometimes described by the specific neurotransmitters on which they act. For example, medicines such as fluoxetine (Prozac), sertraline (Zoloft), and paroxetine (Paxil), which are used to treat depression, anxiety, and some other conditions, are called *selective serotonin reuptake inhibitors* (SSRIs) because they inhibit the reuptake, primarily, of the neurotransmitter serotonin. Likewise, a common antidepressant, venlafaxine (Effexor), is considered a serotonin and norepinephrine reuptake inhibitor (SNRI) because it inhibits reuptake mainly of those two neurotransmitters. Medicines that increase the length of time neurotransmitters are present in the synapse, either by blocking reuptake or by preventing their destruction, make it more likely that enough receptor sites will be stimulated to send a signal to the receiving cell. Other medicines work by stimulating the release of extra neurotransmitters, and some actually enter the synapse and mimic neurotransmitters by themselves stimulating receptor sites. Medicines that function in those ways are called *agonists*.

Still other medications, called *antagonists,* block transmissions from neurons by binding with receptor sites, in effect locking out neurotransmitters so that the receiving cell cannot be stimulated. Whether by inhibiting the reuptake of a neurotransmitter, preventing its destruction by enzymes in the synapse, or by acting as an agonist or antagonist, psychotropic medicines affect thoughts and moods through increasing and decreasing the complex pattern of nerve signals in the brain.

What Are Side Effects?

The desired improvements in behavior and subjective comfort that medicines produce, called *target effects*, result from changes in neuronal transmission at specific locations in the brain. However, because the bloodstream takes medicines throughout the body, medicines can cause unintended physiological changes by stimulating or blocking transmissions of neurons at locations that have nothing to do with the mental disorder that they are intended to treat. The unwanted results that come from the use of medicines are called *side effects*. Side effects can range from mild and inconsequential to so severe that even an otherwise effective medicine cannot be continued for a patient. A medicine may have to be discontinued because the side effects are excessively annoying or cause extreme discomfort, or in some cases, because they medically compromise the patient's survival.

Most psychotropic medicines have some associated side effects.[10] Which side effects are actually experienced depends not only on which neurotransmitters are influenced but also an individual's specific body chemistry. For that reason, the side effects of medicines can differ greatly from one person to another. Some patients will have few, mild side effects that subside in a few days, whereas others taking the same amount of the same medicine can experience much greater and prolonged discomfort. Examples of common side effects some patients may experience include sedation or drowsiness, changes in blood pressure, nausea or other stomach distress, headache, or increased or decreased salivation. Although common side effects of medicines are sometimes annoying, they seldom are of serious medical concern unless their discomfort causes patients to refuse to take the medication.

In some cases, a major consideration in selecting which medicine would be best for a given patient requires balancing probable side effects with the expected benefit. For example, most medicines used to treat disorders such as schizophrenia can produce what are called *extrapyramidal* side effects, which include muscular rigidity, tremor, lethargy, and a shuffling gait. Some of these antipsychotic medicines are less likely to produce extrapyramidal side effects but more likely to produce

---

[10] Sometimes the difference between a target effect and a side effect depends on the reason a medicine is used. For example, diphenhydramine when taken as Benadryl for allergic reactions has the side effect of causing drowsiness. The same medicine as Simply Sleep has the target effect of drowsiness, and dryness of the mouth and nasal passages become side effects.

anticholinergic effects such as dry mouth, constipation, urinary retention, blurred vision, and mental confusion. (Anticholinergic effects occur when transmission of the neurotransmitter acetycholine is blocked.) Another possible side effect from prolonged use of these medicines, called *tardive dyskinesia*, involves abnormal involuntary movements of the hands, trunk, and extremities, occasionally with associated facial contortions or grimaces. Usually tardive dyskinesia will stop with discontinuation of the medication; however, it can become a lifelong condition if the medicine causing it continues to be taken. Tardive dyskinesia often resulted from use of the earliest psychotropic medicines. Unfortunately, there were few choices in medicines, and as the improvement from medication was judged to be preferable to eliminating that treatment, many patients continued to receive the same medicines for many years and developed permanent tardive dyskinesia. You may encounter such patients, particularly if you have an opportunity to observe a setting that serves persons who have a long history of treatment for psychotic disorders.

There are some side effects of medication that are relatively rare but that constitute serious, indeed sometimes deadly, conditions. *Neuroleptic malignancy syndrome* (NMS) is a potentially fatal condition that most often results from antipsychotic medication. The signs and symptoms of NMS include elevated body temperature, confusion, muscle stiffness, irregular heartbeat, and sweating. *Agranulocytosis*, a blood disorder, and *Stevens–Johnson syndrome*, a severe skin reaction, are both life-threatening conditions that can result from a variety of psychotropic medications. The immediate treatment for these serious conditions is discontinuation of the offending medication and the initiation of supportive medical treatment. In the case of Stevens–Johnson syndrome, the destruction of skin cells can be so severe that patients with that condition are sometimes treated in hospital burn units. The many common and rare side effects that can result from psychotropic medications underscore the importance of frequent checks with the health care prescriber as well as the necessity for patients to closely following their prescriber's directions.

How Are Medicines Developed?

As noted earlier in this chapter, it has only been about 50 years since the discovery that medicines can be of significant use in the treatment of mental disorders. Some of the most important of these discoveries have been accidental. For example, in 1952, two French physicians found that chlorpromazine (Thorazine), which had been developed with the hope that it would prevent lowered blood pressure during surgery—which it did not in fact do—greatly reduced the hallucinations and delusions associated with psychosis. Chlorpromazine[11] became the first medicine found to be useful in the treatment of psychotic disorders such as schizophrenia. Soon thereafter, a Swiss pharmaceutical company attempted to modify the chemical structure of chlorpromazine to produce an antipsychotic medicine with fewer side effects. The resulting drug imipramine (Tofranil) did not work at all well for psychotic symptoms, but it was found to be a very effective antidepressant medicine. Even more unexpected was the finding several years later that an ingredient that was being used as a filler for many tablets, valproic acid, was actually very effective in treating seizure disorders.

The early, accidental discovery of effective psychotropic medications started a flood of biochemical research that continues today with the goal of discovering additional medicines that are even more effective and that can treat a greater number of emotional conditions. Researchers today do not have to rely as heavily on accident and luck to determine the usefulness of medicines they are developing. Understanding of the human brain and how it works is greater than even a few years ago, and it is constantly expanding. Improved knowledge of brain function guides research toward the production of newer medicines. The actual effects of new medicines, in turn, give many clues into how the nervous systems work. Certainly knowledge of the biological components of mental disorders has increased dramatically; however, there is still much that is not known. Indeed, biochemists typically are able to tell what a psychotropic medicine may do in the brain, but they are usually unsure exactly how and why it produces its effect. For example, medicines such as the SSRIs were developed as antidepressants, a function they often perform well, although researchers are not sure just why they work. Moreover, researchers have subsequently discovered that some of the SSRIs are also useful in treating conditions such as generalized anxiety, bulimia, and obsessive–compulsive disorder. The challenges for today and for tomorrow will be to continue the study of the brain and to develop medicines that can effectively target selected brain functions while limiting unwanted effects on other unrelated neurological processes.

---

[11] Prolonged use of chlorpromazine was responsible for many cases of tardive dyskinesia.

What About
Herbal Medicines?

The first medicines used by humans to treat illnesses came from plants and herbs that were naturally available. Plants often contain chemical compounds that can be useful in treating diseases. Indeed, many of the most commonly prescribed medicines today have as their active ingredients compounds that were first found in plants. Pharmaceutical companies often extract or synthetically produce those plant compounds to make modern drugs. Medicinal herbs have been used for treatment of mental as well as physical disorders. As an example, rauwolfia, an herb indigenous to India and the East Indies, was used for centuries to treat some mental disorders. In the mid-1900s, a U.S. scientist discovered a compound in rauwolfia called reserpine[12] that was subsequently extracted and used as an early psychotropic.

Herbal medicine continues to be a popular method of treatment in Eastern countries and central Europe. In recent decades, people in the United States have shown an increasing interest in herbal, or so-called "natural," medicines. Today, the marketing of herbs, often in the form of tablets or capsules, is a multimillion dollar industry.

DO HERBAL MEDICINES WORK?

There is no question that most herbal preparations have a physiological effect on the body. There are several concerns and misconceptions, however, about the use of such preparations. Many people falsely believe that because plants are natural, their use for medical treatment is safer than using pharmaceutical products. That assumption is often not the case. Certainly oleander and hemlock are natural plants—and both are quite deadly when taken internally. Plants and herbs can have an extremely complex chemistry. When they are taken orally, the body is exposed to numerous chemical substances, some of which may have benefit and others that may be benign or even quite harmful. The exact chemical compounds or combination of compounds of an herb that produce a desired effect are often unknown. Likewise, dosage ranges for safety and for effectiveness have not been clearly established for most herbal products. Recommended daily amounts, printed on the package labels, often come from speculation or tradition rather than

---

[12] Reserpine had many side effects and was soon replaced by other psychotropics such as chlorpromazine, but it continues to be used to treat some types of hypertension.

rigid research. Definitive scientific study of exactly which components of plants may be useful and how they work is growing as a result of consumer interest but remains limited at this time. In China as well as many Eastern and European countries, the manufacture and sale of herbal preparations are regulated. In the United States, however, those products are marketed not as drugs but as "dietary supplements." That designation avoids regulation by the FDA, and consequently, there is no governmental assurance of content, potency, quality, or even the absence of harmful impurities. Most important, herbals can interact with traditional pharmaceutical drugs. It is essential that patients inform their prescriber of any herbal, or natural, substances they may be taking.

What Medications Are Commonly Prescribed for Mental Disorders?

One common and useful way to group psychotropic medicines is by the type of disorders they have been found to effectively treat, although some medicines, such as the SSRIs noted above, may be used to treat more than one condition (see Table 9.1). Below are listings, brief descriptions, and examples of some of the most commonly used psychotropic medications. It is likely that you will find many of these medicines in use at the treatment programs you have an opportunity to observe.

ANTIDEPRESSANT MEDICATIONS

Tricyclic antidepressants are named for a molecular structure that all have in common.[13] Most work by blocking the reuptake of the neurotransmitters epinephrine and serotonin. Although they take several days to be completely effective, the tricyclics are often very effective in treating depression and are also of value in the treatment of anxiety. Many have been approved for use with children. Disadvantages include dry mouth and urinary retention,[14] potentially fatal overdose, and in rare cases cardiac (heart) toxicity. Examples include imipramine (Tofranil), desipramine (Norpramin), and amitriptyline (Pamelor).

---

[13] The molecular structure is three fused benzene rings.

[14] Urinary retention as a side effect has allowed some tricyclics such as imipramine (Tofranil) to be used to treat nocturnal enuresis (bed wetting).

TABLE 9.1

Common Psychotropic Medications

Medical purpose	Generic name	Brand name
Antidepressant	Bupropion	Wellbutrin
	Mirtazapine	Remeron
	Duloxetine	Cymbalta
	Venlafaxine	Effexor
Antidepressant and antianxiety	Fluoxetine	Prozac
	Paroxetine	Paxil
	Sertraline	Zoloft
	Escitalopram	Lexapro
Antianxiety	Buspirone	BuSpar
	Alprazolam	Xanax
	Lorazepam	Ativan
Antipsychotic	Aripirazole	Abilify
	Clozapine	Clozaril
	Haloperidol	Haldol
	Olanzapine	Zyprexa
	Risperidone	Risperdal
	Quetiapine	Seroquel
	Ziprasidone	Geodon
Mood stabilizing	Lithium	Eskalith
	Lamotrigine	Lamictal
	Carbamazepine	Tegretol
	Gabapentin	Neurontin
	Valproic acid	Depakote

As described earlier, MAOIs produce their effect by changing mono-amine oxidase in the neuronal synapse so that it cannot chemically destroy neurotransmitters. The MAOIs are also very effective antidepressants, but when they are taken in combination with certain foods[15] or other medicines, they can produce life-threatening *hypertension* (high blood pressure) or other dangerous nervous system reactions. Examples include pheneizine (Nardil) and tranylcypromine (Parnate).

As noted above, SSRIs block the reuptake mainly of the neurotransmitter serotonin. The SSRIs have been found to be effective not only in the treatment of depressive disorders but also for generalized anxiety, obsessional disorders, panic disorders, and bulimia. It usually takes about two weeks for them to reach full effectiveness. Examples include fluoxetine (Prozac), paroxetine (Paxil), and sertraline (Zoloft).

---

[15] Specifically, MAOIs are dangerous and can be life threatening when taken in combination with foods containing the substance tryamine.

New antidepressant medications have recently been developed that do not fit the traditional categories above. These include venlafaxine (Effexor), which inhibits the reuptake of both norepinephrine and serotonin; mirtazapine (Remeron), which affects norepinephrine and serotonin by blocking feedback channels so that more neurotransmitters are released; bupropion (Wellbutrin), a norepinephrine and dopamine reuptake inhibitor; and two closely related serotonin reuptake inhibitors, citalopam (Celexa), and escitalopram (Lexapro).

ANXIOLYTIC (ANTIANXIETY) MEDICATIONS

Benzodiazepines are tranquilizers that provide temporary relief for anxiety. As noted earlier, the benzodiazepines easily cross the blood–brain barrier so they work rather quickly. They are often used for acute anxiety attacks or as short-term treatment to allow the other long-term medicines to take effect. These medicines are also sometimes used to treat withdrawal symptoms during alcohol detoxification. The body can develop a tolerance to benzodiazepines, and their prolonged use may actually cause depression. These medicines are relatively safe in overdose, but even modest amounts can be fatal when taken with alcohol. Examples include diazepam (Valium), chlordiazepoxide (Librium), and alprazolam (Xanex).

Buspirone (Buspar) is an antianxiety medication that works in a complicated way by blocking feedback channels in neurons so that they continue to release serotonin. Tricyclic antidepressants and SSRIs, as noted above, are also effective in the long-term treatment of anxiety.

ANTIPSYCHOTIC MEDICATIONS

Medications termed *typical antipsychotics* are used to treat conditions such as schizophrenia. They are usually effective in reducing symptoms such as hallucinations and delusional thought. These medications generally reduce neural transmission by blocking dopamine receptors at receiving neurons (i.e., they are dopamine antagonists). All can produce extrapyramidal or anticholinergic side effects, and all have a risk of tardive dyskinesia with prolonged use. Typical antipsychotics are further classified as having *low potency* or *high potency*.[16] Low-potency antipsychotics such as chlorpromazine (Thorazine) and thioridazine (Mellaril) are less likely to cause extrapyramidal motor side effects, whereas

---

[16] Typical antipsychotics are grouped as high or low potency. Both are equally effective treatments; the difference is in the amount of medication needed to reach therapeutic effect. It takes more of a low-potency medication to have the same treatment effect as a high-potency preparation.

high-potency antipsychotics such as trifluoperazine (Stelazine), thio-thiexene (Navane), and haloperidol (Haldol) tend to have fewer or milder anticholinergic side effects.

Atypical antipsychotics are new medications that function some-what differently than the traditional medications (hence, atypical). In some cases, these new medications produce fewer or milder side effects, and some may bring about improvement not found with typical medi-cines, such as enhanced emotional expression, social interest, and moti-vation. Examples include the dopamine and serotonin agonists rispari-done (Risperdal), olonzapine (Zyprex), and ziprasidone (Geodon) and a dopamine antagonist clozapine (Clozaril). Clozaril has gained much attention since it became available because it not only reduces abnormal behavior in schizophrenia but also promotes more normal emotional expression. Moreover, Clozaril does not seem to produce extrapyrami-dal side effects. Unfortunately, Clozaril can cause seizures, and it is more likely than most medicines to produce agranulocytosis. The potential severity of those side effects limits the medicine's utility and necessitates strict and regular laboratory monitoring when Clozaril is prescribed. An even newer antipsychotic medicine that has only recently received FDA approval is aripiprazole (Abilify). Early information indicates this mediation may compare favorably to Clozaril in effectiveness, perhaps with fewer serious side effects. There is even some indication that Abilify may help improve some cases of tardive dyskinesia that had been thought to be irreversible.

MOOD STABILIZERS

Mood stabilizers are medicines used to treat conditions such as bipolar disorders in which a patient may experience periods of depression and excessive elation (mania), usually separated by periods of relatively less disturbance. The typical medicine used to treat severe cases of such cycling mood disorders is lithium carbonate (e.g., Eskalith and Lithonate). Unlike most medicines, lithium is a metal and is therefore not metabolized by the liver. Blood levels of lithium must reach a certain level to be effective; however, excessive amounts of lithium can produce toxicity and even death. Lithium levels in the blood can change rather rapidly depending on diet, exercise, and other medicines one may be taking. Therefore, close monitoring of blood levels is neces-sary with lithium. Some cyclic mood disorders respond well to treat-ment with antidepressant medications. Additionally, a number of medi-cines developed to control seizures have been found to be effective mood stabilizers as well. Examples include carbamazepine (Tegretol), divalproex (Depakote), and topiramate (Topamax).

PSYCHOSTIMULANTS

Psychostimulants, as their name implies, stimulate neural transmission in the brain. It is thought that they are dopamine agonists. These medications are used to treat conditions such as the sleep disorder narcolepsy and attention-deficit/hyperactivity disorder. Some years ago they were often prescribed as diet aids because of the side effect of reduced appetite (anorexia); however, that use is now uncommon because more effective medicines are available and because psychostimulants can be abused and may produce psychological addiction. Examples include dextroamphetamine (Dexedrine), methylphenidate (Ritalin, Concerta, and Metadate), and amphetamine and dextroamphetamine (Adderall).

How Does a Prescriber Know Which Medicine Is Best for a Patient?

The examples provided above do not include all possible conditions for which psychotropic medications may be used, and they list only a few typical examples of the many medications that are available for use. With so many choices, how do prescribers know which medicines to use for which patients? In addition to considering factors such as a patient's age, overall health, and medical status, many prescribers consider subtle aspects of the emotional disorder and evaluate factors such as possible side effects when selecting a particular psychotropic medicine. Even with the most careful examination, however, the use of psychotropic medicines unavoidably includes an element of trial and error. There is no guarantee that any psychotropic will produce the desired results for a given patient. Likewise, individual differences in body physiology can cause unacceptable side effects for any medication. The usual procedure is to prescribe a medicine thought likely to be effective and then closely monitor how well that medicine is tolerated by the patient and to determine if it is producing the desired improvement. It is this monitoring that often takes place during treatment staff meetings and at med checks. It is not at all uncommon to find that medications will need to be changed or supplemented with the addition of other medicines. It is clear that the need for ongoing study of the biological components of mental disorders and the ways in which medicines can work continues.

Medicine or Psychotherapy?

It is not surprising that the discovery that medicines can be effective in treating mental disorders has caused some to question the need for psychotherapy. Does the finding that biological agents can change mood, emotion, and behavior mean that one should abandon psychotherapy in favor of only physiologically based treatment? The majority of mental health professionals would argue against such a one-sided approach to mental health care. Although it is true that biology is linked to mental functioning, it would be incorrect to assume that all mental disorders necessarily result from biological causes. In many situations, even if medication is helpful, it may be that relative effectiveness in responding to and coping with life events has caused rather than resulted from the changes in physiology. Some mental disorders, such as schizophrenia, seem to result from biological predispositions. However, other conditions, such as posttraumatic stress disorder, are clearly triggered by environmental events. Conditions such as reactive depression can often be treated quite effectively without the use of medication and many anxiety disorders seem to respond best when psychotherapy and medication are used together. Even when there is reason to suspect a biological cause for a mental illness, psychotherapy may shorten the severity and duration of that condition and help patients comply with treatment and cope with their disorders. Both medication and psychotherapy can be of tremendous value in the treatment of mental disorders. Often, treatment is not a matter of choosing between medicine and psychotherapy but rather deciding how best to include both methods into an integrated plan of mental health care.

Summary

During the last 50 years, mental health treatment has experienced the development of an ever-increasing number of medicines that can greatly improve disordered thought and behavior. Medicines are now routinely used as a part of an overall treatment program in most mental health settings. Knowledge of the basics of medicines and familiarity with the types of medications used in mental health treatment are important in understanding a comprehensive plan of treatment.

Current understanding of how each drug produces its effects in the body and ongoing study of how the brain works help prescribers in selecting the proper medicines for each patient. Knowledge of the biological components of mental disorders has increased dramatically, yet there is still much that is not known. The challenges of continuing the study of the brain and developing medicines that effectively treat mental disorders with minimal risk of unpleasant or dangerous side effects remain.

Additional Readings

Johnson, J., & Preston, J. D. (2003). *Clinical psychopharmacology made ridiculously simple* (4th ed.). Miami, FL: MedMaster.

Lawson, G., & Cooperrider, C. A. (Eds.). (2004). *Clinical psychopharmacology: A practical reference for the nonmedical psychotherapists.* Austin, TX: Pro-Ed

Spinella, M. (2001). *The psychopharmacology of herbal medicine: Plant drugs that alter mind, brain, and behavior.* Cambridge, MA: MIT Press.

Stahl, S. M., & Muntner, N. (2001). *Essential psychopharmacology: Neuroscientific basis and practical applications* (2nd ed.). Cambridge, England: Cambridge University Press.

Online Resources

http://www.rxlist.com/
http://www.webmd.com/
http://www.noah-health.org/english/illness/mentalhealth/cornell/medications/psychmed.html

Jean C. Elbert

Special Issues in Working With Children

n this chapter, I provide introductory information for those undergraduate students contemplating future study or work with preschool and school-age children and who may be planning a formal practicum experience or volunteer work in a child setting. Such placements typically include public or private schools, day-care facilities, hospitals, pediatric or mental health clinics, and hospitals or residential settings. I begin with a review of basic information regarding normal development and then provide emphasis on challenges experienced by children who demonstrate emotional or behavioral problems. This information will help you have a better foundation to understand what you see in the applied setting. A predominant frame of reference for understanding behavioral and emotional disturbance (*developmental psychopathology*) in the child is that it is normal development gone awry; that is, failure in certain aspects of development often represents a precursor to subsequent emotional and behavioral problems. It is beyond the scope of this chapter to provide detailed and specific information, and I assume that you will receive information regarding the practices of a particular setting, together with appropriate supervision in working with a particular group of children. However, I provide general comments regarding suggested ways for you to develop rapport, interact with children, and respond to problematic behaviors.

Brief Review of Developmental Issues

THE PRESCHOOL CHILD

Development of Motor, Cognitive, and Language Skills

Table 10.1 provides an overview of the expected milestones in development of preschool children, covering physical as well as cognitive development (Schickendanz, Schickendanz, Forsyth, & Forsyth, 2001). By age 1, most children learn to walk and then begin running and climbing on such playground equipment as ladders and jungle gyms. They are throwing a ball overhand by age 3, and by ages 4 to 5, most are able to ride a tricycle. Fine motor control develops somewhat later; preschool children are usually able to button clothes, string beads, and use a "fist" grip to manipulate markers at 3 or 4. Most children are tying their shoes by age 5 (Kail, 2002; Schickendanz et al., 2001). Observing and interacting with preschool children in a variety of activities will provide you with many examples of physical and motor development.

Prior to age 5 children have what is known as *preoperational* thinking, which is illogical, inflexible, and tied to specific contexts. Young preschool children are initially "egocentric" and believe that others perceive the world as they do. They often confuse appearance with reality, don't yet appreciate that thoughts differ from reality, and don't understand that others can have false beliefs (e.g., conclude that someone who is smiling must be happy). By age 4, the understanding of what others know ("theory of mind") begins to develop, and you can foster this by reading picture books to children, discussing various points of view, and encouraging them to comment on their own thoughts or experiences related to the story (Kail, 2002; Schickendanz et al., 2001). Activities like these will provide many examples of both the child's language and cognitive development (e.g., the degree to which a child can participate in a conversation about the story, as opposed to merely pointing and labeling pictures).

In normally developing preschool children, language develops rapidly, and they will begin to show large increases in vocabulary. Young children initially learn vocabulary through direct association: by attaching a word with something concrete that they can see or touch. Later

TABLE 10.1

Milestones in Preschool Development

Age	Area of development			
	Physical	Cognitive	Language	Social–emotional
3 years	Demonstrates true run with both feet leaving ground; walks upstairs alternating feet; walks downstairs using marked-time climbing; can take most clothes off	Begins to demonstrate pre-operational thinking; knows conventional counting words up to five; can solve nesting cup problem by reversing two cups or by insertion	Understands *in, on,* and *under*; speaks in more complete sentences; distinguishes graphics that are writing versus pictures; begins to overgeneralize rules for creating verb tenses and plurals	May begin preschool; uses physical aggression more than verbal aggression; can remember a prohibition when the parent is absent
3 years, 6 months	Can hop a few steps on preferred foot; can button large buttons; can put easier clothes on	Can't easily distinguish false beliefs; can count five objects before making a partitioning error	Might use syllable hypothesis to create written words; rereads favorite storybooks using picture-governed strategies; often uses scribble writing	Has difficulty generating alternatives in a conflict situation; learns aggressive behavior rapidly if these means succeed
4 years	Appears thinner because of longer trunk; can walk a curved line; walks downstairs alternating feet; can gallop; can cut straight line with scissors	Can make a row of objects equal to another row by matching one to one; understands false beliefs	Creates questions and negative sentences using correct word arrangement; might create "mock" letters	Watches, on average, 2 to 4 hours of TV per day

continued

TABLE 10.1 (Continued)

Milestones in Preschool Development

Age	Area of development			
	Physical	Cognitive	Language	Social–emotional
4 years, 6 months	May begin to hold writing tool in finger grip; leans forward more when jumping from a height; can button smaller buttons	Knows conventional counting up to 15; understands false beliefs	Often reverses letters when writing; understands *beside, between, front,* and *back*	Self-control often depends on removal of temptation
5 years	Can stop and change direction quickly when running; can hop 8 to 10 steps on one foot	Selects own view in three-mountain task; creates classes of objects based on a single defining attribute	Understands passive sentences; may begin to use invented spellings	Inhibitory or effortful control should be well-established for familiar prohibitions
5 years, 6 months	Can connect a zipper on a coat; may be able to tie shoes	Can count 20 objects without making a partitioning error; may display conservation of number	May begin to make print-governed reading attempts with favorite books	

Note. From *Understanding Children and Adolescents* (4th ed., p. 403), by J. A. Schickendanz, D. I. Schickendanz, P. D. Forsyth, and G. A. Forsyth, 2001. Published by Allyn & Bacon, Boston, MA. Copyright © 2001 by Pearson Education. Reprinted by permission of the publisher.

they begin to infer word meaning from both context and word order, with concrete nouns and verbs representing their earliest vocabulary. Words such as prepositions (*in, on, under,* and *beside*) appear later, with *beside, between, in front of,* and *behind* not emerging before 4 to 5 years. In young children, language is often restricted to the "here and now." By age 4, children with sufficient language stimulation begin to follow along with simple stories that have picture cues, rhyming words, and language that they have heard many times. A feature of language development at this stage is the beginning sensitivity to the *phonology* of speech, that is, the sounds that make up words; by age 3, most children should be able to recognize and produce the sounds represented in their native language. This "play" with language (rhyming, taking words apart, and substituting sounds) develops naturally in many children, and engaging them in wordplay is important in encouraging language development. Perhaps more important, this play with sounds in words becomes one of the most important factors in early reading development: Those children who do not develop the sensitivity to sounds in words are known to be at much greater risk for difficulty in mastering beginning reading skills (Kail, 2002; Schickendanz et al., 2001).

Adequate language development is critically important for cognitive and social development as well as later school performance. If you are working with young preschool children, you should be aware of the factors that enhance language development. These include (a) using simple sentences with a slow rate of speech; (b) demonstrating joint attention, for example, commenting on what the child is attending to and encouraging interactive conversation; (c) following the child's lead during play interactions rather than directing; (d) reading to the child, choosing books with multiple repetitions, directing the child to associate words with pictures, and engaging the child in language play by inviting him or her to think of words that rhyme (e.g., "Let's think of words that start with the same sound as . . ."); and (e) asking "what and where" questions and actively engaging the child in a story. The process of language acquisition unfolds quite readily in most young children with adequate stimulation. However, for some children with otherwise normal development, speech and language is delayed. Such children can't find the words to express their needs, leading to considerable frustration, distress, and sometimes, emotional outbursts. Many such children with diagnosed expressive language disorders are known to be at risk for both learning disabilities (because later reading and writing skills build on a foundation in oral language), and emotional disorders (involving frustration, social anxiety, or noncompliance). In children from different linguistic and cultural backgrounds, second-language learning obviously develops more slowly, and they tend to mix vocabulary from both languages. However, by preschool age, bilingual children typically are able to separate the two languages, and by school entry, many are proficient in both languages and even begin to surpass monolingual children in some language skills (Kail, 2002). For those children who have not learned English prior to school entry, research suggests that they do best when given instruction in English while simultaneously being taught their other subjects in their native language (Padilla et al., 1991).

Social and Emotional Development

To better understand the behavior of young children, you should be aware of those critical elements of development that shape healthy, positive social relationships. First, both a child's biological traits (nature) and the environment created by parents, extended family, caretakers, teachers, and significant others (nurture) combine to jointly influence emotional development and social behavior in children. One primary aspect of these influences is *attachment,* the emotional bond that exists between the infant and primary caregiver. This bond emerges as parents respond to signals of their infant's distress, and these early experiences with parenting set the stage for development of trust in others. Attachment typically develops by the middle of the first year of life and is characterized by responding differently to familiar and unfamiliar people and showing wariness of strangers. The primary attachment person provides a secure base from which the infant can explore the environment. When working with toddlers or preschool children, you should have some basic understanding of the patterns of attachment, which typically develop between 12 to 18 months. On the basis of observations of children's reactions to their mothers' absence and to the introduction of a stranger, several patterns of attachment have been reported. Children with a *secure* attachment may be moderately distressed by their mother's absence but are usually comforted when she returns. These children tend to be more social and are better apt to develop empathy. *Insecure/avoidant* attachment describes those young children who tend to have poor exploration, who are often highly distressed at their mother's absence, and who then may actually resist efforts at comfort when she returns (Kail, 2002). Important for later emotional development is the extensive body of work showing that mothers who respond to their infants abruptly, who are unresponsive, or who pace their behavior to their own needs and schedules tend to foster the development of an anxious or ambivalent attachment characterized by excessive anger, clinging, or avoidance behavior on the part of the infant (Campbell, 2002). An excellent way of understanding attachment patterns in preschool children is to observe the interactions between children and their working parent(s) when the child is dropped off in a day-care setting. Although most children will require some time to adjust to new caretakers, there are some children who will be highly stressed by separation, are very difficult to console, and may show moderate to extreme irritability.

The parents' ability to interpret and adjust to their young child's signals is often a predictor of the child's later behavior. Insecurely attached infants tend to cry more, play less often, have more frequent tantrums, and show aggression, emotional dependence, and need for support as children (Kail, 2002; Schickendanz et al., 2001). Other evidence for the later effects of disturbed attachment comes from examples of children raised in institutional settings in which bonding with caretakers has not been adequately fostered (e.g., in recent years exemplified by the experience of the many children adopted from Eastern European orphanages). We know that many of these children respond indiscriminately to others and fail to form lasting relationships. This issue of attachment is certainly important for the increasing number of young children in day care. A large national study indicated that child care, per se, does not appear to affect the development of secure mother–infant attachment (National Institute of Child Health and Human Development [NICHD], 1997). However, infants whose mothers are insensitive and unresponsive to their needs are more likely to develop insecure attachment when placed in poor quality child care. Thus, if you were to seek a practicum experience in a child-care setting, you would do well to inquire about the extent and quality of staff training and the child to adult ratio.

Finally, although disturbed attachment is a significant general risk factor for later disturbances in emotional responses and problem behavior, both positive and negative changes in the parents' situation (e.g., increase or reduction in life stressors, mental health problems, and individual stability) will clearly influence the attachment relationship.

A second major influence on a child's development is *temperament,* a child's consistent mood and individual style of interaction with the environment. Infants and toddlers differ with respect to how strongly they react emotionally, how easily they become calm again, their general physical activity level, and their ease and preference in being with people. Early studies of infants and preschool children (e.g., Kagan, 1997) identified three general types of temperament in infants that appear to be fairly stable in young preschool children: "easy" (adaptable), "slow to warm up," and "difficult" (having more intense moods, frequent crying, higher levels of irritability, and slow to accept change). Infants with a difficult temperament have been shown to frequently withdraw from new experiences, display a negative mood, and be slow in adapting to new situations. Such infants are more difficult to parent and are at risk for problems in controlling their behavior. Sensitive parenting helps many difficult infants outgrow this phase. However, those with "negative emotionality" and those whose parents are impatient or intolerant are at considerable risk for later depression and behavioral problems (Garrison & Earls, 1987; Kail, 2002; Schickendanz et al., 2001).

An important aspect of temperament is *self-regulation*—the process by which young children actively try to control their emotions, motor activity levels, and attention. Some experts believe that the development of self-control may be the most important variable in later social and behavior problems. The child who has poor control of emotions and behavior is more apt to have a later psychiatric diagnosis and may also be at major risk for being either victim or perpetrator of physical abuse. For example, poor control of bodily functions is a frequent precursor to later serious eating and elimination disorders (e.g., obesity, anorexia and bulimia, and enuresis and encopresis). You should be aware that obesity is now recognized as being one of the most significant health problems in the United States, with more than 15% of children over the age of 6 being overweight. The American Academy of Pediatrics (2003) has recommended that those involved in the care of children can play an important role in preventing childhood obesity by encouraging parents to instill healthy eating patterns, routinely promote physical activity, include unstructured play, and limit the child's sedentary time in watching television and videos.

By age 2 to 3 years, children typically begin to learn which behaviors are acceptable and unacceptable. This is when most children have developed the cognitive and language skills to respond to verbal commands and to exercise self-control. Young children begin to mimic a parent's directives and respond to reward and punishment, which then leads to internalizing the parent's values. You can see this in young preschool children who may actually verbalize a parent's command (i.e., "No, No!"). When does the young child develop conscience? Although some 3-year-old children begin to say "I'm sorry," it is not until later that they are able to use true self-appraisal. This aspect of development becomes extremely important; those children who don't develop the ability to appraise their own behavior are at risk for excessive anxiety, guilt, later obsessive–compulsive behaviors, and depression, or alternatively, acting out and antisocial behaviors (Wenar & Kerig, 2000).

Developing Rapport With Preschool Children

A child's temperament and comfort with new people will vary, but it is important for you to learn to "read" a child's signals. For example, when approaching children for the first time, if they avert eye contact and appear shy, it is very important to provide time for these slow-to-warm-up children to adjust. Offering them an interesting toy, commenting on what they are doing (e.g., "nice digging in the sand"), and following their lead rather than directing them are good ways to initiate contact. In contrast, direct questions or commands may be intimidating to some children. Children are typically quite sensitive to facial expression; a pleasant smile and quiet demeanor may be encouraging to the child, whereas a loud voice or laughter can intimidate the shy child. When first meeting a child, it is often helpful to join an activity including another familiar child or adult, thus allowing a shy child a chance to "look over" the new person. You will also need to be sensitive to different cultural expectations that influence a child's behavior. For example, making direct eye contact varies across cultures; children from Native American and some Latin American and Asian cultures are not socialized to make direct eye contact in the same way as children from the dominant Caucasian culture and may be taught to believe that this is impolite.

THE SCHOOL-AGE CHILD

Development of Motor, Cognitive, Language, and Academic Skills

Table 10.2 provides an overview of growth and development in the school-age child. Physical growth slows, with the average child's height increasing by 2 to 3 inches per year and weight by 5 to 7 pounds per year. Girls tend to begin their preadolescent growth spurt at age 10 to 11, with boys maturing somewhat later, at the beginning of their teens. We noted previously that obesity often has its roots in preschool; however, this stage of rapid physical development in school-age children increases the risk for obesity. Overweight children are often rejected by peers and tend to have lowered academic performance, poor self-esteem, and increased behavior problems and are at increased risk for depression. Finally, poor weight control in children clearly puts them at risk for food binging and purging and serious eating disorders, particularly in young preadolescent girls (Schroeder & Gordon, 2002).

Some children will have difficulty with gross motor control, balance, and physical coordination, and you should be sensitive to these weaknesses, particularly if you are to be involved in directing children's sports or physical activity. Fine motor skills show accelerated development in 6 to 8 year olds. By early school age, children develop a more mature grip and develop the fine motor skills necessary for writing; it is also at this age that children with fine motor difficulty are identified.

TABLE 10.2

Milestones in School-Age Development

Age (in years)	Area of development			
	Physical	Cognitive	Language	Social-emotional
6	Has 90% of adult-size brain; reaches about 2/3 of adult height; begins to lose baby teeth; moves a writing or drawing tool with the fingers while the side of the hand rests on the table top	Begins to demonstrate concrete operational thinking; demonstrates conservation of number on Piaget's conservation tasks; can create series operationally rather than by trial and error	Might use a letter-name spelling strategy, thus creating many invented spellings; appreciates jokes and riddles based on pho-nological ambiguity	Feels one way only about a situation; has some difficulty detecting intentions in situations in which damage occurs; demonstrates Kohlberg's preconventional moral thinking
7	Is able to make small, controlled marks with pencils or pens because of more refined finger dexterity; has longer face; continues to lose baby teeth	Begins to use some rehearsal strategies as an aid to memory; becomes much better able to play strategy games; may demonstrate conservation of area	Sorts out some of the more difficult syntactic difficulties, such as *ask* and *tell*; more conventional speller; more fluent reader	May express two emotions about one situation, but these will be same valence; demonstrates Kohlberg's conventional thinking; understands gender constancy
8	Plays jacks and other games requiring considerable fine motor skill and good reaction time; jumps rope skillfully; throws and bats a ball more skillfully	Still has great difficulty judging if a passage is relevant to specific theme; may demonstrate conservation of specific area	Sorts out some of the more difficult syntactic difficulties, such as *ask* and *tell*; more conventional speller; more fluent reader	Expresses two same-valence emotions about different targets; understands that people may interpret situations differently but thinks it's because of different information
9	Enjoys hobbies requiring high levels of fine motor skill (sewing, weaving, and model building)	May demonstrate conservation of weight		Can think about own thinking or another person's thinking but not both at the same time

10	May begin to menstruate	Begins to make better judgments about relevance of a text; begins to delete unimportant information when summarizing		Can take own view and view of another as if a disinterested third party
11	May begin preadolescent growth spurt if female	May demonstrate conservation of volume	Begins to appreciate jokes and riddles based on syntactic ability	Still has trouble detecting deception; spends more time with friends
12	Has reached about 80% of adult height if male, 90% if female; has all permanent teeth except for two sets of molars; plays ball more skillfully because of improved reaction time; begins to menstruate	Shows much greater skill in summarizing and outlining; may begin to demonstrate formal operational thinking		May begin to demonstrate Kohlberg's postconventional moral thinking

Note. From *Understanding Children and Adolescents* (4th ed., p. 545), by J. A. Schickendanz, D. I. Schickendanz, P. D. Forsyth, and G. A. Forsyth, 2001. Published by Allyn & Bacon, Boston, MA. Copyright © 2001 by Pearson Education. Reprinted by permission of the publisher.

In elementary school, children begin involvement in organized play, which provides opportunities for development of motor skills. Organized sports, jumping rope, bicycling, and throwing all support gross motor development, whereas marbles, legos, and arts and crafts help to increase fine motor development (Kail, 2002; Schickendanz et al., 2001).

School-age children make significant gains in cognitive development: They first begin to use mental operations to solve problems, and thinking becomes more logical; for example, they are not as bound by physical appearances and develop the important ability for *perspective taking*. Between ages 7 to 12, children begin to understand that others have different ideas, feelings, and behaviors from their own. This ability to take another's perspective is critically important in developing healthy social skills. Cognitive development involves the child's growing ability to *process information*, which can be viewed as a hierarchy including the following levels from simple to complex: (a) *perception*, the ability to recognize differences in bits of sensory information, beginning with recognition of faces to later visual discrimination of letters and numbers (*u/n* and *b/d*) and recognizing different sounds in spoken words (*ban* and *pan*); (b) *memory*, the ability to retain and store what is heard or seen for higher level processing; and (c) *conceptualization*, higher level thinking and logical reasoning. Children's memory skills improve rapidly during the elementary school years as they begin to use more effective strategies to aid memory: rehearsal, elaboration, chunking and organizing information, and linking new information to their own previous experience. Inadequate development in any of these cognitive processes can reflect various types of *learning disabilities* that subsequently affect the child's development of the academic skills of reading, written language, and math. If you are working with children on their schoolwork, you can assist them by teaching some strategies for remembering information.

Language and communication skills greatly expand in school-age children. Their vocabulary increases when they begin to grasp multiple meanings and root words that help to expand concepts (e.g., happy and then unhappy, happiness, and happier). School becomes a child's major "work," and school success becomes a major factor in developing self-esteem. Learning to read becomes prominent and is a skill that involves the integration of many different subskills. Understanding that reading involves getting meaning from the printed word initially requires the perceptual abilities to recognize, distinguish, and label letters of the alphabet, learning specific letter–sound correspondence, and recognizing that in English there is not perfect correspondence between letters and sounds. Good vocabulary and oral language background are essential for children to understand that reading is a *psycho-*

linguistic guessing game whereby one's previous oral communication skills (depth and breadth of vocabulary and understanding word endings) aid one to make decisions about unknown written words (Kail, 2002; Schickendanz et al., 2001). It is important to mention that the particular method of reading instruction is now known to be very important in the ease with which children develop reading skill. Although methods of teaching reading have varied over time, research has now clearly demonstrated that direct and systematic instruction in the structure and phonology of written words (e.g., their letter–sound correspondence) is essential in teaching children to recognize ("decode") written words. With frequent exposure to words, children learn to recognize familiar spelling patterns (e.g.,"ight") and associate those with known words, which then allows them to sound out and recognize unfamiliar words. Following this initial word recognition stage, reading comprehension skill is strongly associated with the child's ability to understand spoken language (Shaywitz, 2003). Depending on the particular city or state, bilingual education classes may be available so that a child is able to learn new information in his or her native language or be assisted by a translator while learning English as a second language.

Written language is often considered to be the most complex communication task. It presumes knowledge of correct spelling, understanding the rules of grammar and formal sentence construction, that is, the ability to appropriately organize and sequence words within a sentence and sentences within a paragraph, and at a higher level, to organize ideas. Thus, most children with learning disabilities or children with English as a second language will have difficulty in this area. In learning math, children progress from using a counting strategy for simple computation to using mental operations involving memory. By third or fourth grade, most children have memorized addition and subtraction "math facts."

Social and Emotional Development

An important aspect of healthy social development in the school-age child is the growth of *social cognition,* the ability to think about a situation from another's point of view and thereby understand the other person's behavior and also how he or she might feel, that is, *empathy.* Showing concern for others and communicating through both body language and spoken language are important ingredients in social acceptance. Popular children tend to be skilled in both the language and social aspects of communicating; they are able to join into others' play and conversation, are good at appraising how their behavior affects others, and are more likely to share and cooperate. In contrast, those children with poor verbal or nonverbal communication skills are often left out, ignored, teased, or rejected (Kail, 2002; Schickendanz et al., 2001). Peer acceptance clearly factors into the child's emotional stability. Rejected children often have histories of inconsistent parental discipline and parents whose own social skills are poorly developed; thus, they likely have had poor models for developing appropriate social skills. The development of negative behaviors varies with age and gender in children. Younger children are more likely to use bullying behaviors; by school age, girls are more apt to use verbal aggression and gossip, whereas boys tend more toward physical aggression.

The development of self-esteem typically is shaped during school age when children are able to be more introspective and begin to compare themselves and their skills with peers'. Those with healthy self-esteem can be objective about their abilities in different areas, such as schoolwork, sports, and music. They may be aware they don't excel in all areas; yet, they are generally able to maintain a healthy self-esteem. In contrast, children with poor self-esteem are unable to be objective, judge themselves harshly, and view poor skill levels (i.e., in academics or athletics) to mean they have less value as a person. Self-esteem is based in part on how children are viewed by those around them; those with nurturing, accepting parents and teachers are more likely to have healthy self-esteem. Parents who set rules, provide structure and discipline, and reward compliance tend to have children with higher self-esteem. Children with low self-esteem are known to be at risk for a variety of developmental problems, including poor peer relationships and depression (Wenar & Kerig, 2000). If you are working with school-age children with low self-esteem, several aspects of child care are important in enhancing self-esteem: (a) providing an atmosphere in which verbal and physical aggression are not tolerated; (b) using opportunities to reinforce the importance of effort and fair play (e.g., "I really liked how you helped out there!"); and (c) commenting to a self-critical child, "You are being quite hard on yourself."

Developing Rapport With School-Age Children

Prior to meeting children, it will be helpful for you to learn something about them: their interests, likes and dislikes, and particular strengths and weaknesses. With children who are shy, or have limited language communication, you should refrain from excessive questioning. Such children will feel more comfortable when they are invited to choose an activity or game, and the choice of activity may reveal a child's skill level, competitiveness, and level of self-confidence. If you may be involved in tutoring children, you will want to encourage and reward attempts without being judgmental or reinforcing negative self-appraisal (e.g., "Good trying; that was a really hard one"). Most children are able to relate to someone who is accepting and lets them take the lead but who also is able to set clear limits regarding aggressive behaviors. It is also important to be aware of cultural differences among school-age children. For example, more direct physical interaction may be accepted in African American children but be less accepted in Asian or Native American children.

Issues Regarding the Family Context

A number of issues related to the context of the family are important to understand in working with children, among them: parent discipline, parent conflict, divorce, and blended families. The process of change and adaptation surrounding parents' conflict and divorce can obviously have major consequences for the child and family, particularly when this is prolonged (Schroeder & Gordon, 2002). A child must deal with the loss of a parent, adapt to remarriage, and adjust to a foster parent or family. In addition, as the custodial parent, mothers often experience reduced income, which may create stress for both parent and children. The possibility of ongoing parental conflict and custody arrangements are additional stressors. A child's age, temperament, and ability to regulate feelings (anger, sadness, happiness, and fear) are all relevant factors in how well the child will cope with parents' divorce. Younger children are more apt to try to control parents' disputes; older children tend to take sides; and the largest fraction of children often appear to cope by avoidance and withdrawal. When divorced parents remarry and construct new "blended" families, these most often include a stepfather because mothers are more often granted custody of children. Whereas school-age boys may benefit from a positive relationship with an involved stepfather, girls are more apt to sense a disruption in the close relationship with their mothers, often making adjustment more difficult for them (Schroeder & Gordon, 2002).

Finally, parents and siblings may play a large role in cultivating aggressive behavior in children. Families in which parents use physical punishment and siblings respond to conflict with physical fights clearly serve as models for aggressive behavior to the child. In addition to physical punishment, parents who are coercive, unresponsive, and not emotionally engaged or invested in their children are likely to have aggressive children.

Children With Special Challenges: Introduction to Childhood Disorders

The following sections deal very briefly with several of the most common types of developmental disorders and emotional and behavioral disorders in children. I refer you to Batshaw (2002) for a comprehensive review of children's neurodevelopmental disorders and to Mash and Wolfe (2002) and Gelfand and Drew (2003) for reviews of major childhood emotional and behavioral disorders. In addition, Web sites including information about children and adolescents are included in a list of online sources at the end of this chapter.

Many potential child practicum sites involve programs for exceptional or challenged children, and you would benefit from background information regarding primary delays and disorders in development that place some children at particular risk. Exhibit 10.1 lists the primary childhood disorders, each of which is also a recognized category of special education. Thus, children who meet eligibility criteria for any of these disorders must be provided appropriate special education services in the "least restrictive environment," that is, they are to be included with normally achieving peers to the extent possible.

Children with a specific learning disability represent the largest of these categories and include children who, in spite of adequate intelligence, experience significant difficulty in mastering basic academic skills of reading, math, and written language. Those children with reading disability (*dyslexia*) represent the largest category of learning disabilities, and research in the past 10 years has shown that brains of individuals with dyslexia do not process information as efficiently as do normal readers; moreover, this disability is known to be inherited in many individuals. Learning disability has traditionally used a *discrepancy model* for diagnosis, based on the assumption that there must be a significant discrepancy between a child's assessed intelligence and his or her actual level of academic achievement. However, this model has been fraught with problems, primary among them that children not meeting arbitrary criteria for discrepancy are often ineligible to receive needed specialized instruction until they have experienced several years of failure. The federal law that defines learning disability and the criteria for special education eligibility was revised in 2004. As an alternative

EXHIBIT 10.1

Definitions of Common Childhood Disorders

Mental retardation: Children may experience significant delay in cognitive development that is typically assessed by an intelligence quotient (IQ) of below 70, which is accompanied by similar delays in adaptive functioning (how effectively the child can cope with ordinary life demands). Such cognitive delays are often accompanied by similar delays in physical and language development. There is wide variation in a child's functioning, ranging from children who function quite well in school and the community to others whose physical and cognitive impairments require high levels of care.

Communication disorders: Children may experience delay or disorder in oral language development, that is, the ability to comprehend (receptive language) or to produce speech (expressive language). There are several types of expressive disorder characterized by the child who (a) has difficulty with the motor pattern in articulating sounds or words, reducing the intelligibility of speech (*phonological disorder*); (b) stutters; or (c) has difficulty in using proper grammar and word order (*syntax*) or processing (*semantics*).

Specific learning disability: Children may experience significant delays in achievement of age-appropriate academic achievement in reading (word recognition and comprehension), writing (spelling and written language), or math, which are not *primarily* a function of mental retardation. The most frequent type of learning disability is *dyslexia*, a specific difficulty in mastering word-decoding skills. This disorder often has a genetic basis and is characterized by difficulty in phonological awareness, the understanding that words are composed of sequences of sounds. Children with oral language disorders often also exhibit disabilities in reading and written language. Children with math disabilities often have problems with spatial orientation and associated visuomotor disorders.

Sensory disorders: Children may experience impaired vision or hearing acuity that may range from mild visual problems correctable by glasses or mild hearing loss correctable by sound amplification or hearing aids to total deafness or blindness. Although children with severe sensory impairment require highly specialized educational settings and training, children with milder impairments may be expected to have mild to moderate difficulty in various aspects of communication/language and thinking/reasoning.

Physical and motor impairments: Children may experience a wide variety of fine and gross motor skill disorders, ranging from mild finger dexterity to severe *cerebral palsy* (brain injury from birth, which may result in generalized impairment in the part of the brain controlling large- and small-muscle movement and coordination). Such children may require a wheelchair, be unable to speak, and have little use of coordinated hand and finger movements but , may have quite normal thinking, reasoning, and language comprehension abilities.

continued

to requiring that a child must demonstrate a significant discrepancy between intelligence and achievement, it is possible for school systems to diagnose a learning disability if a child fails to respond to research-based instruction (Individuals With Disabilities Education Improvement Act, 2004). This change will help to mandate appropriate

EXHIBIT 10.1 (Continued)

Definitions of Common Childhood Disorders

Pervasive developmental disorders (PDD): Children may experience developmental disorders characterized by abnormalities in social functioning, language, and communication and unusual behaviors and interests. *Autism* is the more severe form of PDD that is caused by disorder in brain development that results in generalized impairment in complex information-processing abilities, most often with severe impairments in language development. Once thought to be rare, the incidence of *autistic spectrum disorders* has been found to be steadily increasing, with a sizeable fraction of children functioning within the mentally retarded range of ability. Children with *Asperger's* disorder have a milder form of the disorder, which includes difficulties in social interaction and unusual, restricted, and stereotyped patterns of behavior but with relatively intact cognitive and communication skills. Some children with PDD have highly developed but isolated skills in reading, math, and music, and are regarded as *savants* (children who have generalized developmental delays but specialized abilities in only selected areas of their development).

Emotional and behavioral disorders: Children with psychiatric disorders experience a variety of problems related to the ability to regulate emotional experience and to control their behavior. Childhood disorders are typically divided into two categories: *internalizing* disorders that involve distress for the child (e.g., anxiety and depression), and *externalizing* disorders that involve outward-directed behaviors (e.g., overactive, oppositional, or aggressive behaviors). Management and treatment of these disorders typically involves psychotherapy or behavior management approaches, and the various behavioral approaches often have well-supported evidence for their effectiveness.

---

early instruction as well as to make needed services available to a child early in elementary school. Federally sponsored research has clearly demonstrated that dyslexic children need carefully sequenced instruction in *phonological awareness* together with highly structured, systematic instruction in word decoding. It is expected that early diagnosis and early and appropriate instruction for such children may result in many fewer children diagnosed with dyslexia, or reading disability.

Although it is beyond the scope of the chapter to discuss the different categories of disability, you should be aware that any child with a disability may often cope with significant feelings of frustration, lowered self-esteem, and not infrequently, associated behavior disorders. Finally, there is considerable (20%–30%) overlap between learning disability and attention-deficit/hyperactivity disorder (ADHD). The nature of this overlap is not clear, although there may be some shared genetic variation; significant attentional disorders may interfere with mastering reading, or alternatively, persistent academic failure may lead to restlessness and inattention in the classroom.

COMMON EMOTIONAL DISORDERS IN CHILDREN: INTERNALIZING DISORDERS

The term *internalizing* refers to conditions that primarily produce stress in the child and have less obvious impact on others: for example, the child who experiences worry or stress, is overly anxious, or is sad. Preschool children are most frequently fearful of strangers, animals, being hurt, and the dark. A shy or inhibited (slow-to-warm-up) child experiences more than usual anxiety and discomfort when separated from the parent. When working with these children, you should know that they will need considerable time to adjust to new surroundings and adults. For some young children, separation from the parent can precipitate extreme panic and distress (i.e., prolonged crying and extreme irritability). When day care is necessary for such a child, introduction to a new setting and caregiver must be gradual. As a caregiver, you should ask the parent to provide a familiar toy or blanket and a favorite snack as "transitional" objects to help comfort the child. In developing rapport with such a child, you will want to let the child take the lead and respect his or her need to "warm up." For young children placed in day care, slowly introducing activities, speaking softly, and showing patience often helps to calm a fearful child. In situations in which the child shows marked distress on separation from the parent (e.g., prolonged crying and extreme irritability), the parent–child relationship likely needs to be addressed by a professional, for example, by teaching the parents effective means to comfort their child while similarly providing the needed encouragement to trust other caretakers.

For a school-age child experiencing diagnosable anxiety or depression, recognized treatments by psychologists typically involve psychotherapy, with *behavioral therapy* and *cognitive–behavioral therapy* approaches demonstrated to be most successful. Many children with very specific fears and phobias require skilled treatment in *desensitizing* them; for example, children with irrational animal phobias are taught to master fear by means of developing a *fear hierarchy*, or graded sequence of things they fear, followed by gradually exposing them to feared animals in very small increments. This process is coupled with teaching children methods to reduce the physical symptoms of anxiety through relaxation resulting in *systematic desensitization*. Child therapists practicing cognitive–behavioral therapy believe that a child's thoughts, beliefs, and feelings are important and require as much modification as the child's environment. Excessive separation anxiety in school-age children can often be severe, for example, leading to the child's refusal to leave home or go to school (Mash & Wolfe, 2002).

Children who constantly appear unhappy and who show little enthusiasm for normal age-appropriate activities often have mood disorders (depression) that can affect many areas of their functioning. Such children often feel inadequate, are preoccupied with their own inner feelings, and may experience physical changes such as loss of appetite and fatigue. These are often the children who have poor regulation of their emotions and poor skills in coping with new situations (Gelfand & Drew, 2003). Recognizing these symptoms in a child, you should ask supervisors about making an appropriate referral to a mental health professional.

COMMON BEHAVIORAL DISORDERS IN CHILDREN: EXTERNALIZING DISORDERS

In contrast to internalizing problems, children with externalizing problems tend to direct their behaviors outwardly, that is, toward other people. Depending on a child's individual temperament, the development of autonomy (the "terrible twos") is a normal process for toddlers and preschool children. However, when this process goes awry, the irritability and negativism may become extreme, resulting in "disruptive behavior disorders" in children (American Psychiatric Association [APA], 2000). Such children exhibit problems that annoy and disrupt others: temper outbursts, arguing, deliberately annoying others, and noncompliance, which may be consistent with *oppositional defiant disorder*. Interventions for these children typically involve special programs to train social and cognitive skills (aimed at remediating deficient problem-solving skills) and to train parents in methods of behavior management. A subset of these children with high levels of aggression may meet diagnostic criteria for *conduct disorder* in which clearly antisocial behavior occurs (e.g., stealing, fire setting, involvement with drugs, physical aggression, and gang-related activity). Such children clearly are in need of highly structured therapeutic programs and may be referred for management in residential facilities administered through the juvenile justice system.

Many young children with disruptive behavior disorders also exhibit the core symptoms for ADHD: inattention, impulsivity, and overactive behaviors (APA, 2000). Of the school-age population, 3% to 5% is estimated to have this disorder, which is more prevalent in boys than in girls. Their impulsivity frequently leads these children to behave inappropriately, talk out of turn, and have difficulty waiting. Such behavior often provokes reprimands from others (i.e., peers, parents, and teachers who often inadvertently reinforce inappropriate behaviors by their negative attention). Although the majority of children with ADHD display the characteristic impulsiveness and difficulty in modulating their behavior, a smaller subset of children diagnosed with ADHD have a *primarily inattentive* subtype. In contrast to the hyperactive child, these children often appear "spacy," disorganized, and "hypoactive," or slow to respond. Similar to those with hyperactivity, these children seem not to listen and often have difficulty processing and understanding language; unlike hyperactive children, they are more apt to exhibit internalizing disorders of anxiety or depression.

Symptoms reflect an interaction of biology (e.g., temperament), which sets the risk, and environment (e.g., how parents, families, teachers, and others respond to the child's behavior), which can serve to both increase and reduce the symptoms. The primary treatments for ADHD include medication, parent training programs, and behavioral interventions for children (see Gelfand & Drew, 2003, for discussion of stimulant medications). Although medications may effectively reduce symptoms of ADHD, they are not a "cure" for the disorder, which must be managed by modeling and reinforcing the child's appropriate behaviors. Thus, the preferred and more comprehensive approach to working with the child with ADHD also includes behavior-based interventions; "contingency management," structured to provide specific consequences for the child's behavior (rewards for compliance and punishment for noncompliance). For most children with ADHD, behavioral management involves setting up well-designed behavioral contracts in which behaviors are carefully specified, followed by rewards for compliance. Frequently the rewards are points or tokens ("token economy" system) that are redeemable in favorite activities tailored to the child (e.g., a video game, time with a favorite toy, or spending money) Exhibit 10.2 provides some practical suggestions if you are involved in working with children having symptoms of ADHD (Mather & Goldstein, 2001).

The child with extreme oppositional or aggressive behaviors clearly requires specialized management. One behavioral approach for treating young children that has a record of success by professionally trained therapists with extensive training is Parent–Child Interaction Therapy (PCIT; Eyberg, 1988; Hembree-Kigin & McNeil, 1995). Although it is emphasized that this treatment method requires highly specialized training, some of the principles followed may be useful in dealing with disruptive behaviors. Giving children *negative attention* for disruptive behavior (e.g., verbal reprimands) may actually serve to increase the behavior; alternatively, it is important to clearly describe or demonstrate the desired behavior, then reward the child for compliance. The following practices are useful in modifying difficult behavior: (a) practicing minding by making *direct* commands and describing *specific* behavior, followed immediately with *labeled praise* for compliance (e.g., "Thanks for putting your bike in the garage when I asked you to; good

EXHIBIT 10.2

Suggestions for Working With Children With Attention-Deficit/Hyperactivity Disorder

1. **Be positive.** This involves giving directives to the child (e.g., "I want you to sit in this chair" versus "Stop teasing Jamie").
2. **Give clear directions.** Make instructions simple and brief and have the child repeat them.
3. **State the rules.** Have a brief list of rules (written for school-age children who can read) for expected procedures in the particular child practicum setting; go over them with the child, and ask him or her to repeat them.
4. **Provide cues.** For older school-age children in a classroom or doing seat work, external cues have been found to be helpful in assisting children to monitor their on-task behavior (e.g., running a tape on which a beep sounds at programmed intervals and having the child make a check on a chart when he or she was on task).
5. **Structure and minimize transitions.** The child with attention-deficit/hyperactivity disorder (ADHD) does best when the environment is formal, focused, and structured.
6. **Provide a consistent routine.** A consistent schedule and plan for children with ADHD is much preferable to varying the sequence of activities.
7. **Keep things changing.** Within the consistent routine, the child with ADHD functions best when given multiple shortened work periods together with opportunities for choices of both tasks and reinforcers.
8. **Offer feedback.** Immediate, specific, and labeled feedback for compliance (e.g., "I like the way you sat down in your seat right after I asked you to").
9. **Prepare the child for changes.** Specifically mention any change in routine and the amount of time remaining for a specific activity.
10. **Use preventive strategies.** Anticipate potential problems by considering the task demands and the child's skills and develop preventative rather than reactionary strategies.

Note. Adapted from *Learning Disabilities and Challenging Behaviors: A Guide to Intervention and Classroom Management* (pp. 71–75), by N. Mather and S. Goldstein, 2001, Baltimore: Paul H. Brookes Publishing Co. Copyright 2001 by Paul H. Brookes Publishing Co. Adapted with permission.

minding!"); (b) demonstrating and modeling the skills; (c) using *selective ignoring* of such inappropriate behaviors as whining, nagging, and tantrums; (d) imitating and praising appropriate play; and (e) using *strategic attention* (e.g., for playing *gently*, using an *indoor* voice, sharing, and taking turns). For students working with children who demonstrate seriously aggressive or destructive behaviors, it is paramount that you be provided with specialized training in methods of safe restraint and that you receive careful supervision in using such methods. Hembree-Kigin and McNeil (1995, p. 68) recommended a brief wrist restraint in which the caretaker gives a briefly stated rule (e.g., "no hurting"), averts his or her eyes while gently holding the child's forearms for approximately 20 seconds, and then says "I'm going to let you go now; remember, no more hurting"). You would then draw the child into more a prosocial activity by initiating appropriate play. It is emphasized that you *must* receive clear permission from the particular governing agency to use any method of physical restraint of a child.

Treatment Settings for Children

You will find that potential practicum sites for gaining experience with children will vary greatly and include a wide variety of settings, both inpatient or residential (children's hospitals, pediatric units in general hospitals, and residential treatment centers) and outpatient (private or public schools, day-care centers, after-school programs, Head Start programs, private preschool programs, outpatient child development and child mental health clinics, child study centers, or with mental health providers in private practice settings). If you are planning a practicum experience, it is recommended that you meet with an under graduate advisor who frequently sponsors such student placements and who may have a list of prospective sites in the area. The following issues should be considered when beginning to seek a practicum experience with children: (a) the age range of children (preschool, school-age, or adolescents), (b) whether the experience will involve actual interaction with children versus observation or errand running, (c) the extent of training and supervision that will be provided in the setting, and (d) the amount and quality of prior experience with children expected by the site.

Lyman and Campbell (1996) have provided a thorough discussion of residential and inpatient treatment settings for children and youth with emotional and behavioral problems. Child mental health treatment settings reflect a continuum of care, from least to most restrictive. Outpatient settings might involve 1 to 3 hours weekly of private individual psychotherapy, family therapy, and behavioral therapy, with school and community activities minimally affected. In-home interventions involve direct treatment in the child's home: establishing a treatment, modeling behaviors, and instructing parents in the procedures. Examples include crisis intervention and the growing number of private agencies that provide intensive behavioral treatments for young autistic children. These latter services most often involve *discrete trial training,* that is, systematically shaping appropriate behaviors with primary reinforcers such as food, verbal praise, or physical contact. Such experience is excellent background if you may be planning graduate study in areas such as clinical child or school psychology. However, you should be aware that the degree and quality of training can be quite variable, and you would be advised to inquire about the nature and extent of training and supervision. College students are often used as assistants in day treatment and in regular education, special education, and after-school therapeutic programs. Some children are placed in residential or inpatient care for brief periods (generally less than 2 weeks) to stabilize them during a crisis; others may be removed from home and placed in foster care. Group homes are often operated as part of child-care agencies and employ "house parents."

Legal and Ethical Issues

Finally, it is important that as a practicum student involved with children and youth, you are aware of the professional code of ethics (American Psychological Association, 2002; see also http://apa.org/ethics) including *informed consent, confidentiality, duty to protect,* and *duty to report* (Brems, 2002). Specific procedures may differ across various practicum settings (pediatric hospital, psychiatric facility, therapeutic clinic, or day care), and you should be informed of the specific practices in a particular setting. However, there are some general principles of ethical conduct and legal requirements in working with children.

Signed informed consent indicating that the parent (custodial parent in the case of divorce) is informed of all relevant information regarding the evaluation and treatment of his or her child is necessary prior to mental health treatment. This includes video- or audiotaping and observation, risks and benefits of treatment, and the limits of confidentiality and duty to report, that is, mandated reporting of information relating to harmful neglect or abuse of a child.

A therapist or agency has a *duty to warn* a potential victim if a client has acknowledged the threat of harm to others (see chap. 4, this volume, for a discussion of the duty to warn). Although this would typically not be relevant with child clients, it could apply in the case of adolescents. Finally, parents of children are guaranteed the security and privacy of information regarding themselves and their children. Agencies involved with children must disclose how information regarding children and families will be used, develop specific procedures for how privacy regarding diagnostic and therapeutic practices will be protected, and state how long personal records and files will be maintained and how and when they will be destroyed.

Summary

Experience in working with both normally developing children and adolescents as well as those who present challenges of development and behavior is now expected for students applying for admission into many applied graduate programs. If you are planning to enter such fields as clinical child psychology, school psychology, applied developmental psychology, or social work, experience in working with a wide age range of children and adolescents is highly desirable. In this chapter, I outlined some of the primary aspects of normal physical, cognitive, language, and social–emotional development and provided a brief introduction to those children exhibiting learning and behavior disorders. It is my hope that with this introduction together with additional readings, you may be better informed in selecting a practicum setting that suits your goals and interests. This introduction outlines such important skills as developing rapport, engaging children, and appreciating how appropriate behaviors are reinforced by adult praise and encouragement. It is also very important that you become an educated consumer of potential training experiences, that is, that you are conscious of the need for supervision, particularly with children with serious emotional or behavioral disorders, and that you have an appreciation of ethical standards in the care of children.

Online Resources

American Academy of Child and Adolescent Psychiatry: http://aacap.org/

American Academy of Pediatrics: http://aap.org/

Child Development Institute: http://childdevelopmentinfo.com/

Children and Adults With Attention Deficit Disorder (CHADD): http://www.chadd.org/

Children With Disabilities: http://childrenwithdisabilities.ncjrs.org/

Council for Exceptional Children: http://www.cec.sped.org/

ERIC Clearinghouse on Disabilities and Gifted Education: http://ericec.org/

Individuals With Disabilities Education Improvement Act (H.R. 1350): http://edworkforce.house.gov/issues/108th/education/idea/1350confsummary.htm

Learning Disabilities Online: http://www.ldonline.org/

National Center for Learning Disabilities: http://www.ld.org/
National Information Center for Children and Youth With Disabilities:
http://nichy.org/

References

American Academy of Pediatrics, Policy Statement, Committee on Nutrition. (2003). Prevention of pediatric overweight and obesity. *Pediatrics, 112,* 424–430.

American Psychiatric Association. (2000). *Diagnostic and statistical manual of mental disorders* (4th ed., text rev.). Washington, DC: Author.

American Psychological Association. (2002). Ethical principles of psychologists and code of conduct. *American Psychologist, 57,* 1060–1073. Also available at http://www.apa.org/ethics

Batshaw, M. L. (2002). *Children with disabilities* (5th ed). Baltimore: Brookes Publishing.

Brems, C. (2002). *A comprehensive guide to child psychotherapy* (2nd ed.). Boston: Allyn & Bacon.

Campbell, S. B. (2002). *Behavior problems in preschool children* (2nd ed.). New York: Guilford Press.

Eyberg, S. (1988). Parent–child interaction therapy: Integration of traditional and behavioral concerns. *Child and Family Behavior Therapy, 10,* 33–46.

Garrison, W. T., & Earls, F. J. (1987). *Temperament and child psychopathology* (Vol. 12). Newbury Park, CA: Sage.

Gelfand, D. M., & Drew, C. J. (2003). *Understanding child behavior disorders* (4th ed.). Belmont, CA: Wadsworth.

Hembree-Kigin, T. L., & McNeil, C. B. (1995). *Parent–child interaction therapy.* New York: Plenum.

Individuals With Disabilities Education Improvement Act. (2004, November 17). *Strengthening and renewing special education: The Individuals With Disabilities Education Improvement Act* (H.R. 1350 Conference Report). Retrieved July 1, 2005, from http://edworkforce.house.gov/issues/108th/education/idea/1350confsummary.htm

Kagan, J. (1997). Temperamental contributions to social behavior. *American Psychologist, 44,* 668–674.

Kail, R. V. (2002). *Children.* Upper Saddle River, NJ: Prentice Hall.

Lyman, R. D., & Campbell, N. R. (1996). *Treating children and adolescents in residential and inpatient settings.* Thousand Oaks, CA: Sage.

Mash, E. J., & Wolfe, D. A. (2002). *Abnormal child psychology.* Belmont, CA: Wadsworth.

Mather, N., & Goldstein, S. (2001). *Learning disabilities and challenging behaviors: A guide to intervention and classroom management.* Baltimore: Brookes Publishing.

National Institute of Child Health and Development, Early Child Care Research Network. (1997). The effects of infant childcare on infant–mother attachment security: Results of the NICHD Study of Early Child Care. *Child Development, 68,* 860–879.

Padilla, A. M., Lindholm, K. J., Chen, A., Duran, R., Hakuta, K., Lambert, W., & Tucker, G. R. (1991). The English-only movement. Myths, reality, and implications for psychology. *American Psychologist, 46,* 120–130.

Schickendanz, J. A., Schickendanz, D. I., Forsyth, P. D., & Forsyth, G. A. (2001). *Understanding children and adolescents* (4th ed.) Boston: Allyn & Bacon.

Schroeder, C. S., & Gordon, B. N. (2002). *Assessment and treatment of childhood problems* (2nd ed.). New York: Guilford Press.

Shaywitz, S. (2003). *Overcoming dyslexia.* New York: Knopf.

Wenar, C., & Kerig, P. (2000). *Developmental psychopathology: From infancy through adolescence* (4th ed.). Boston: McGraw-Hill.

Janet R. Matthews and C. Eugene Walker

Mental Health Professions | 11

Optimal treatment for individuals with emotional problems requires a wide range of services. Service providers are trained in many different mental health professions. Over the years, cost cutting reductions in staff have blurred the lines in terms of who provides what type of service. Similar cost considerations have led many treatment centers to rely heavily on the use of medication rather than psychological treatments that often require more professional time. Although they do keep costs down, such measures do not necessarily provide the best treatment for those in need of care. As you read this chapter, you will learn some general information about the training and professional activities of many different professions. For those students who want to obtain further information about any of these professions, we have provided resources at the end of this chapter to assist your search. An undergraduate degree in psychology can provide a good foundation for pursuing most of these other occupations in addition to being the basis for furthering your education in psychology.

Each facility has different staffing needs and budgetary support. Thus, you will not necessarily meet people from each of the professions we are describing. You may also meet people who have different titles at your placement and yet seem to be doing the type of work we describe here.

This situation is related to the "blurring" of jobs we mentioned above. Depending on the nature of your facility, you may also meet other mental health professionals we have not described. Because there are so many professions involved today in mental health services, we cannot cover all of them in this chapter. We have selected those professions with whom our students most often have interactions. You may find other professions by doing an Internet search of mental health professions. We suggest that you interview some of these people to find out what training they have had and what their role is and to obtain their perspective on the job satisfactions and frustrations in their profession. It is important to learn not only about the tasks and rewards of a career but also the types of things that can make a professional upset with his or her role. Although you do not want to dwell on the negative side of any career, you do want to have some idea about whether you will have difficulty with certain facets of the career. For example, if a particular position requires a considerable amount of paperwork with very tight deadlines and you already know that you are not comfortable with meeting tight timelines, this is probably not the job for you. Be sure to be respectful in your questioning and let them know that you are interested in knowing more about the different professions as you plan for your future career. The information you receive may well help you decide on what you want to do professionally.

Psychologists

Psychologists in mental health settings are generally clinical or counseling psychologists. Theoretically, clinical psychologists are trained to work with more severe forms of mental illness, whereas counseling psychologists work with less severe emotional problems and attempt to help people optimize their ability to cope with life problems. In practice, however, these distinctions are artificial, and there is almost total overlap in the functioning of the two specialties in job settings. These psychologists have a doctoral degree (PhD, doctor of philosophy; PsyD, doctor of psychology; or EdD, doctor of education) in psychology, with specialization in the areas of personality, psychopathology, diagnostic evaluation, treatment of people with emotional disturbances, methods of scientific research, and related areas. The clinical or counseling psychologist must complete four years of undergraduate training in psychology and at least four or more years of graduate training in psychology. During the graduate training, in addition to relevant courses, the graduate student in psychology works in treatment settings such as hospitals and clinics under the supervision of experienced psychologists. He or she then completes a year of internship prior to receiving the doctoral degree and then undergoes an additional year or more of supervision after the doctoral degree is awarded. At this point, the psychologist-in-training can be licensed to offer services on an independent basis to the public as well as use the term *psychologist*. The title of psychologist is restricted to doctorally trained professionals who have a license to practice the profession in that state, territory, or Canadian province. When a psychologist moves from one state to another, a new license must be obtained, and the person is not permitted to use the title in the new state until meeting that jurisdiction's requirements. Individuals with master's level training in psychology often qualify for certification or licensing in various areas of counseling but may not refer to themselves as psychologists. Some common titles for master's level practitioners in the United States are licensed professional counselor, psychological assistant, and marriage and family therapist. We discuss some of these professions later in the chapter.

Clinical as well as counseling psychologists are trained and experienced in the basic sciences pertaining to diagnosis and treatment of emotional disturbances. In addition, they have a significant amount of training in research methods and procedures, which enables them to conduct research that adds to our understanding of mental illness and its treatment. A major difference between those psychologists with a PhD degree and those with a PsyD degree is the balance between the research and applied portions of their training. The PsyD programs place greater emphasis on the applied work, such as practicums, than on the science of psychology. Psychologists trained in PsyD programs have received training in the broad background of psychology in addition to their practical experiences. Psychologists trained in PhD programs are more likely to have been required to produce a research dissertation as part of their doctoral training requirements than psychologists from the PsyD programs. In the PsyD programs, the research requirement might be met through an intensive case study or publishable quality literature review.

Psychiatrists

Psychiatrists are physicians who specialize in treating emotional rather than physical disorders. After graduating from medical school, these physicians do a residency in which they are trained to work with people whose behavior is sufficiently distressing to themselves or others to be labeled a mental illness. The general psychiatry residency usually lasts four years after completing medical school. Some psychiatrists specialize by the age of the patients they see, such as working with children (child psychiatry) or the elderly (geropsychiatry). Such specialty training often requires one or more additional years of training after the general psychiatry residency. Some psychiatrists specialize in particular types of disorder, such as depression. Like their colleagues in other fields of medicine, some psychiatrists elect to have general practices in which they see a range of both ages and disorders.

Within the U.S. mental health system, psychiatrists may serve as medical director, program director, hospital administrator, and consultant to special programs. Traditionally, psychiatrists have emphasized the use of medication for the treatment of emotional problems. Historically, the development and administration of psychotropic medication was cited as a major reason for the deinstitutionalization movement. Before these medications were available, many patients exhibited such disordered behavior that they could expect to spend most if not all of their lives as inpatients. They were sent to long-term care facilities often located great distances from their homes. Thus, it was difficult for family members to participate in their treatment or even to visit them regularly. Today, patients with these same behaviors may be given medication, stabilized on it, and released to outpatient treatment in a week or less.

Over time, medications have been developed for far less severe forms of disordered behavior. Television ads for antianxiety and antidepressant medications are now common. Thus, although psychiatrists are trained to prescribe as well as to perform more traditional forms of psychotherapy, they often find their practices consisting of mental status evaluations, prescription of medications, and evaluation of medication dosage level. Very few psychiatrists currently spend a significant amount of their time doing psychotherapy. This is generally left to other professionals such as psychologists, counselors, and social workers.

Social Workers

In July 2002, the International Federation of Social Workers adopted a new definition of their profession. According to this definition,

> The social work profession promotes social change, problem solving in human relationships and the empowerment and liberation of people to enhance well-being. Utilizing theories of human behavior and social systems, social work intervenes at

the points where people interact with their environments. Principles of human rights and social justice are fundamental to social work.

Social workers receive their postbaccalaureate training in social work. This profession has its own body of knowledge and code of ethics. Most professionals working in psychiatric settings as social workers have an MSW degree (master's of social work) and are then certified after practicing for two years (3,000 hours) under the supervision of an experienced social worker and passing a national test. Social workers may also enter the profession with a bachelor's degree and a small number have doctoral degrees in social work. Those with doctoral degrees have more training in research and are generally interested in academic and research careers. When you read a chart note signed by a social worker who has the initials BCSW after his or her name, that means the person is a board-certified social worker. The designation LCSW refers to a licensed clinical social worker, and ACSW stands for accredited clinical social worker. These are equivalent to BCSW.

Social workers are trained to conceptualize emotional problems from the perspective of how they interact with the person's social functioning. To be able to do this they are trained to consider how factors such as poverty, racism, and unemployment affect mental health and how one's mental health determines the role one plays in daily life. They tend to view a patient's problems in the context of the family or community rather than from an individual basis the way the *Diagnostic and Statistical Manual of Mental Disorders, Fourth Edition, Text Revision* (*DSM–IV–TR*; American Psychiatric Association, 2000) system is designed.

Academic training in social work includes courses in behavioral science, research, social work theory, and therapeutic interventions. In addition, a major part of the training is supervised fieldwork. This fieldwork is done in facilities such as community agencies and psychiatric hospitals when the student is interested in becoming a psychiatric social worker. Social work has been one of the leading professions in the use of supervised fieldwork as part of the educational process. In contrast to the training of psychologists, social workers do not have a focus on formal psychological testing procedures although certain forms of assessment, mostly based on interview, are part of their education. Similarly, research training is included in social work programs, but it does not receive the emphasis it does in psychology programs.

Traditionally, social workers were the members of the mental health team who took the patient's history and made arrangements for follow-up care in the community after discharge from the hospital. They may also do follow-up home visits to check on the patient after discharge from the hospital. They receive training in working with a range of community agencies and thus may help patients receive many different community services.

Today, social workers are also primary therapists for patients, serve as unit administrators, and maintain independent private practices. They work with individuals, groups, families, and communities. Their interventions include assessment and diagnosis of emotional problems, crisis intervention, psychosocial and educational interventions, and both brief and long-term psychotherapy. For example, according to Minnesota statutes,

> Social work practice is the application of social work theory, knowledge, methods, and ethics to restore or enhance social, psychosocial, or biopsychosocial functioning of individuals, couples, families, groups, organizations, and communities, with particular attention to the person-in-environment configuration. (Retrieved June 18, 2003, from http:// www.socialwork.state.mn.us/Default.aspx?tabid=434)

In Minnesota, social workers that are licensed to practice at the independent level both diagnose and treat emotional disorders. Social work appears to be a growing profession. Trull and Phares (2001) noted that social workers at the beginning of the 21st century were providing about half of all mental health services in the United States. Enrollment in social work training programs has grown to support this profession. By 2005, the number of social workers is predicted to increase by 34% (Clay, 1998).

Counselors

Different titles are used for counselors depending on state law where they practice. Some common professional titles are licensed professional counselor (LPC), marriage, family, and child counselor (MFCC), and licensed mental health counselor (LMHC). There are a number of others in various states. Educationally, these individuals most often have a master's degree requiring 1 to 2 years of study after the undergraduate degree followed by supervised practical experience. Their bachelor's degree may have been in any of the behavioral sciences or even unrelated areas such as English literature, chemistry, or history. These individuals have a specialty license from the state to provide counseling services to individuals, groups, and families. Regardless of the type of setting, some mental health facilities also have specialty counselors known as pastoral counselors. Because this term tends to be used across various states, we are providing additional information about this profession. This example illustrates one of the roles counselors may have within the mental health service delivery system.

PASTORAL COUNSELORS

Today there are over 3,000 counselors in the United States who identify themselves as *pastoral counselors*. Some of these counselors are members of the clergy of various religions, but others are individuals who have received graduate education integrating theology and psychology. According to the American Association of Pastoral Counselors, "pastoral counseling is a unique form of psychotherapy which uses spiritual resources as well as psychological understanding for healing and growth" (American Association of Pastoral Counselors, n.d). Pastoral counselors provide individual, group, and family counseling on both an inpatient and outpatient basis. Their approach to emotional problems is to discuss them within a spiritual context.

A 1992 Gallup poll of 1,000 people reported that 66% of the respondents preferred to receive counseling from a person who represented their spiritual values. Thus, it is not surprising that people experiencing distress seek assistance from their clergy. Many members of the clergy have neither the time nor the training to provide extensive work with these individuals. Pastoral counselors are one alternative for people who wish to have the clinical services they receive include a spiritual component. Depending on the pastoral counselor, reading scripture, prayer, and other religious activities may be combined with more traditional forms of psychotherapy. To provide a more standardized form of training for pastoral counselors, the American Association of Pastoral Counselors (see the Web site listed at the end of this chapter for information) accredits training programs for pastoral counselors and is currently developing a national licensing exam for them. In mental health facilities, the chaplain may include pastoral counseling as a part of his or her duties or may choose to limit practice to traditional religious duties.

Psychiatric Nurses

Psychiatric nursing is a specialty area within the nursing profession. Although a person can become a registered nurse (RN) with a specialized 2-year degree, today many of the psychiatric nurses working in hospitals have not only a bachelor's degree based on four years of training but also a master's degree, which requires an additional two years. There are also specialty training programs in which people who have undergraduate degrees in related fields, such as psychology, can enter nursing programs and gain the added training to join this profession. Psychiatric nurses are often employed in inpatient psychiatry settings. They function as unit coordinators and administrators as well as staff members. They often work closely with the psychiatrist on managing the dosage of psychotropic medication prescribed by the psychiatrist. They may also provide individual, group, and family psychotherapy. During their specialty training, they learn about psychiatric diagnosis and psychotherapy in much the same way as other mental health professionals do.

Creative Arts Therapists

A general term often used to describe therapists with a range of specialties is *creative arts therapist*. The term *expressive therapy* is also sometimes used. The National Coalition of Arts Therapies Associations includes six specialty groups: art, dance or movement, drama, music, poetry therapists, and psychodramatists. We have provided Web site addresses for many of these professions at the end of this chapter so you can get information about training programs and career options. Although many hospitals have one staff member who provides services overlapping many of these specialties, each has its own organization and curriculum. We provide brief descriptions of a few of them to illustrate these fields.

ART THERAPISTS

The belief that the creative process involved in making various art products allows one to express and deal with emotions is the basis for art therapy. Art therapists do patient assessment, treatment, and research in psychiatric settings. They also provide consultation to other professionals in these settings. Art therapy is conducted with individuals, groups, families, and communities. Art therapists must have a solid foundation in human development and psychological theory. Most art therapists have master's degrees. The first graduate degree programs in art therapy appeared in the 1970s. By 2002, there were 27 nationally accredited master's degree programs in art therapy. To be listed as a registered art therapist, the person must have successfully passed a national exam.

Historically, mental health professionals have studied patients' art work to better understand both patients' pathology and treatment reactions. Likewise, art educators found that people's spontaneous art often symbolically reflected personal issues. These two streams of interest contributed to the development of formal training programs in art therapy. Art therapists use both talking about art and the actual production of art as part of their therapy. Art therapists may select specific media such as charcoal or ceramics for the patient depending on the patient's issues. With increased use of technology, art therapists are also using videotaping and computer graphics to help their patients express emotional needs (Wadeson, Durkin, & Perach, 1989).

DANCE THERAPISTS

Dance or movement therapy is the psychotherapeutic use of movement to assist in emotional expression and integration by the patient. Its foundation is in the expressive nature of dance that allows patients to experience themselves through their bodies. Among the goals of dance therapy are catharsis, mood elevation, and improvement of self-esteem and body image. Training for this profession is on the graduate level, with undergraduate coursework in psychology providing a good basis for graduate training. Graduates of approved master's degree programs in dance or movement therapy may become registered as a DTR (dance therapist registered). Dance therapy is used on both an individual and group basis in both inpatient and outpatient mental health treatment settings.

DRAMA THERAPISTS

Drama therapy uses both processes and products of theater to relieve patient symptoms and assist in personality integration. Drama therapists help patients express feelings, gain insight, and facilitate growth. Many different drama forms are used. Although patients may play standard roles in published plays, more often they are encouraged to reenact previous traumatic life events and to role-play effective coping behaviors. Other techniques include puppetry, mime, improv, and similar theatrical modalities. A pioneer in this field was J. L. Moreno who coined the term *psychodrama* and developed many of the techniques still used today (Ehrenwald, 1976). Drama therapists are trained in theories of personality and developmental psychology in addition to the theater arts.

MUSIC THERAPISTS

Modern music therapy started in the 20th century at VA hospitals. Musicians were visiting the veterans to play for them. When the professional staff noted patient improvement following these visits, the professional staff asked that some musicians be hired as regular hospital employees. It soon became apparent that these new employees needed education regarding the etiology and characteristics of the patients' problems. Thus, suitable college curricula were developed. Today certified music therapists (CMT) have at least a bachelor's degree in music therapy or its equivalent from an approved training program. Their training includes a 900-hour clinical internship. The first music therapy degree program was founded in 1944 at Michigan State University. Their approach to treating emotionally disturbed people is a combination of many forms of psychotherapy combined with various music modalities. Just as psychologists differ in their theoretical orientation and methods of doing therapy, so do music therapists. Music therapists use their relationship with the patient to help the patient address problems in much the same way as psychologists, social workers, and others. Although they use various forms of music in their work, music therapists do not need to have a professional level of music ability. They do, however, need to have some musical ability as well as an appreciation of several forms of music. The patient does not need to have any musical ability to benefit from this form of treatment.

Music therapy has been used with patients of all ages. It has been used with a range of mental disorders including Alzheimer's disease, substance abuse, and developmental disabilities. Music therapists assist in both the assessment and treatment process with these patients. Music therapy is used in both individual and group sessions. The techniques may involve receptive listening to music, performance of various forms of music, music improvisation, and discussion of the lyrics of songs. The music therapist helps the patient explore personal feelings, practice problem solving, and make positive emotional changes.

Music has been found to assist in stress reduction. Because stress is a common component in emotional problems, reduction of stress is often a useful part of the treatment program. To illustrate the use of music therapy in a clinical setting, consider the approach Rogers developed for use with sexually abused children (Rogers, 1993). In this approach, different musical instruments are designated as representing different people in the child's life. The child helps the music therapist select which instruments represent which people. The music therapist uses the size of the instruments as well as their relative placement and which are played with which others to help understand the child's trauma. This approach is quite similar to the use child psychologists make of toys when working with children.

Occupational and Recreational Therapists

Therapists in these two specialties use their skills not only to assist in the assessment and treatment of emotional problems but also try to provide the patients with the opportunity to develop new interests that can be used throughout their lives. Both of these professions work with people across the lifespan on both an inpatient and an outpatient basis.

OCCUPATIONAL THERAPISTS

The occupational therapist helps the patient learn new ways to approach the job setting so that it is not experienced as overwhelming. Occupational therapists help patients learn time management skills, how to work productively with others, and how to enjoy leisure time. In some cases, the occupational therapist may help the patient change employment settings because the current one does not meet the patient's emotional needs. Some inpatients may not be able to return to former positions because those jobs are no longer available.

Currently, people serving as occupational therapists may have a bachelor's, master's, or doctoral degree. Recently, the American Occupational Therapy Association (AOTA) has established qualifications for this title. Starting January 1, 2007, new occupational therapists must have education beyond the undergraduate degree. A list of accredited programs can be found on the AOTA Web site listed at the end of the chapter.

RECREATIONAL THERAPISTS

The recreational therapist involves the patient in selected active experiences such as games, sports, and other activities intended to aid in recovery as well as promote wellness in the future. The Web site (http://www.atra-tr.org/atra.htm) of the largest organization of recreational therapists, the American Therapeutic Recreation Association, states that "recreational therapy utilizes various activities as a form of active treatment to improve the physical, cognitive, emotional and social functioning and to increase independence in life activities of persons disabled as a result of trauma or disease." These activities are designed to teach positive self-esteem and encourage interpersonal relations to facilitate growth. The specific activities used vary depending on the facility and the reason for referral. Ideally, these activities can be used as part of the person's leisure activities in the future. Among the activities used by recreational therapists are aquatic exercises, horticulture, various handicrafts such as ceramics and macramé, and a range of individual and team sports. Participation in these activities may also allow the patient to feel sufficiently comfortable to talk about issues not yet revealed in more traditional forms of therapy. The recreational therapist may then share this information with the patient's primary therapist. There are national standards for certification as a recreational therapist. They are available on the Web site listed at the end of the chapter.

Case Managers

Many agencies have a position called "case manager." This title can be used for people from many different professions. For example, a social worker might be assigned to be the case manager for one patient, and a psychiatric nurse might be assigned to be the case manager for another patient in that same program. Because it is such a commonly used title, we are including it in our description of professions. Case managers' responsibility is to facilitate and coordinate all aspects of the treatment plan for those individuals assigned to them. One of their primary tasks is to see that all treatment provided is properly documented in the patient's chart. They also see that required paperwork for payment for treatment is submitted to the insurance company or party paying for the treatment, unless insurance filing is handled by the business office of the facility. Inpatient settings frequently use this title for members of the professions typically found in the facility. The role of the case manager may include making referrals to specialists outside the unit both during hospitalization and for follow-up care after discharge and assuring that all aspects of the planned treatment program are being addressed. For example, if a psychiatric patient needs to see an orthopedic specialist for a knee problem, the person acting as the case manager would arrange for this consultation. The case manager would also be the one to arrange follow-up visits with an employment counselor if this is part of a treatment plan. The title tends to be used in a somewhat different way in outpatient settings. Rather than the case manager being one of the professionals in the facility, this term is often used for bachelor's degree employees who are hired specifically for this duty. They are responsible for arranging the community needs of the individuals who come to the agency.

Summary

In this chapter, we have introduced you to a range of mental health professions. There are many others that might have been included. We did not provide an exhaustive description of any of them but rather attempted to illustrate the field as it currently functions. Students who are interested in further exploration of these related professions are encouraged to visit some of the Web sites listed at the end of the chapter as well as to do their own Internet searches for additional professions. We have also provided the names of two books that contain such career information. One of these books deals with issues faced by students doing graduate study in any of the helping professions, and the other addresses various career paths within psychology. Once again, these are just two of the many books available.

Additional Reading

Students who are considering careers in one of the mental health fields may want to do further reading in addition to asking questions of the professionals with whom they are interacting in the course of their field placement experience. Below are two sources that may be helpful.

Echterling, L. G., Cowan, E., Evans, W. F., Staton, A. R., Viere, G., McKee, J. E., et al. (2002). *Thriving: A manual for students in the helping professions.* Boston: Lahaska Press.

The information in this book is designed for students in graduate school for any of the "helping" professions. Chapters address personal issues faced by students who are in the process of integrating their personal and professional identities. It also provides ethics codes for several of the helping professions as well as references on counseling.

Sternberg, R. J. (Ed.). (1997). *Career paths in psychology: Where your degree can take you.* Washington, DC: American Psychological Association.

This book provides descriptions of a number of different careers within psychology. A number of psychologists provide information about what they do on a regular basis in their jobs and how you get started doing the type of work they do.

Online Resources

American Art Therapy Association: http://www.arttherapy.org
American Association of Pastoral Counselors: http://www.aapc.org
American Dance Therapy Association: http://www.adta.org
American Music Therapy Association: http://www.musictherapy.org
American Occupational Therapy Association: http://www.aota.org
American Therapeutic Recreation Association: www.atra-tr.org/
    benefitscost.htm
International Federation of Social Workers: http://www.ifsw.org
National Association for Drama Therapy: http://www.nadt.org
National Association for Poetry Therapy: http://www.poetry
    therapy.org
National Association of Social Workers: http://www.nasw.org
National Coalition of Arts Therapies Associations: http://www.
    ncata.com

References

American Association of Pastoral Counselors. (n.d.) *About pastoral counseling*. Retrieved June 18, 2005, from http://www.aapc.org/about.cfm

American Psychiatric Association. (2000). *Diagnostic and statistical manual of mental disorders* (4th ed., text rev.). Washington, DC: Author.

Clay, R. A. (1998, September). Mental health professions vie for position in the next decade. *Monitor on Psychology, 29,* 20–21.

Ehrenwald, J. (1976). *The history of psychotherapy: From healing magic to encounter*. New York: Jason Aronson.

International Federation of Social Workers. (2000, August). *Definition of social work*. Retrieved September 9, 2005, from http://www.ifsw.org/Publications/4.6e.pub.html

Rogers, P. (1993). Research in music therapy with sexually abused clients. In H. Payne (Ed.), *Handbook of inquiry in the arts therapies: One river many currents* (pp. 197–217). London: Kingsley.

Trull, T. J., & Phares, E. J. (2001). *Clinical psychology* (6th ed.). Belmont, CA: Wadsworth.

Wadeson, H., Durkin, J., & Perach, D. (Eds.). (1989). *Advances in art therapy.* New York: Wiley.

Medical Abbreviations Glossary

From *Medical Abbreviations Glossary* at http://www.jdmd.com/glossary/jdmd_glossary.pdf by JD.MD, Inc. Reprinted with permission. Glossary is updated daily.

Medical Abbreviations Glossary

These medical abbreviations are commonly used in hospital, medical, and dental records. There are many others, rarely used, and some doctors and hospitals create their own. If you cannot locate an abbreviation in this glossary, contact us for assistance.

A

a	artery, before
aa	equal part of each
AA	affected area
AAA	abdominal aortic aneurysm
A2	aortic second sound
AAL	acute lymphoblastic, leukemia, anterior axillary line
ab	antibody
AB	abortion
abd	abdomen
ABG	arterial blood gasses
ABN	abnormal
ABP	arterial blood pressure
abs	absent
a.c.	before meals (ante sebum)
Ac	acute
AC	anterior chamber
acc	accident
accom.	accommodation
acid phos.	acid phosphate
ACL	anterior cruciate ligament
ACTH	adrenocorticotrophic hormone
AD	right ear
add.	abductor or abduction
ADH	antidiruetic hormone
ADL	activites of daily living
ad lib	as desired
adm.	admission
AE	above elbow
AEA	above elbow amputation
AF	atrial fibrillation, afebrile
AFB	acid fast bacilli
AFO	ankle-foot orthosis
AFP	alpha fetoprotein
A/G	albumin globulin ratio (blood)
AGA	appropriate gestational age
AI	aortic insufficiency
AIDS	acquired immunodeficiency syndrome
AJ	ankle jerk
a.k.	above knee
aka	alcoholic ketoacidosis
AKA	above knee amputation

alb.	albumin
alc.	alcohol
alk. phos.	alkaline phosphate
ALL	acute lymphocytic leukemia
ALS	amyotrophic lateral sclerosis
ALT	alternating with, alanine aminotransferase (formerly SGPT)
AMA	against medical advice
amb.	ambulating, ambulatory
AMI	acute myocardial infarction
AML	acute myeloid leukemia
amnio	amniocentesis
amp.	amputation, ampule
ANA	antinuclear antibody
anes.	anesthesia
ann. fib.	annulus fibrosis
ANS	autonomic nervous system
ant.	anterior
ante	before
ANUG	acute necrotizing ulcerative gingivitis
Anxty	anxiety
A/O	alert and oriented
AOB	alcohol on breath
AODM	adult onset diabetes mellitus
AP	ante partum
A&P	auscultation and percussion
A-P	anteroposterior
APC	atrial premature contractions
aph	aphasia
A-P & lat	anteroposterior and lateral
AP resection	abdominal perineal resection of the rectum
aq.	water
AR	aortic regurgitation
ARD	acute respiratory distress
ARDS	adult respiratory distress syndrome
ARF	acute respiratory failure, acute rheumatic fever
AROM	artificial rupture of membranes
art	arterial
AS	left ear, aortic stenosis
ASA	acetylsalicylic acid, aspirin
A.S.A.	American Society of Anesthesiologists

Only an expert case evaluation, performed by a qualified physician or dentist, can tell you what you need to know. Before you accept a case, be sure the odds are in your favor. Let JD.MD evaluate it.

☎ 800-225-JDMD or e-✉ information@jdmd.com

Medical Abbreviations Glossary

A.S.A. 1	normal healthy patient
A.S.A. 2	patient with mild systemic disease
A.S.A. 3	patient with severe systemic disease
A.S.A. 4	patient with incapacitating systemic disease that is constant threat to life
ASAP	as soon as possible
ASCVD	atherosclerotic cardiovascular disease
ASD	atrial septal defect
ASHD	arteriosclerotic heart disease
at. Flutter	atrial flutter
ATN	acute tubular necrosis
ATNR	asymmetrical tonic neck reflex
AU	both ears
aud.	auditory
Aur. Fib	auricular fibrillation
A-V	arteriovenous
AVF	arteriovenous fistula
AVR	aortic valve replacement
A&W	alive and well
Ax.	axilla, axillary
A.Z.	Ascheim-Zondek test

B

B.	bath
BA	barium
Bab.	Babinski sign
Ba.E	barium enema
Bas.	basal, basilar
baso	basophile
BBB	bundle branch block
BBT	basal body temperature
BCA	basal cell atypia
BCD	basal cell dysplasia
BCE	basal cell epithelioma
BCG	bacillus Calmette-Guerin vaccine (tuberculosis vaccine)
BDC	burn dressing change
BE	below elbow, barium enema
BEA	below elbow amputation
BFP	biological false positive
Bic.	biceps
b.i.d.	twice daily
BIH	bilateral inguinal hernia
bilat.	Bilateral, bilaterally
bili	bilirubin
b.i.n.	twice a night

BiW	twice weekly
BJ	biceps reflex
bk.	back
BK	below knee
BKA	below knee amputation
bl cult	blood culture
bld.	blood
Bl.T	bleeding time
BM	black male, bone marrow, bowel movement
BMR	basal metabolic rate
body wt.	body weight
BOMA	otitis media, both ears, acute
BOW	bag of water
BP	blood pressure
BPD	bronchopulmonary dysplasia
BPH	benign prostatic hypertrophy
BPM	beats per minute
Br.	breech presentation
BR	bedrest, bathroom
brach.	brachial
BrBx.	breast biopsy
broncho	bronchoscopy
BRP	bathroom privileges
BS	blood sugar, bowel sounds
B.S.	breath sounds
BSA	body surface area
BSB	bedside bag
BSC	bedside commode
BSD	bedside drainage
BSO	bilateral salpingooophorectomy
BST	blood serologic test
BT	bleeding time
BTL	bilateral tubal ligation
BUN	blood urea nitrogen
BW	birth weight
Bx.	biopsy

C

c.	with
C	cervical, Caucasian
C.	centigrade, Celsius complement
CI-XII	1st to 12th cranial nerve
C-1 to C-7	cervical vertebrae
Ca	calcium
CA	carcinoma, cancer

 **Medical Abbreviations Glossary**

CABG	coronary artery bypass graft
CAD	coronary artery disease
CAHD	coronary atherosclerotic heart disease
Cal	calorie, calories
CAPD	continuous ambulatory peritoneal dialysis
Caps	capsules
car.	carotid
card.	cardiac
Card Cath	cardiac catheterization
CAT	computerized axial tomography
cath	catheterization, catheter
CB	Cesarean birth
CBC	complete blood count
CBD	common bile duct
CBF	cerebral blood flow
CBG	capillary blood gas
CBR	complete bed rest
cc.	cubic centimeter
CC	chief complaint
CCU	coronary care unit
CD	cardiac disease, contagious disease
CEA	carcinoembryonic antigen
Cerv.	cervix, cervical
CF	cardiac failure, cystic fibrosis
CHD	congenital heart disease, coronary heart disease
Chem.	chemotherapy
CHF	congestive heart failure
CHO	carbohydrate
Chol	cholesterol
Chr	chronic
C.I	color index
CI	cardiac insufficiency, cardiac index
CIS	carcinoma in situ
CK	creatinine kinase
Cl	chlorine, chloride
Clav.	clavicle
cldy	cloudy
CLL	chronic lymphocytic leukemia
Cl.T	clotting time
cm.	centimeter
CML	chronic myeloid leukemia
CMV	cytomegalovirus
CN	cranial nerve

CNS	central nervous system
cnst.	constipation
c/o	complains of, complaints
Co2	carbon dioxide
comb.	combine, combination
comm.	communicable
comp.	compound, compress
conc.	concentrated
cons.	consultation
cont.	contractions, continued
COPD	chronic obstructive pulmonary disease
Cor	heart
CPAP	continuous positive airway pressure
CPC	clinicopathological conference
CPD	cephalo-pelvic disproportion
CPK	creatinine phosphokinase
CPPB	continuous positive pressure breathing
CPR	cardiopulmonary resuscitation
CPT	chest physical therapy
CR	closed reduction
cran.	cranial
CRD	chronic respiratory disease
creat.	creatinine
CRF	chronic renal failure
C/S, CS	Cesarean section
C&S	culture and sensitivity
CSF	cerebrospinal fluid
C-spine	cervical spine
CT	computed axial tomography
C-V	cardiovascular
CVA	cerebrovascular accident, costovertebral angle
CVL	central venous line
CVP	central venous pressure
CVS	cardiovascular system
Cx	cervix, culture
CxR	chest x-ray
Cysto	cystoscopy

D _____

DAP	distal airway pressure
db.	decibel
DBE	deep breathing exercise
d/c	discontinue

*At JD.MD reliability means performing consistently and meeting your expectations every time.
Our medical and dental malpractice case evaluations are on target and on time.*

☎ 800-225-JDMD or e-✉ information@jdmd.com

Medical Abbreviations Glossary

DC	discharges, discontinue
D&C	dilation and curettage
DD	discharge diagnosis
D/DW	dextrose, distilled water
DDx	differential diagnosis
D&E	dilation and evacuation
decr.	decreased
dehyd.	dehydrated
Derm.	Dermatology
DES	Diethylstilbestrol
D5RL	5% dextrose and lactated ringers
D5W	5% dextrose and sterile water
DI	diabetes insipidus, diagnostic imaging
DIAG.	diagnosis
diam.	diameter
DIC	disseminated intravascular coagulation, disseminated coagulopathy
diff.	differential
dil.	dilute
dim.	diminished
DIP	distal interphalangeal (joint)
dis.	disease
disch.	discharge
disp.	disposition
dist.	distilled, distal
DIU	death in utero
div.	divorced
DJD	degenerative joint disease
DKA	diabetic ketoacidosis
DLE	disseminated lupus erythematosis
D/L DI	decilter
DM	diabetes mellitus, diastolic murmur
DNA	deoxyribonucleic acid
DNKA	did not keep appointment
DOA	dead on arrival
DOB	date of birth
DOE	dyspnea on exertion
Dors	dorsal
D.P.	dorsal pedia
DPT	diphtheria, pertussis, tetanus vaccine
DR	delivery room
D&R	dilation and radium implant
drsg.	dressing
D/S	discharge summary
DTR	deep tendon reflexes
DT's	delirium tremens
DU	duodenal ulcer

DUB	dysfunctional uterine bleeding
DUI	driving under influence
D/W	dextrose in water
Dx	diagnosis

E

e	without
EBL	estimated blood loss
EBV	Epstein-Barr virus
ECF	extended care facility, extracellular fluid
ECG	electrocardiogram
ECHO	enterocytopathogenic human orphan virus
E.coli	Escherichia coli
ECS	endocervical scrape
ECT	electroconvulsive
ED	emergency department
EDC	estimated date of confinement
EDOD	estimated date of delivery
EEG	electroencephalogram
EENT	eyes, ears, nose, throat
EEX	electrodiagnosis
EGA	estimated gestational age
EGD	esophago-gastroduodenoscopy
EKG	electrocardiogram
elev.	elevated
ELF	elective low forceps
EmBx	endometrial biopsy
EMG	electromyogram
EMS	endometrial scrape, emergency medical service
En.	enema
ENT	ears, nose, throat
Eos.	eosinophiles
EOM	extraocular movement
Epis.	episiotomy
Epis. LML	left mediolateral episiotomy
Epis. Med.	medial episiotomy
Epis. RML	right mediolateral episiotomy
ERCP	endoscopic retrograde cholangiopancreatography
ESR	erythrocyte sedimentation rate
EST	electroshock therapy
ETIOL.	etiology
ETOH	ethanol
EUA	examine under anesthesia
EVAL	evaluation
ex.	exercise, example

Medical Abbreviations Glossary

expir	expiration, expiratory
Exp. Lap	exploratory laparotomy
ext.	extremities, external
ext. gen.	external genitalia

F

F	finger, female, Fahrenheit
FA	fluorescent antibody
F.A.	first aid
F.B.	foreign body
FBS	fasting blood sugar
FD	fully dilated
FDA	Food and Drug Administration
FDP	flexor digitorum profundus
Fe def.	iron deficiency
FEF	forced expiratory flow
FEKG	fetal electrocardiogram
fem.	femoral
fem. pop.	femoral popliteal
fet.	fetal
FEV	forced expiratory volume
f.f.	force fluid
FFP	fresh frozen plasma
fh	fundal height
FH	family history, fetal heart
FHR	fetal heart rate
FHR-UC	fetal heart rate-uterine contraction
FHT	fetal heart tones
FiO2	faction of inspired oxygen concentration
fl.	fluids
flac.	flaccid
flex.	flexor, flexion
fl. oz.	fluid ounce
FM	finger movement
FPAL	full term premature abortion living
fract.	fractional
FRC	functional residual capacity
FS	finger stick
FSH	follicle stimulating hormone
FT	full term
FTD	failure to descend
FTND	full term normal delivery
FTT	failure to thrive
FUB	functional uterine bleeding
F/U,F-U,F.U.	follow-up
FUO	fever of unknown origin
FVC	forced vital capacity

FW	fetal weight
Fx	fracture

G

G	gravida
G.A.	general anesthesia
GB	gallbladder
GBS	gallbladder series
G.C.	gonococcus
GCS	Glasgow Coma Scale
GE	Gastroenterology
G/E	gastroenteritis
gen, genl.	general
gest.	gestation
GFR	glomerulo filtration rate
G.H.	growth hormone
G.I.	gastrointestinal
gluc	glucose
gm	gram
Gm+	gram positive
Gm-	gram negative
gm.%	grams per 100 c.c.
GMA	grand mal attack
GNC	general nursing care
GP	General Practitioner, general paralysis
gr.	grain, grains (dosage)
Grav.	pregnancy
gt.	drop
Gt.tr.	gait training
gtts.	drops
GSW	gunshot wound
GTT	glucose tolerance test
GU	genitourinary
G/W	glucose and water
GYN	Gynecology

H

h	hour
H	hydrogen history, hour, hypodermic
H/A	headache
HAF	hyperalimentation fluid
HASCVD	hypertensive arteriosclerotic cardiovascular disease
Hb., Hgb	hemoglobin
HB	heart block
HBP	high blood pressure
HC	head circumference

JD.MD provides you with medical and dental malpractice case evaluations performed by appropriate Board Certified Specialists.

☎ 800-225-JDMD or e-✉ information@jdmd.com

 **Medical Abbreviations Glossary**

H&C	hot and cold
HCG	human chorionic gonadotropin
HCO3	bicarbonate
Hct.	hematocrit
HCVD	hypertensive cardiovascular disease
h.d.	at bedtime
Hd	head, Hodgkin's disease
HDI	high density lipids
HEENT	head, eyes, ears, nose, throat
hern.	hernia
Hem	Hematology
Hem Pro	hematology profile
Hep. Lock	Heparin lock
HGO	hepatic glucose output
HH	hard of hearing
HIDA(scan)	hepatobiliary scan
HIE	hypoxic ischemic encephalopathy
hist.	history, histology
HIV	human immunodeficiency virus
HKAFO	hip knee ankle foot orthosis
HLA	human leukocyte group A, histocompatibility leukocyte focus
HM	hand movement
HMD	hyaline membrane disease
HMG	human menopausal gonadotropin
HNP	herniated nucleus pulposus
h/o	history of
H.O.	house officer
HOB	head of bed
horiz.	horizontal
H&P	history and physical
hpf	high power field
HPI	history of present illness
HPL	human placental lactogen
HR	heart rate
H.R.S.T.	heat, reddening, swelling, tenderness
HS	bedtime
HSG	hysterosalpingography
H2O	water
H2O2	hydrogen peroxide
Ht	height, heart
HVD	hypertensive vascular disease
Hx	history

Hyperal.	hyperalimenation
Hz	hertz (cycles/second)

I _____

I	radioactive iodine
IA	intra-arterially
IABP	intra-aortic balloon pump
i.c.	intracutaneous(ly)
ICCU	intensive coronary care unit
ICF	intracellular fluid
ICS	intercostal space
ICT	insulin coma therapy
ICU	intensive care unit
i.d.	during the day
ID	intradermal, identification, Infectious Disease
I&D	incision and drainage
IDDM	insulin dependent diabetes mellitus
I/E	inspiratory, expiratory
Ig	immunoglobulin
IGA	immunoglobulin A
IGE	immunoglobulin E
IGG	immunoglobulin gamma G(Globulin)
IGM	immunoglobulin M
IH	infectious hepatitis
IHD	ischemic heart disease
IM	intramuscular, intramedullary
IMCU	intermediate medical care unit
imp.	impression
IMP	inpatient multidimensional psych scale
IMV	intermittent mandatory ventilation
In.	inches
Inc. AB	incomplete abortion
incr.	increased (ing)
Inev. AB	inevitable abortion
inf	infusion, inferior
inj	injured, injection
INR	coagulant response time
inspir	inspiration, inspiratory
int.	internal
INTHC	intrathecally

JD.MD. is Performance...

☎ 800-225-JDMD or e-✉ information@jdmd.com

Medical Abbreviations Glossary

IO	inferior oblique
I&O	intake and output
IOP	intraocular pressure
IP	intraperitoneal
IPJ	interphalangeal joint
IPPB	intermittent positive pressure breathing
IQ	intelligence quota
IRDS	idiopathic respiratory distress syndrome
irreg.	Irregular
IS	intercostal space
IST	insulin shock therapy
ITP	idiopathic thrombocytopenic purpura
I.U., IU	International Unit
IUC	intrauterine catheter
IUCP	intrauterine contraceptive device
IUD	intrauterine device
IUFD	intrauterine fetal death
IUGR	intrauterine growth retardation
IUP	intrauterine pregnancy
IUTP	intrauterine term pregnancy
IV	intravenous(ly)
IVC	inferior vena cava, intravenous cholangiogram
IVD	intervertebral disc
IVP	intravenous pyelogram
IVPB	intravenous piggy back
IVU	intravenous urogram

J

J	joint
J-P	Jackson Pratt drain
JRA	juvenile rheumatoid arthritis
jt.	joint
JVP	jugular venous pulse

K

K	potassium, kidney
KC1	potassium chloride
Kcal.	Kilocalorie, calorie
Kg., kg.	kilogram
KJ, K-J	knee jerk
KK	knee kick
17 KS	17 keto steroids

KUB	kidney, ureter, bladder (X-rays)
KVO	keep vein open

L

L	left, liver, liter, lower, light, lumbar
L2,L3	second, third lumbar vertebrae
LA	left antrum
lab.	laboratory
lac.	laceration
lacr.	lacrimal
lact.	lactic
LAD	left anterior descending coronary artery
L&D	labor and delivery
LAE	left atrial enlargement
lam.	laminectomy
lap.	laparotomy
lat.	lateral
LAVH	laparoscopic assisted vaginal hysterectomy
lax	laxative
lb.	pound
LB	large bowel
LBBB	left bundle branch block
LBP	lower back pain
LBW	low birth weight
LCA	left coronary artery
L.D.	lethal dose
LDH	lactic dehydrogenase
LDL	low density lipids
LE	lupus erythematosus
L.E.	lower extremities
leuc.	leukocytes
LF	low forceps, low flap
LFA	left frontoanterior
LFD	low forceps delivery
LFP	left frontoposterior
LFT	left frontotransverse, liver function test
lg	large, leg
LGA	large for gestational age
LGV	lymphogranuloma venereum
LH	luteinizing hormone
LHT	left hypertrophia
LICS	left intercostal space
lig.	ligament
LIH	left inguinal hernia

JD.MD maintains a complete roster of highly qualified health-care experts. JD.MD handles the medical or dental side of your malpractice case, leaving you to do what you do best...

☎ 800-225-JDMD or e-✉ information@jdmd.com

Medical Abbreviations Glossary

liq.	liquid
LKS	liver, kidneys, spleen
LL	lower lid
LLE	left lower extremity
LLG	left lateral gaze
LLL	left lower lobe
LLQ	left lower quadrant
LMA	left mentoanterior
LMD	family doctor
l/min	liter per minute
LML	left mediolateral
LMP	left mentoposterior, last menstrual period
LMT	left mentotransverse
L.N.	lymph node
LNMP	last normal menstrual period
LOA	left occiput anterior
L.O.C.	loss of consciousness, level of consciousness, laxative of choice
LOM	left otitis media
LOP	left occipital posterior
LOS	length of stay
LOT	left occiput anterior
LP	lumbar puncture, light perception
lpf	low power field
LPN	licensed practical nurse
LR	labor room, lateral rectus, light reflex
LRQ	lower right quadrant
Ls.	loose
L.S.	lumbosacral
LSA	lateral sacrum anterior
LSB	left sternal border
LSCS	lower segment Cesarean section
LSK	liver, spleen, kidneys
LSO	left salpingo-oophorectomy
LSP	left sacrum posterior
LST	left sacrum transverse
Lt.	left, light
LTCS	low transverse Cesarean section
LUE	left upper extremity
LUL	left upper lobe
LUQ	left upper quadrant
LV	left ventricle
LVEDP	left ventricular end diastolic pressure
LVF	left ventricular failure

LVH	left ventricular hypertrophy
L & W	living and well
LWCT	Lee-White Clotting Time, coagulation time
Lymphs	lymphocytes
lytes	electrolytes

M

m.	minim
m,M	married, male, mother, murmur, meter mass, molar
MA	mental age
macro.	macrocytic, macroscopic
MAP	mean arterial pressure
max.	maximum, maxillary
MBC	maximum breathing capacity
mcg.	microgram
MCH	mean corpuscular hemoglobin
MCHC	mean corpuscular hemoglobin concentration
MCL	midclavicular line
MCP	metacarpophalangeal joint
MCV	mean corpuscular volume
MD	muscular dystrophy
MDI	metered dose inhaler
Mdnt.	midnight
ME	middle ear, medical examiner
MEC	medical emergency clinic
Med.	medicine
MEq./L	milliequivalents per liter
Mets.	metastasis
mg.	milligram
Mg.	magnesium
MG	myasthenia gravis
mg/dl	milligrams per deciliter
mg.%	milligrams per 100 cc
m.g.r.	murmurs, gallops, or rubs
MH	marital history
MI	myocardial infarction, mitral insufficiency
micro	microcytic, microscopic
MICU	medical intensive care unit
min	minute
Mitr.I	mitral insufficiency
ml.	milliliter
MLF	medial longitudinal fasciculus

JD.MD is Service...

☎ 800-225-JDMD or e-✉ information@jdmd.com

Medical Abbreviations Glossary

mm	millimeter
mm.	muscles
MM	mucous membrane
MMPI	Minnesota Multiphasic Personality Inventory
Mn.	manganese, midnight
mod	moderate
MOM	milk of magnesia
mono.	monocyte
MP	metacarpophalangea, metacarpophalangeal
MPA	malpractice attorney
MR	medial rectus, mental retardation, mitral regurgitation
MRI	magnetic resonance imaging
MRM	modified radical mastectomy
ms	mitral stenosis
Ms	murmurs
MS	mitral stenosis, multiple sclerosis, morphine sulfate
MSL	midsternal line
mss	massage
MT	metacarpophalangeal (joint)
M.T.	muscles and tendons
MVA	motor vehicle accident
MVP	mitral valve prolapse
MVR	mitral valve replacement
MW	maximum voluntary ventilation

N

n.	nerve
N2	nitrogen
N2O	nitrous oxide (anesthetic)
Na	sodium
NaCl	sodium chloride
NAD	no apparent distress
nb	note well
NB	newborn
NBM	nothing by mouth
NBS	normal bowel sounds, normal breath sounds
NED	no evidence of disease
neg.	negative
NER	no evidence of recurrence
NERD	no evidence of recurrent disease
Neur.	Neurology

NG	nasogastric tube
NI	no insurance
NIC	neonatal intensive care
NICU	neonatal intensive care unit
NIDDM	noninsulin dependent diabetes mellitus
NKA	no known allergies
NM	neuromuscular
NMR	nuclear magnetic resonance
noct.	nocturnal
NOS	not otherwise specified
NP	neuropsychiatric
N.P.	Neuropsychiatry
NPH	NPH insulin (Neutral Protamine Zinc)
NPN	nonprotein nitrogen
NPO	nothing by mouth
Ns.	nerves
N.S.	nervous system
NSA	no significant abnormality
NSAID	nonsteriodal anti-inflammatory drug
NSD	normal spontaneous delivery
NSR	normal sinus rhythm
NST	non-stress test
N&V	nausea and vomiting
NS	Neurosurgery
NSVD	normal spontaneous vaginal delivery
NTG	nitroglycerine
NTP	normal temperature and pressure
nullip	never gave birth
NVD	nausea, vomiting, diarrhea
N&W	normal and well
NWB	non-weight bearing
NYD	not yet diagnosed

O

o	none, without
O	oral
O2	oxygen
O2 cap.	oxygen capacity
O2 sat.	oxygen saturation
OA	osteoarthritis
OB, OBG	Obstetrics
OB/GYN	Obstetrics and Gynecology
Obs	observation
OBS	organic brain syndrome
OCC.	occipital, occasional
OD	right eye
O/E	on examination

JD.MD takes the burden of finding a qualified medical or dental expert off your shoulders.
Using JD.MD's resources lets you concentrate on your case, not on finding an expert.

☎ 800-225-JDMD or e-✉ information@jdmd.com

Medical Abbreviations Glossary

OH	occupational history
17 OH	17 hydroxy steroid
OHD	organic heart disease
oint.	ointment
O.M.	otitis media
OMS	organic mental syndrome
OOB	out of bed
Op.	operation
OPC	outpatient clinic
OPD	outpatient department
Ophth.	Ophthalmology
OR	operating room, open reduction
OR-IF	open reduction with internal fixation
ORT	operating room technician
Ortho.	Orthopaedic Surgery
os	opening, mouth, bone
OS	left eye
ot.	ear
Oto	Otolaryngology
OTC	over-the-counter (pharmaceuticals)
O.T.	occupational therapy, old tuberculin
OU	both eyes
OV	office visit
oz.	ounce

P

P	after, phosphorus pulse
P2	pulmonic second heart sound
PA	physician's assistant
P-A	posteroanterior
p & a	percussion and auscultation
PAC	premature atrial, auricular contraction
PaCO2	arterial carbon dioxide tension pressure
PACU	post anesthesia care unit
PAF	paroxysmal atrial fibrillation
palp.	palpate, palpated, palpable
PaO2	alveolar oxygen pressure
Pap	Papanicolaou test (pap smear)
Para	prior births, paraplegic
PARU	post anesthesia recovery unit
PAS	pulmonary artery systolic pressure
PAT	pregnancy at term, paroxysm atrial tachycardia
Path.	Pathology
PA view	posterioranterior view on x-ray
Pb	lead
PB	peripheral blood

PBI	protein bound iodine
p/c., p.c.	after meals
PCL	posterior cruciate ligament
PCO2	carbon dioxide concentration
PCV	packed cell volume (of blood)
PD	pupillary distance, peritoneal dialysis
PDA	patent ductus arteriosus
pdr.	powder
PDR	Physician's Desk Reference
PDN	private duty nurse
PE	physical examination, pulmonary embolism
Ped.	Pediatrics
PEEP	positive end expiratory pressure
PEG	pneumoencephalogram
PEN	Penicillin
PERRLA	pupils equal, round, reactive to light and accommodation (normal)
PET	positron emission tomography
PF	push fluids
PFC	persistent fetal circulation
PFT	pulmonary function test
pH	hydrogen ion concentration
PH	past history
pharm	pharmacy
PHYS.	physical, physiology
PI	present illness, pulmonary insufficiency
PICA	posterior inferior coronary artery
PICU	pulmonary intensive care unit
PID	pelvic inflammatory disease
PIP	proximal interphalangeal
Pit.	Pitocin
PKU	phenylkentonuria
Plac.	placenta
plts.	platelets
PM	petit mal
P.M.	afternoon, post-mortem
PMH	past medical history
PMN	polymorphonuclear (leukocytes)
PM&R	Physical Medicine and Rehabilitation
PN	poorly nourished, practical nurse
P&N	Psychiatry and Neurology
PNC	prenatal clinic, premature nodal contraction
PND	paroxysmal nocturnal dyspnea, post nasal drip
pneu.	pneumo, pneumonia

The quality of our service will save you time & effort.

☎ 800-225-JDMD or e-☒ information@jdmd.com

Medical Abbreviations Glossary

PNI	peripheral nerve injury
PNX	pneumothorax
p.o.	by mouth
PO2	oxygen pressure (or tension)
POC	product of conception
p.o.d.	postoperative day
polys	polymorphonuclear leukocytes
POMR	problem-oriented medical record
poplit.	popliteal
pos.	positive
post.	posterior
POSTOP.	postoperative
pot. or potass.	potassium
pp	post partum, post prandial
PPBS	post prandial blood sugar
PPD	purified protein derivative
PPF	protein plasma fractional
PPH	post partum hemorrhage
ppm	parts per million
PPPG	post prandial plasma glucose
p.r.	per rectum
PR	Proctology
PRBC	packed red blood cells
PRE	progressive resistive exercise
prem	premature
pre-op	preoperative
prep.	prepare for
primip.	first pregnancy
p.r.m.	according to circumstances
p.r.n., PRN	as often as necessary
prod.	productive
Prog.	prognosis
PROM	passive range of motion, premature rupture of membranes
pron.	pronator, pronation
pros.	prostate, prostatic
prosth.	prosthesis
prot.	protein, Protestant
pro.time	prothrombin time
PS	pulmonary stenosis, psychotic, Plastic Surgery
PSH	past surgical history
psi	pounds per square inch
PSMA	progressive spinal muscular atrophy
Psych.	Psychiatry
pt., Pt.	patient

PT	physical therapy
P.T.	physical therapy, posterior tibial artery pulse
PTA	prior to admission, percutaneous transluminal angioplasty
PTB	patellar tendon bearing
PTCA	percutaneous transvenous coronary angioplasty (balloon angioplasty)
PU	pregnancy urine
PUD	peptic ulcer disease
PUPPP	pruritic urticarial papules & plaques of pregnancy
PV	plasma volume, peripheral vascular
PVC	premature ventricular contraction
PVD	peripheral vascular disease
PVR	pulmonary vascular resistance
PVT	previous trouble
PWB%	partial weight bearing with percent
Px, PX	physical examination

Q

q	every
q.d.	every day
q.h.	every hour
q2H	every two hours
q4H	every four hours
q.i.d.	four times a day
q.i.w.	four times a week
q.l.	as much as desired
qn, q.n.	every night
q.n.s., QNS	quantity not sufficient
q.o.d.	every other day
q.o.n.	every other night
q.p.	as much as you please
q.q., Q.Q.	each, every
q.q.h.	every four hours
q.s.	quantity, sufficient
qt.	quart
qts.	drops
quad.	quadriplegic
quant.	quantitative or quantity
q.v.	as much as you wish
q.w.	every week

We screen our medical and dental experts to maintain the high levels of professionalism and credibility you expect.

☎ 800-225-JDMD or e-✉ information@jdmd.com

Medical Abbreviations Glossary

R

r., R	right, rectal, roentgen, x-ray
R.	rub, rectal temperature
Ra	radium
RA	rheumatoid arthritis, right atrium
rad.	radial
RAI	radioactive iodine
r.a.m.	rapid alternating movements
R.A.S.	right arm sitting
RAtx	radiation therapy
RBBB	right bundle branch block
rbc/RBC	red blood cell, red blood count
RCA	right coronary artery
RCS	reticulum cell sarcoma
RCU	respiratory care unit
RD	respiratory distress, reaction to degeneration
RDS	respiratory distress syndrome
RE	reconditioning exercise
rect.	rectum, rectal (ly), rectus muscle
reg.	regular
rehab.	rehabilitation
resp.	respiratory, respirations
RF	rheumatic fever
RFA	right frontoanterior
RFP	right frontoposterior
RFT	right frontotransverse
Rh, Rh.	rhesus blood factor
RHI	right hyperphoria
RHD	rheumatic heart disease
RHF	right heart failure
RHT	right hypertrophia
RIH	right inguinal hernia
RLA	Rancho Los Amigo Scale
R to L&A	react to light and accommodation
RLE	right lower extremity
RLF	retrolental fibroplasia
RLL	right lower lobe
RLQ	right lower quadrant
RMA	right mentoanterior
RML	right mediolateral, right middle lobe
RMP	right mentoposterior
RMSF	Rocky Mountain Spotted Fever
RMT	right mentotransverse
RNA	ribonucleic acid
RO, R/O	rule out

ROA	right occipital anterior
ROM	range of motion, rupture of membranes, right otitis media
ROP	right occipital posterior
ROS	review of systems
ROT	right occipital transverse
RP	retrograde pyelogram
RQ	respiratory quotient
RR	recovery room
RRE, RR&E	round, regular, and equal
RSO	right salpingo-oophorectomy
RSA	right sacrum anterior
RSD	reflex sympathetic dystrophy
RSP	right sacrum posterior
RSR	regular sinus rhythm
RST	right sacrum transverse
Rt.	right
RT	radiation therapy, respiratory therapy
RTC	return to clinic
RUC	regular uterine contraction
RUE	right upper extremity
RUL	right upper lobe
RUQ	right upper quadrant
RV	residual volume
RVH	right ventricular hypertrophy
Rx	therapy, prescription

S

s	without
S	sensation, sensitive, serum
Sa.	Saline
S&A	sugar and acetone
SAH	systemic arterial hypertension
SaO2	arterial oxygen saturation
SB	stillborn
SBE	subacute bacterial endocarditis
SBFT	small bowel follow through (x-ray)
SBO	small bowel obstruction
s.c.	subcutaneous(ly)
SC	sickle cell
SCC	sickle cell crisis
SCD	sudden cardiac death
schiz	schizophrenia
SCU	special care unit
sec	second
sed. rate	erythrocyte sedimentation rate

JD.MD maintains an extensive roster of U.S. and Canadian experts in all medical and dental specialties and geographic locations.

☎ 800-225-JDMD or e-✉ information@jdmd.com

Medical Abbreviations Glossary

sem. ves	seminal vesicles
Sens.	sensory, sensation
sep.	separated
Sept. AB	septic abortion
Serol.	serology, serological test
SGA	small for gestational age
s.gl.	without correction (without glasses)
SGOT,SGO-T	serum glutamic oxalacetic transaminase
SH	social history, serum hepatitis
SI	sacroiliac joint, stroke index
sib.	sibling
SICU	surgical intensive care unit
SIDS	sudden infant death syndrome
skel.	skeletal
Sl.	slightly
SL	under the tongue
SLE	systemic lupus erythematosus
SLR	straight leg raising
sm	small
SMA-14	routine admission chemistry
SNS	sympathetic nervous system
SO	superior oblique
SO4	sulfate
S.O.A.P.	subjective, objective assessment plan
SOB	shortness of breath
sod.	sodium
Sol.	solution
sono.	sonogram
S.O.S.	repeat once if urgent
sp.	spine, spinal
S/P	status post (previous condition)
sp.cd.	spinal cord
spec.	specimen
sp.fl.	spinal fluid
spg.	sponge
sp.gr	specific gravity
sp&H	speech and hearing
spin.	spine, spinal
spont.	spontaneous
SR	system review, superior rectus muscle, sedimentation rate, stimulus response
SROM	spontaneous rupture of membranes
SS	social service
SSE	soap suds enema
st	stage (of disease)
st.	stomach
Staph, Staph.	staphylococcus

stat.,STAT	immediately
STD	sexually transmitted disease
stom, st.	stomach
strep.	streptococcus
S.T.S.	serological test for syphilis
subcut.	subcutaneous
subling.	sublingual
sulf.	sulfate
sup.	superior
supin.	supination
supp	suppository
surg.	surgery, surgical
SVC	superior vena cava
SVD	spontaneous vaginal delivery
SVR	systemic vascular resistance
SVT	supra ventricular tachycardia
SWD	short wave diathermy
Sx	symptoms
sys.	system
syst.	systolic

T

T3	triodothyronine
T4	total serum thyroxine
TA	tendon Achilles
T&A	tonsils and adenoids, tonsillectomy and adenoidectomy
T&C	type and crossmatch
tab.	tablet
TAB	therapeutic abortion
TAH	total abdominal hysterectomy
T.A.T.	tetanus antitoxin
TB	tuberculosis
TBI	total body irradiation
TBLC	term birth living child
tbsp.	tablespoon
TCDB	turn, cough, deep breathe
TEE	transesophageal echocardiography
temp	temperature
TENS	transient electric nerve stimulation
TESD	total end systolic diameter
T.F.	tuning fork
T of F	tetralogy of Fallot
TGA	transposition great vessels
THERAP.	therapy, therapeutic
thor.	thorax, thoracic
THR	total hip replacement

Expedited service is available on all medical and dental malpractice case evaluations and experts' reports.
For complete details on fees, contact us, and ask for our free Attorney Information Packet.

☎ 800-225-JDMD or e-✉ information@jdmd.com

Medical Abbreviations Glossary

TI	tricuspid insufficiency
TIA	transient ischemic shock, transient ischemic attack
t.i.d.	three times a day
TIP	terminal interphalangeal (joint)
TIUP	term intrauterine pregnancy
t.i.w.	three times per week
TJ	triceps reflex
TKR	total knee replacement
TLC	tender loving care, total lung capacity
T.M.	tympanum membrani (ear drum)
TMJ	temporomandibular joint
TNI	total nodal irradiation
TNM	tumor, nodes, and metastases
TO	telephone order
TOA	tubo-ovarian abscess
to AA	to affected areas
T, OD	tension, right eye
TORCH (titer)	toxoplamosis others (hepatitis, beta strep, flu, mumps, etc.) rubella, cytomegalovirus (CMV), herpes virus II
TP	term pregnancy
TPA	thrombo proteolytic activity
TPN	total parenteral nutrition
TPR	temperature, pulse, respiration
tr	trace
trach	tracheostomy
TS	tricuspid stenosis
TSH	thyroid stimulating hormone
tsp.	teaspoon
TSS	toxic shock syndrome
T,T.	temperature, thoracic
TTI	total thromboplastin index
TTP	thrombotic thrombocytopenia purpura
T-Tube	cholangiogram
TUR	transurethral resection
TURB	transurethral resection of the bladder
TURP	transurethral resection of the prostate
TV	tidal volume
TVH	total vaginal hysterectomy
TVR	tricuspid valve replacement
Tx	treatment, traction

U

U.	unit

U/A	urinalysis
UC	uterine contractions
UCD	usual childhood diseases
UCG	urinary chorionic gonadotropin
UCHD	usual childhood diseases
UG	upward gaze
UGI	upper gastrointestinal series (x-rays), upper gastrointestinal tract
UL	upper lid
uln	ulnar
ULQ	upper left quadrant
ung.	ointment
unilat.	unilateral
u/o	under observation for, urine output
Ur.	urine
URD	upper respiratory disease
URI	upper respiratory infection
Urol.	Urology
URQ	upper right quadrant
u/s, US	ultrasound
USI	urinary stress incontinence
USN	ultrasonic nebulizer
USP.	United States Pharmacy
USPHA	United States Public Health Administration
ut.	uterus, uterine
UTI	urinary tract infection
UVL	ultraviolet light

V

V	vein
VA	visual acuity
vag	vagina, vaginal
VC, (vit.cap)	vital capacity
VCS	vasoconstrictor substance
VCU	voiding cystourethrogram
Vd	void
VD	venereal disease
VDRL	blood test for syphilis
vent.	ventilator
vert.	vertical
VF	visual fields, ventricular fibrillation
VG	vein graft
VHD	valvular heart disease
VI	volume index
V.I.	vaginal irrigation
Via	by way of

Medical Abbreviations Glossary

VIPS	voluntary interruption of pregnancy and sterilization service
vit.	vitamin
VLDL	very low density lipoproteins
VM	vestibular membrane
VN	visiting nurse
VO	verbal order
VOD	vision right eye
vol	volume
VOS	vision left eye
VP	venous pressure
VPC	ventricular premature contraction
VS, V.S.	vital signs
VSA	vital signs absent
VSD	ventricular septal defect
VSS	vital signs stable
VT, V Tach	ventricular tachycardia
V & T	volume and tension (pulse)
VTX	vertex
Vx.	vertex presentation

W

W	widowed, white
W/A	while awake
Wass.	Wasserman
WB	whole blood
wbc, WBC	white blood cells, white blood count
W/C, wh.ch.	wheelchair
WBT	weight bearing to tolerance
WDWN	well developed, well nourished
WE	wide excision
WF	white female
wk	week
WM	white male
w/n	within
WN	well nourished
WNL	within normal limits
WP	whirlpool
wt.	weight
w/u	workup

X

x	times
X	exophoria distance
XT	exotrophia distance

Y

y.o.	years old
yrs.	years

Index

A

AARS (Adolescent Anger Rating Scale), 144
Ablon, J. S., 96
Acceptance, fostering, 51–54
Accidental meetings with clients, 56
Accountability, professional, 158
Acetylcholine, 195
Achievement tests, 131, 140, 147–148
Action potential, 195
Active listening, 33–34, 45
Active metabolites, 193
Active phase (schizophrenia), 113
ADHD. *See* Attention-deficit/hyperactivity disorder
Adjustment disorders, 123
Adler, Alfred, 85
Administration (of medicines), 191, 193–195
Administrative director, 43
Adolescent Anger Rating Scale (AARS), 144
Adolescents, 37. *See also* Children
Adults, helping skills applied to, 37
Aggressive behavior, 52
Agnosia, 116
Agonists, 196, 204
Agoraphobia, 106, 163
Agranulocytosis, 198
Alcohol abuse and dependence, 115, 165–168
Alogia, 113
Alprazolam, 203
Alsobrook, J. M., 28
Alzheimer's Disease, 50, 117
American Academy of Family Physicians, 95
American Academy of Pediatrics, 216
American Association of Pastoral Counselors, 243

American Occupational Therapy Association (AOTA), 247
American Psychiatric Association (APA), 86, 105, 157
American Psychological Association (APA), 61–63, 86, 99, 100
American Therapeutic Recreation Association, 247–248
Amitriptyline, 201
Amnesia, dissociative, 120
Amnestic disorders, 117
Amphetamine, 204
Animal magnetism, 170
Anorexia nervosa, 109–110
Antagonists, 196
Anterior cingulotomy, 171
Anterograde amnesia, 117
Antianxiety medications, 202
Anticholinergic side effects, 198
Antidepressant medications, 193–194, 201–203
Antipsychotic drugs, 168, 176, 202
Antipsychotic medications, 203–204
Antisocial personality disorder, 123
Anxiety, adjustment disorder with, 123
Anxiety disorders, 106–108, 162–165
Anxiolytic medications, 203
AOTA (American Occupational Therapy Association), 247
APA. *See* American Psychiatric Association; American Psychological Association
APA Ethics Code. *See* "Ethical Standards of Psychologists and Code of Conduct"
Aphasia, 116
Aripiprazone, 204
The Art of Helping in the 21st Century (Robert Carkhuff), 29, 32

Art therapists, 244–245
Asperger's disorder, 125
Assessment. *See* Psychological assessment(s)
Asylums, 83–84, 87
Attachment, 214–215
Attending, 33–34
Attention and concentration tasks, 131
Attention and concentration tests, 138–139, 145
Attention-deficit/hyperactivity disorder (ADHD), 124, 226, 228–230
Attitudes, societal, 90–91
Atypical antipsychotics, 204
Auditory hallucinations, 53, 112
Authority, lines of, 43
Autistic disorder, 125
Avoidance behavior, 214
Axis I, 96, 106
Axis II, 106, 124
Axis III, 106
Axis IV, 106

B
BAI. *See* Beck Anxiety Inventory
Bayley Scales of Infant Development— Second Edition (BSID–II), 147
BCSWs (board-certified social workers), 43
BDI–II. *See* Beck Depression Inventory—II
Beck, Aaron, 92, 161–162
Beck Anxiety Inventory (BAI), 140–141
Beck Depression Inventory—II (BDI–II), 131, 140
Beery–Buktenica Developmental Test of Visual Motor Integration—Fourth Edition (VMI), 149
Behavioral coping strategies, 163
Behavioral marital therapy, 166
Behavioral redirection, 160–161
Behavioral tests, 144, 151–152
Behavioral therapy, 227
Behavior modification programs, 168
Behavior therapy, 85
Bender Visual–Motor Gestalt Test (BG), 131, 141–142
Benzodiazepines, 88, 194
BG. *See* Bender Visual–Motor Gestalt Test
Bilingual education, 221
Bipolar I disorder, 111, 160
Bipolar II disorder, 111, 160
Bipolar mood disorders, 110, 160–161
Birch, John, 82
Blood–brain barrier, 194
Bloodletting, 83, 84
Board-certified social workers (BCSWs), 43
Body dysmorphic disorder, 119
Body piercings, 42
Borderline personality disorder, 123

Bornstein, R. F., 93
Boston Psychopathic Asylum, 87
Boundaries, professional, 69–71
Brain surgery, 86–87
Brand names (of medicine), 189–191
Breathing-related sleep disorder, 122
Briefer therapies, 92, 98
Brief psychotic disorders, 114
Bright light therapy, 174
BSID–II (Bayley Scales of Infant Development—Second Edition), 147
Bulimia nervosa, 109, 110
Bupropion, 203
Buspirone, 203

C
California, 67
California Verbal Learning Test—Second Edition (CVLT–2), 143
Campbell, N. R., 231
Carbamazepine, 204
CARE (College ADHD Response Evaluation), 152
Careers. *See* Mental health professions
Carkhuff, Robert, 29–34
Case managers, 248–249
CAT. *See* Creative arts therapist
Catatonic behavior, disorganized and, 113
Catatonic stupor, 113
CBCL/6-18 (Child Behavior Checklist), 152
CBT. *See* Cognitive–behavioral therapy
Charge nurse, 43
Chemical name (of medicine), 189
Child abuse, discussing and reporting suspected, 66–67
Child Behavior Checklist (CBCL/6-18), 152
Childhood disintegrative disorder, 125
Childhood disorders, 224–231
    externalizing disorders, 228–231
    internalizing disorders, 227–228
Children, 209–234
    aggressive behavior in, 52
    attachment behavior in, toward therapist, 54
    building rapport with, 216–217, 222–223
    in context of family, 223
    development of motor/cognitive/ language skills in, 210, 213–214, 217, 220–221
    disorders usually first diagnosed in, 124–126
    helping skills applied to, 36–37
    legal and ethical issues in working with, 52, 232
    obligation to protect, 68–69
    preschool, 210–217
    school-age, 217–223

social and emotional development in, 214–216, 221–222
treatment settings for, 231–232
Chlordiazepoxide, 203
Chlorpromazine, 199, 203
Cingulotomy, anterior, 171
Circadian rhythm sleep disorder, 122
CISD. *See* Critical Incident Stress Debriefing
Citalopam, 203
Client(s)
accidental offsite meetings with, 56
attachment of, to therapist, 53–54
first session with, 48–49
fostering acceptance with, 51–54
greeting former, 65
history of aggressive behavior in, 52
multiple relationships with, 69–71
protecting privacy of, 65
starting/maintaining conversation with, 49–51
Client-Centered Therapy (Carl Rogers), 86
Client confidentiality. *See* Confidentiality
Clinical psychologists, 239
Clozapine, 204
"The Cochran Collaboration," 95
The COGNISTAT, 137–138
Cognitive–behavioral coping-skills therapy, 166
Cognitive–behavioral therapy (CBT), 160–161, 163–165, 227
Cognitive development, 210–212, 218–220
Cognitive disorders, 116–117
Cognitive restructuring, 160–161
Cognitive tests. *See* Intellectual and cognitive tests
Cognitive therapies, 92
College ADHD Response Evaluation (CARE), 152
Communications disorders, 125–126, 225
Communication skills, 29–30, 221–222
Community care, 88–90
Community Mental Health Centers Act of 1963, 88, 90
Community reinforcement, 165
Competence, professional, 74–75
Compulsions, 107
Concentration tests. *See* Attention and concentration tests
Conduct disorder, 125, 228
Confidentiality, 45–46, 49, 63–72
in assessment, 73
and informed consent, 71–72
legitimate breaches of, 67–69
and professional boundaries, 69–71
Confrontation, 55
Conners Rating Scales—Revised (CRS–R), 132, 152
Consent, informed, 71–72, 232

Construct validity, 133–134
Consultants, 43–44
Content, poverty of, 113
Content validity, 133
Continuous Performance Test—Second Edition (CPT–II), 131, 145
Contracts, practicum, 14–15, 18–19
Conversation, starting and maintaining, 49–51
Conversion disorder, 119
Coping-skills therapy, cognitive–behavioral, 166
Coping strategies, behavioral, 163
Counseling psychologists, 239
Counselors, 242–243
Coworkers
diversity in, 10–13
relationships with, 9–10
CPT (current procedural terminology), 99
CPT–II. *See* Continuous Performance Test—Second Edition
Creative arts therapist (CAT), 43, 244–247
Crisis intervention, 91
Criterion validity, 133
Critical Incident Stress Debriefing (CISD), 91–92
CRS–R. *See* Conners Rating Scales—Revised
Cultural differences, 12–13
Current procedural terminology (CPT), 99
Cut scores (cutoff scores), 134
CVLT–2 (California Verbal Learning Test—Second Edition), 143

D
Dance therapists, 245
Decision making, ethical, 62–63
Decision trees, 46
DeLeon, Patrick, 97–98
Delirium, 116
Delusional disorders, 114
Delusional thinking, 52–53
Delusion of persecution, 112
Delusion of reference, 112
Dementia, 116–117
Dementia Rating Scale—2 (DRS–2), 138
Dendrites, 192
Depersonalization disorder, 120
Depressed mood, adjustment disorder with, 123
Depression, 110–112, 161–162
Desensitization, systematic, 227
Desipramine, 201
Dextroamphetamine, 204
Diagnostic and Statistic Manual of Mental Disorders, Fourth Edition (DSM–IV), 96, 105–106, 113, 114, 118, 123, 124, 126, 157, 158, 165, 173, 241
Diazepam, 203

Disclose, duty to, 68
Discrepancy models, 224
Disorganized and catatonic behavior, 113
Disorganized speech and thinking, 112–113
Dissociative amnesia, 120
Dissociative disorders, 120
Dissociative fugue, 120
Dissociative identity disorder, 120
Divalproex, 204
Diversity (in work environment), 10–13
Dix, Dorothea, 84
Dopamine, 195, 204
Dopamine theory of schizophrenia, 113–114
Down Syndrome, 118
Drama therapists, 245
Dress, appropriate, 42
DRS–2 (Dementia Rating Scale—2), 138
DSM–IV. See Diagnostic and Statistic Manual of
     Mental Disorders, Fourth Edition
Duty to disclose, 68
Duty to inform, 67–68
Duty to warn, 67, 232
Dyslexia, 224
Dyssomnias, 121–122
Dysthymic disorder, 111

E
Eating disorders, 109–110
ECT. See Electroconvulsive therapy
Efficacy studies, 92–93
Egan, Gerard, 33, 34
Electroconvulsive therapy (ECT), 82, 159,
     171–173, 176
Ellis, Albert, 92
EMDR. See Eye Movement Desensitization
     Response
Empathy, 30, 34–36
Empirically supported treatments
     for alcohol abuse and dependence,
          165–168
     for anxiety disorders, 162–165
     for mood disorders, 160–162
     for schizophrenia, 168–169
Empirically validated therapies, 94
Encopresis, 126
End organs, 195
Enuresis, 126
EOWPVT–2000 (Expressive One-Word
     Picture Vocabulary Test), 142
Escitalopram, 203
Establishing yourself (in the practicum),
     6–8
Ethical issue(s), 61–78. See also
     Confidentiality
     assessment as, 72–74
     boundary violations as, 69–71
     competence as, 74–75

duty to warn/protect/disclose as, 67–69
and ethical decision making, 62–63
informed consent as, 71–72
multiple roles as, 69–71
and reporting, 77
in supervision of practicum students,
     75–77
in working with children, 232
"Ethical Standards of Psychologists and Code
     of Conduct," x, 8, 61–63
Ethics codes, x
Ethnic differences, 12
Evidence-based treatment(s), 95–98,
     158–159
Exercise therapy, 174–176
Exhibitionism, 121
Exposure and ritual/response prevention
     (EX/RP), 164
Exposure-based procedures/treatments, 163,
     164
Expressed emotion, theory of, 114
Expressive One-Word Picture Vocabulary
     Test (EOWPVT–2000), 142
Expressive therapy, 244
EX/RP (exposure and ritual/response
     prevention), 164
Externalizing disorders (in children), 226,
     228–231
Extrapyramidal side effects, 197–198
Eye contact, 50, 217
Eye Movement Desensitization Response
     (EMDR), 164

F
Face validity, 133
Factitious disorders, 119–120
Family context, children in, 223
Family programs, structured, 169
FDA. See Food and Drug Administration
Fear hierarchy, 227
Feedback, receiving and giving, 56, 76
Fetishism, 121
Field placement programs, 57–58
Fine motor control, development of, 210–
     212, 217–220
First impressions, 41–42
Fixed batteries, 132
Flat affect, 113
Flexible batteries, 132
Fluoxetine, 190, 193–194, 196, 202
Food and Drug Administration (FDA), 190,
     191, 201, 204
Fragile X syndrome, 118
Freeman, Walter, 86, 170–171
Freud, Sigmund, 85, 187
Friends' Asylum, 84
Frotteurism, 121

Full battery assessments, 129–130, 135
Future goals, 4

G
GAD. *See* Generalized anxiety disorder
Gambling, pathological, 122
Garfield, S. L., 94
Gender identity disorder, 121
Gender role expectations, 11–12
Generalized anxiety disorder (GAD), 108, 163–164
Generic medicines, 191–192
Generic name (of medicine), 189
Genuineness, 30
Geriatric clients. *See* Older adults
Goals, future, 4

H
Hallucinations, 53, 112
Halstead–Reitan Neuropsychological Test Composite Battery, 151
Hamilton Depression Inventory (HDI), 141
Health-engendering persons (HEPs), 28
Health Insurance Portability and Accountability Act of 2003 (HIPAA), 45
"Health" treatments, 93–97
Hedges, M., 98
Helping and Human Relations (Robert Carkhuff), 30
Helping relationships, 23–38
    and basic helping skills, 29–30
    checklist for, 28–29
    and definition of helping, 24–25
    discriminating between helpful and unhelpful responses in, 30–31
    guidelines for success in, 25–26
    practice exercises, 31–36
    and stages of life, 36–38
    unhelpful vs., 27–28
HEPs (health-engendering persons), 28
Herbal medicines, 200–201
High-potency antipsychotics, 203–204
HIPAA (Health Insurance Portability and Accountability Act of 2003), 45
History of treatment of mental illness, 81–101
    in ancient and medieval times, 81–82
    behavior therapy, 85
    brain surgery, 86–87
    briefer therapies, 92
    community care, 88–90
    crisis intervention, 91
    Critical Incident Stress Debriefing (CISD), 91–92
    and current trends in psychiatric treatment, 97–100
    efficacy studies, 92–93

    in 18th-century United States, 82–83
    empirically validated therapies, 94
    evidence-based treatment, 95–97
    and expansion of professional roles, 85–86
    "health" treatments, 93–97
    hydrotherapy, 87
    insulin coma therapy, 87
    manual-based treatments, 94–95
    in 19th-century United States, 83–84
    psychoanalysis, 85
    psychotropic medications, 88
    self-help therapies, 90–91
Histrionic personality disorder, 123
House–Tree–Person Technique (H-T-P), 149
Huntington's disease, 117
Hydrotherapy, 87
Hypersomnia, 122
Hypertension, 202
Hypnotherapy, 170
Hypomania, 111

I
ICD (*Manual of the International Statistical Classification of Diseases, Injuries, and Causes of Death*), 105
ILS (Independent Living Scales), 144
IM (intramuscular) administration, 194
Imipramine, 193–194, 199, 201
Impressions, first, 41–42
Impulse control disorders, 122
Independent Living Scales (ILS), 144
Inducers, 114
Inform, duty to, 67–68
Information processing, 220
Informed consent, 71–72, 232
Initial assessment, 46
Inpatient practicum settings, 4–5
Insecure/avoidant attachment, 214
Insomnia, 122
Insulin coma therapy, 87
Intellectual and cognitive tasks, 131
Intellectual and cognitive tests, 139–140, 146–147
Intelligent quotient (IQ), 117–118, 126, 131, 139
Intermittent explosive disorder, 122
Internalizing disorders (in children), 226–228
International Federation of Social Workers, 240–241
Interpersonal therapy for depression (IPT), 162
Interviewing
    as assessment, 130
    of clients, 46–47
    for information about future employment, 4

Intoxication, substance, 116
Intramuscular (IM) administration, 194
Intravenous (IV) administration, 194
IPT. *See* Interpersonal therapy for depression
IQ. *See* Intelligent quotient
IV (intravenous) administration, 194

J
Jarvis, Edward, 83
Jet lag, 174
Johnson, Norine G., 99
Journal of the American Medical Association, 95
Jung, Carl, 85

K
Kaufman Assessment Battery for Children—
    Second Edition (KABC–II), 147
Kaufman Brief Intelligence Test (K–BIT),
    139
Kaufman Short Neuropsychological Assess-
    ment Procedure (K–SNAP), 143
K–BIT (Kaufman Brief Intelligence Test),
    139
Kendall, P. C., 94
Kirkbride, Thomas, 84
Kleptomania, 122
Kraus, H. H., 28
K–SNAP (Kaufman Short Neuropsycho-
    logical Assessment Procedure), 143

L
Labeled praise, 229, 230
Language development, 210–213, 218–221
Language tests, 131, 142, 150
Learning disabilities, 220, 221, 224–226
Learning disorders, 125–126
Legal issues, 52, 67–68, 232
Leiter International Performance Scale—
    Revised (Leiter–R), 147
Leucotomy. *See* Lobotomy
Licensed practical nurses (LPNs), 43
Light box therapy, 174
Limited intellectual ability, adults with, 37
Listening, active, 33–34, 45
Lithium carbonate, 160, 204
Liver, 193
LNNB. *See* Luria–Nebraska Neuropsycho-
    logical Battery
Lobotomy (leucotomy), 86, 87, 170–171
Loose associations, 112–113
Loughary, J. W., 28–29
Low-potency antipsychotics, 203
Low self-esteem, 222
LPNs (licensed practical nurses), 43
Luria–Nebraska Neuropsychological Battery
    (LNNB), 132, 142–143, 151
Lyman, R. D., 231

M
Magnetic seizure therapy (MST), 176
Magnetic stimulation, transcranial, 176
Major depressive disorder (MDD), 110–111,
    161–162
Malingering, 119
Managed care, 92, 136
Mania, 204
Manic episodes, 111
Manual-based treatments, 94–95
*Manual of the International Statistical Classifica-
    tion of Diseases, Injuries, and Causes of
    Death* (ICD), 105
MAO (monoamine oxidase), 196
MAOIs. *See* Monoamine oxidase inhibitors
Marci, C., 96
Marital and family therapy, 161
Marital therapy, behavioral, 166
McClean Asylum, 84
MCMI–III (Millon Clinical Multiaxial
    Inventory—III), 148
MDD. *See* Major depressive disorder
"Med checks," 189
Medical abbreviations (list), 252–265
Medical director, 43
Medical treatment, psychiatric treatment as,
    99–100
Medicines (in treatment of mental disorders),
    187–207
    administration and metabolizing of,
        193–195
    antidepressant medications, 201–203
    antipsychotic medications, 203–204
    anxiolytic medications, 203
    development of, 198–199
    generic, 191–192
    herbal, 200–201
    mood stabilizers, 204
    names of, 189–191
    and nerve transmissions, 195–196
    and nervous system, 192
    prescription of appropriate, 205
    psychostimulants, 205
    psychotherapy as alternative to, 206
    side effects of, 197–198
    understanding, 188–189
Memory, 220
Memory tests, 131, 142–143, 150–151
Mental disorders, treatments for, 157–159
Mental health professions, 237–249
    case managers, 248–249
    counselors, 242–243
    creative arts therapists, 244–247
    occupational therapists, 247
    psychiatric nurses, 243–244
    psychiatrists, 239–240
    psychologists, 238–239

recreational therapists, 247–248
social workers, 240–242
Mental retardation, 117–119, 225
Mental Status Examination in Neurology, 137
Mental status exams, 130–131, 137–138
Mesmer, Anton, 170
Mesmerism, 170
MET. *See* Motivational enhancement therapy
Metabolites, 193
Metabolizing (of medicines), 193–195
Methylphenidate, 204
Mild mental retardation, 118
Millon Clinical Multiaxial Inventory—III (MCMI–III), 148
Mini-Mental Status Examination (MMSE), 137
Minnesota Multiphasic Personality Inventory—2 (MMPI–2), 72, 131, 148
Minnesota Multiphasic Personality Inventory—Adolescent (MMPI–A), 148
Minors, duty to inform when dealing with, 67–69
Mirtazapine, 203
MMPI–2. *See* Minnesota Multiphasic Personality Inventory—2
MMPI–A (Minnesota Multiphasic Personality Inventory—Adolescent), 148
MMSE (Mini-Mental Status Examination), 137
Moderate mental retardation, 118
Monitor on Psychology, 99
Moniz, Antonio De Egas, 86
Monoamine oxidase (MAO), 196
Monoamine oxidase inhibitors (MAOIs), 196, 202
Mood and personality tests, 131, 140–141, 148–149
Mood disorders, 110–112, 160–162
Mood stabilizers, 202, 204
Moreno, J. L., 245
Motivational enhancement therapy (MET), 166–167
Motor control, development of, 210–212, 217–220
Motor impairments (in children), 225
MST (magnetic seizure therapy), 176
Multicompetent cognitive–behavioral treatment, 163
Multidisciplinary team, 188
Multiple personality disorder, 120
Multiple roles, 69–71
Munchausen's by proxy, 120
Munchausen's syndrome, 119–120

Music therapists, 246
Mutism, selective, 126

N
Narcissistic personality disorder, 123
Narcolepsy, 122
National Coalition of Arts Therapies Associations, 244
Negative attention, 229
Negative symptoms, 112
Neologisms, 113
Nervous systems, medications and, 192, 195–196
Neuroleptic malignancy syndrome (NMS), 198
Neurons, 192
Neuropsychological tests, 143, 151
Neurotransmitters, 195–196
Newton, M., 28
Nightmare disorder, 122
NMS (neuroleptic malignancy syndrome), 198
Nonjudgmental, being, 45
Nonpsychological tests, 132
Nonverbal behavior, 36–37
Nonverbal cues, 44–45
Norcross, J. C., 98
Norepinephrine, 195
Normative sample (norms), 134
Nurses, psychiatric, 243–244
Nursing director, unit, 43

O
Objective personality testing, 131
Objective tests, 131
Obsessions, 107
Obsessive–compulsive disorder (OCD), 86–87, 107, 108, 164
Occupational therapists, 247
OCD. *See* Obsessive–compulsive disorder
Older adults
access of, to mental health care, 99–100
helping skills applied to, 37–38
Olonzapine, 204
Open-ended questions, asking, 45
Operant conditioning, 85
Operant Conditioning (B. F. Skinner), 86
Oppositional defiant disorder, 124–125, 228
Oral administration, 193–194
Orgasmic disorders, 121
Outpatient practicum settings, 5
Outpatient treatments, 189

P
Pain disorder, 119
Panic attacks, 106
Panic disorder, 106, 163

Paraphilias, 121
Paraphrasing, 45
Parasomnias, 122
Parent–Child Interaction Therapy (PCIT), 229
Parkinson's disease, 117
Paroxetine, 196, 202
Participant-observer, being a, 47–48
Pastoral counselors, 243
Pathological gambling, 122
Patients. *See* Client(s)
PCIT (Parent–Child Interaction Therapy), 229
PDD (pervasive developmental disorders), 226
Peabody Individual Achievement Test—Revised/Normative Update PIAT–R/NU), 147–148
Peabody Picture Vocabulary Test—3 (PPVT–3), 131, 142
Pedophilia, 121
Perception, 220
Perseverations, 113
Personality disorders, 123–124
Personality tests. *See* Mood and personality tests
Perspective taking, 220
Pervasive developmental disorders (PDD), 226
PFC (prefrontal cortex), 171
Pheneizine, 202
Phenylketonuria (PKU), 118
Phobias, 107, 163
Phonological awareness, 226
Phototherapy, 173–174
Physical attending, 33
Physical impairments (in children), 225
Pica, 126
Pinel, Philippe, 84
PKU (phenylketonuria), 118
Placement in field, 57–58
Poddar, Prosenjit, 67
Positive symptoms, 112
Postpartum depression, 111
Posttraumatic stress disorder (PTSD), 107–108, 164–165
Posture, 44
Poverty of content, 113
Poverty of speech, 113
PPVT–3. *See* Peabody Picture Vocabulary Test—3
PIAT–R/NU. *See* Peabody Individual Achievement Test—Revised/Normative Update
Practicum, 3–16
 and appropriateness of placement, 75
 contract, practicum, 14–15, 18–19

establishing yourself in, 6–8
 issues when leaving, 57–58
 as new work environment, 8–13
 site selection for, 3–6
 supervisory relationship in, 13–15
Practitioner, your role as, 7–8
Praise, labeled, 229, 230
Predictive validity, 133
Prefrontal cortex (PFC), 171
Prehelping, 33
Preoperational thinking, 210
Preschool children, developmental issues with, 210–217
Prescription (of medication), 205
Prisons, 89
Privacy, 45–46, 65–66
Prochaska, J. O., 98
Prodromal phase (schizophrenia), 113
Professional, your role as, 7
Professional accountability, 158
Professional boundaries, 69–71
Professional roles, expansion of, 85–86
Professions in mental health. *See* Mental health professions
Profound mental retardation, 118
Program director, 43
Projective personality testing, 131
Project MATCH, 166–167
Protein-bound medicines, 194
Prozac, 88
Psychiatric hospitals, 89. *See also* Asylums
Psychiatric nurses, 243–244
Psychiatric technicians, unit, 43
Psychiatrists, 86, 239–240
Psychiatry (as profession), 83
Psychoanalysis, 85
Psychodrama, 245
Psychoeducation, 160
Psychological assessment(s), 129–135, 145–152. *See also* Psychological screening(s)
 achievement tests, 147–148
 attention and concentration tests, 145
 behavioral tests, 151–152
 confidentiality issues in, 73
 as ethical issue, 72–74
 full battery assessments, 135
 initial, 46
 intellectual and cognitive tests, 146–147
 language tests, 150
 memory tests, 150–151
 mood and personality tests, 148–149
 neuropsychological tests, 151
 and reliability, 132, 134
 types of, 130–132
 and validity, 133–134
 visual spatial tests, 149–150
Psychological screening(s), 134, 137–144

achievement tests, 140
attention and concentration tests, 138–139
behavioral tests, 144
intellectual and cognitive tests, 139–140
language tests, 142
memory tests, 142–143
mental status exams, 137–138
mood and personality tests, 140–141
neuropsychological tests, 143
visual spatial tests, 141–142
Psychologists, 238–239
Psychopathologies, 105–126. *See also* Treatment(s)
adjustment disorders, 123
anxiety disorders, 106–108
childhood disorders, 224–231
in children and adolescents, 124–126
cognitive disorders, 116–117
dissociative disorders, 120
eating disorders, 109–110
factitious disorders, 119–120
impulse control disorders, 122
mental retardation, 117–119
mood disorders, 110–112
personality disorders, 123–124
psychotic disorders, 112–114
sexual and gender identity disorders, 120–121
sleep disorders, 121–122
somatoform disorders, 119
substance-related disorders, 114–116
Psychostimulants, 205
Psychosurgery, 170–171
Psychotherapy, 187, 206
Psychotic disorders, 112–114
Psychotropic medications, 88, 196–198. *See also* Medicines
PTSD. *See* Posttraumatic stress disorder
Purgative treatments, 83
Pyromania, 122

Q
Questions
open-ended, 45
and rate of speech, 49–50

R
RADS–2 (Reynolds Adolescent Depression Scale—Second Edition), 141
Rapport, building, 44–45, 216–217, 222–223
Rauwolfia, 200
RBANS (Repeatable Battery for the Assessment of Neuropsychological Status), 138
RCDS (Reynolds Child Depression Scale), 141

RCFT. *See* Rey Complex Figure Test and Recognition Trial
RCMAS (Revised Children's Manifest Anxiety Scale), 141
Reading, 220–221
Reason and Emotion in Psychotherapy (Albert Ellis), 92
Receivers, 114
Receptive One-Word Picture Vocabulary Test (ROWPVT–2000), 150
Receptor sites, 195
Recreational therapists, 247–248
Registered nurses (RNs), 43, 243–244
Relationship(s). *See also* Helping relationships
with coworkers, 9–10
multiple, 69–71
with practicum supervisor, 13–15, 55–56
prohibited sexual, 71
unhelpful, 27–28
Relaxation training, 163
Reliability, 132, 134
Reliability coefficient, 132
Repeatable Battery for the Assessment of Neuropsychological Status (RBANS), 138
Reporting
of ethical violations, 77
of suspected child abuse, 66
Reserpine, 200
Residual phase (schizophrenia), 113
Respect, 30
Responding, 34
Retrograde amnesia, 117
Rett's disorder, 125
Reuptake, 196
Reuptake inhibitors, 196
Revised Children's Manifest Anxiety Scale (RCMAS), 141
Rey Complex Figure Test and Recognition Trial (RCFT), 149–150
Reynolds Adolescent Depression Scale— Second Edition (RADS–2), 141
Reynolds Child Depression Scale (RCDS), 141
Ripley, T. M., 28–29
Risparidone, 204
RNs. *See* Registered nurses
Rogers, Carl, 27, *29*, 86, 246
Role(s)
gender, 11–12
historical expansion of professional, 85–86
multiple, 69–71
of practicum supervisee, 13–14
of practicum supervisor, 13
of students, 47–48
taking on new, 7–8

Role ambiguity, 14
Role conflict, 14–15
Rorschach Inkblot Technique, 131, 149
ROWPVT–2000 (Receptive One-Word Picture Vocabulary Test), 150
Rush, Benjamin, 84

S
Safety issues, 100
Sakel, Manfred, 87
Satel, Sally, 89
SB–5. *See* Stanford-Binet Intelligence Scale—Fifth Edition
Scaturo, D. J., 95, 97
Schizophrenia, 112–114, 168–169, 204
Schizophreniform disorders, 114
School-age children, developmental issues with, 217–223
SCL–90–R (Symptom Checklist—90—Revised), 148
Screenings. *See* Psychological screening(s)
Secure attachment, 214, 215
Sedatives, 88
Selected items, 136
Selective ignoring, 230
Selective mutism, 126
Selective serotonin reuptake inhibitors (SSRIs), 196, 199, 201, 202
Selective subtests, 136
Self-esteem, development of, 222
Self-help therapies, 90–91
Self-regulation, 216
Semistructured interviews, 46
Sensory disorders (in children), 225
Separation anxiety disorder, 126
Serotonin, 195, 196, 204
Serotonin and norepinephrine reuptake inhibitors (SNRIs), 196
Sertraline, 196, 202
Session(s), first, 48–49
Severe mental retardation, 118
Sexual desire disorders, 121
Sexual disorders, 120–121
Sexual dysfunctions, 120–121
Sexual masochism, 121
Sexual pain disorders, 121
Sexual relationships, prohibited, 71
Sexual sadism, 121
Shared psychotic disorders, 114
Shipley Institute of Living Scale (SIL), 129, 139–140
Short Category Test, Booklet Format, 151
Shorter, E., 98
Short-term therapies. *See* Briefer therapies
Side effects (of medication), 197–198
SIL. *See* Shipley Institute of Living Scale
Sit, how to, 44–45

SIT–3 (Slosson Intelligence Scale—3), 140
Site selection, practicum, 3–6
  criteria for, 6
  and individual training needs, 4
  information resources for, 5–6
  and potentially dangerous neighborhoods, 55
  and types of sites, 4–5
Situational in vivo exposure, 163
Skills
  communication, 29–30, 221–222
  helping, 29–30, 36–37
  social, 163, 165
Skinner, B. F., 85, 86
Sleep disorders, 121–122
Sleep terror disorder, 122
Sleepwalking disorder, 122
Slosson Intelligence Scale—3 (SIT–3), 140
SNRIs (serotonin and norepinephrine reuptake inhibitors), 196
Social cognition, 221
Social-emotional development, 211–212, 214–216, 218–219, 221–222
Social phobia, 107, 163
Social skills training, 163, 165
Social workers, 43, 240–242
Societal attitudes, 90–91
Somatic delusion, 112
Somatic interventions, 169–177
  anterior cingulotomy, 171
  early examples of, 169–170
  electroconvulsive therapy, 171–173
  exercise therapy, 174–176
  lobotomy, 170–171
  magnetic seizure therapy, 176
  phototherapy, 173–174
  psychosurgery, 170–171
  transcranial magnetic stimulation, 176
  vagus nerve stimulation, 176–177
Somatization disorder, 119
Somatoform disorders, 119
Sonnenstein Asylum, 87
Special education, 224
Specific phobias, 107, 163
Speech
  disorganized, 112–113
  poverty of, 113
  rate of (with clients), 49–50
Split-half reliability, 132
SPS (Suicide Probability Scale), 141
SSRIs. *See* Selective serotonin reuptake inhibitors
Staff, relationships with practicum, 9–10
Staffings, 188
Stages of life, helping relationships during, 36–38
STAI (State–Trait Anxiety Inventory), 141

Stanford-Binet Intelligence Scale—Fifth Edition (SB–5), 131, 146
State–Trait Anxiety Inventory (STAI), 141
Stein, Leonard, 89
Stevens–Johnson syndrome, 198
Stigmas, 126
Strategic attention, 230
Stroop Color and Word Test, 139
Structured family programs, 169
Structured interviews, 46
Students, practicum
    ethical issues in supervision of, 75–77
    role of, 47–48
Stupor, catatonic, 113
Sublingual administration, 194
Substance abuse, 115
Substance dependence, 115
Substance-induced disorders, 116
Substance intoxication, 116
Substance-related disorders, 114–116
Substance use disorders, 115
Substance withdrawal, 116
Suicide Probability Scale (SPS), 141
Summarizing, 45
Supervisee, practicum, 13–14
Supervisor, practicum
    deciding what to tell, 54–55
    discussing confidential matters with, 66
    initial meeting with, 43
    potential problems and solutions with, 14–15
    relationship with, 13–15, 55–56
    roles of, 13
    and roles of supervisee, 13–14
    routine meetings with, 55
Symptom Checklist—90—Revised (SCL–90–R), 148
Symptoms, positive vs. negative, 112
Synapses, 195
Synaptic transmission, 195
Systematic desensitization, 227

T
Tactile hallucinations, 112
Tarasoff, Tatiana, 67
Tarasoff v. Board of Regents, 67
Tardive dyskinesia, 198, 203, 204
Target effects, 197
TAT. *See* Thematic Apperception Test
Test of Achievement and Adult Language—Third Edition (TOAL), 150
Test of Memory and Learning (TOMAL), 150
Test of Visual Perceptual Skills (non-motor)—Revised (TVPS(n-m)–R), 142
Thematic Apperception Test (TAT), 131, 149
Thinking
    delusional, 52–53
    disorganized, 112–113
    preoperational, 210
Thinking and Depression (Aaron Beck), 92
Thioridazine, 203
Third parties, duty to protect, 67
Thorazine, 88, 199
Tic disorders, 126
TMS (transcranial magnetic stimulation), 176
TOAL (Test of Achievement and Adult Language—Third Edition), 150
Token economy, 168
Tolerance, substance, 115
TOMAL (Test of Memory and Learning), 150
Tone of voice, 50
Topiramate, 204
Trail-Making Test, 145
"Training in the Community," 89
Training opportunities
    maximizing your, 9
    and practicum site selection, 4
Tranquilizers, 88
Transcranial magnetic stimulation (TMS), 176
Translator, acting as, 72–73
Transvestic fetishism, 121
Tranylcypromine, 202
Treatment(s), 157–179
    for alcohol abuse and dependence, 165–168
    for anxiety disorders, 162–165
    evidence-based, 95–97
    "health," 93–97
    history of. *See* History of treatment of mental illness
    manual-based, 94–95
    for mental disorders, 157–159
    for mood disorders, 160–162
    for schizophrenia, 168–169
    somatic, 169–177
Treatment settings (for children), 231–232
Treatment team, 188
Trichotillomania, 122
Tricyclic antidepressants, 201
Truax, C. B., 28
TSF (twelve-step facilitation therapy), 167
Tuke, William, 84
TVPS(n-m)–R (Test of Visual Perceptual Skills (non-motor)—Revised), 142
Twelve-step facilitation therapy (TSF), 167
Typical antipsychotics, 203–204

U
Unhelpful relationships, 27–28
Unipolar mood disorders, 110
United States, history of mental illness treatment in. *See* History of treatment of mental illness

Unit nursing director, 43
Unit psychiatric technicians, 43
U.S. Department of Health and Human Services, 45

V
Vagus nerve stimulation (VNS), 176–177
Validity, 133–134
Values, culture-specific, 12–13
Vascular dementia, 117
Venlafaxine, 196, 203
Veterans Affairs Treatment Studies, 166–168
Vineland Adaptive Behavior Scales, 132, 151–152
Viscous medicines, 194
Visual hallucinations, 53, 112
Visual spatial tests, 131, 141–142, 149–150
VMI (Beery–Buktenica Developmental Test of Visual Motor Integration—Fourth Edition), 149
VNS. See Vagus nerve stimulation
Voice, tone of, 50
Voyeurism, 121

W
WAIS–III. See Wechsler Adult Intelligence Scale—III
Warn, duty to, 67, 232
WASI. See Wechsler Abbreviated Scale of Intelligence
Watson, John, 85
Watts, James, 86
Wechsler Abbreviated Scale of Intelligence (WASI), 131, 139
Wechsler Adult Intelligence Scale—III (WAIS–III), 130, 131, 138–139, 146
Wechsler Individual Achievement Test—II (WIAT–II), 147
Wechsler Intelligence Scale for Children—IV (WISC–IV), 131, 146

Wechsler Memory Scale—III (WMS–III), 131, 150
Wechsler Memory Scale—III Abbreviated (WMS–III–A), 143
Wechsler Preschool and Primary Scales of Intelligence—III (WPPSI–III), 131, 146
Westen, D., 96, 97
WHO (World Health Organization), 105
WIAT–II (Wechsler Individual Achievement Test—II), 147
Wide Range Achievement Test—3 (WRAT–3), 131, 140
Wide Range Assessment of Memory and Learning—Second Edition (WRAML–2), 150–151
Withdrawal, 115, 116
WMS–III. See Wechsler Memory Scale—III
WMS–III–A (Wechsler Memory Scale—III Abbreviated), 143
Woodcock–Johnson III, 146–147
Work environment, 8–13
    dealing with diversity in, 10–13
    maximizing your training opportunities in, 9
    practicum as new, 8–13
    and practicum site services/activities/policies, 8–9
    relationships with staff in, 9–10
World Health Organization (WHO), 105
Wortes, Joseph, 87
WPPSI–III. See Wechsler Preschool and Primary Scales of Intelligence—III
WRAML–2. See Wide Range Assessment of Memory and Learning—Second Edition
"Wrap around services," 89–90
WRAT–3. See Wide Range Achievement Test—3

Z
Ziprasidone, 204

About the Editors

Janet R. Matthews, PhD, ABPP, received her PhD in clinical psychology from the University of Mississippi following an internship at the University of Oklahoma Health Sciences Center. Her postdoctoral fellowship in clinical and neuropsychological assessment was at the Nebraska Psychiatric Institute. She is a licensed and board certified clinical psychologist and tenured professor of psychology at Loyola University of New Orleans where she has been teaching an undergraduate practicum course for more than 20 years. Prior to joining Loyola's faculty, Dr. Matthews was a tenured psychology faculty member at Creighton University. Her professional activities include 5 years on her state licensing board as well as service on many boards, committees, and task forces of the American Psychological Association (APA). Dr. Matthews has served on both the Council of Representatives and the Board of Directors of the American Psychological Association (APA). She is a past president of APA Division 2 (Society for the Teaching of Psychology) and Division 12, Section IV (Society of Clinical Psychology; Clinical Psychology of Women) as well as of the Southwestern Psychological Association. Currently, Dr. Matthews is a member of APA's Policy and Planning Board, is completing her term as president of Division 12, Section IX (Society of Clinical Psychology; Assessment Psychology), and serves as a member of the Board of Directors of the American Board of Assessment

Psychology. She is a fellow in nine APA divisions. In addition, Dr. Matthews is a consulting editor for *Teaching of Psychology*. Her publications have appeared in *Professional Psychology, Teaching of Psychology, Contemporary Psychology,* and *Journal of Personality Assessment*. This is the second book she has coedited with Dr. Walker. Dr. Matthews has received many honors, including a mentoring award from APA Division 12, Section IV; an APA Presidential Citation for her lifetime contributions to the Southwestern Psychological Association; and an award for her enduring commitment to clinical psychology from APA Division 12, Section IX. She is married to Lee H. Matthews, a clinical psychologist, with whom she is partner in a private practice.

C. (Clarence) Eugene Walker, PhD, received his PhD in 1965 from Purdue University with a major in clinical psychology and minors in experimental psychology and sociology. His psychology internship was completed at West Tenth Street Veteran's Administration Hospital and Riley Children's Hospital, both in Indianapolis, Indiana. Dr. Walker taught at Westmont College in Santa Barbara, California from 1964 to 1968, where he was an assistant professor and chair of the Division of Psychology, Education, and Physical Education and an athletic director. From 1968 to 1974 he was an assistant, then an associate professor at Baylor University in Waco, Texas. From 1974 to 1995 he was at the University of Oklahoma Medical School in Oklahoma City where he became director of training in pediatric psychology and cochief of mental health services for Children's Hospital of Oklahoma. On retirement, Dr. Walker was named professor emeritus from the medical school and formed a corporation, Psychological Consultants, Inc., located in Edmond, Oklahoma. Dr. Walker has published over 100 articles, reviews, and chapters and more than 20 books on research and clinical practice with children and adults. His early work involved research on psychological testing and measurement. Later work involved behavioral approaches to psychotherapy and effects of pornography on behavior. Other interests include hyperactive behavior in children, child abuse, and juvenile and adolescent sex offenders.

Dr. Walker is a leading expert on the treatment of enuresis and encopresis, treatment of young sex offenders, and behavioral approaches to psychotherapy. Active on many professional committees of APA, Dr. Walker is on the editorial board of numerous journals and was a member of the founding editorial board of *Professional Psychology* and of the *Journal of Clinical Psychology in Medical Settings*. He was president of the Central Texas Psychological Association (1973); Section for Continuing Professional Development in Division 12 (Society of Clinical Psychology) of APA (1973); Southwestern Psychological Association (1977); Oklahoma Psychological Association (1983); and, Society of Pediatric Psychology (1986). He was chair of the Corresponding Committee of Fifty for Division 12 from 1970 to 1973. He is a fellow of the APA, listed in *Who's Who in America* and *Who's Who in the World* as well as numerous other reference works.